# The **ACT**
# Course Book

## MATHEMATICS & SCIENCE

SUMMIT
EDUCATIONAL
GROUP

Focusing on the Individual Student

## Copyright Statement

The ACT Course Book, along with all Summit Educational Group Course Materials, is protected by copyright. Under no circumstances may any Summit materials be reproduced, distributed, published, or licensed by any means.

Summit Educational Group reserves the right to refuse to sell materials to any individual, school, district, or organization that fails to comply with our copyright policies.

Third party materials used to supplement Summit Course Materials are subject to copyright protection vested in their respective publishers. These materials are likewise not reproducible under any circumstances.

## Ownership of Trademarks

Summit Educational Group is the owner of the trademarks "Summit Educational Group" and the pictured Summit logo, as well as other marks that the Company may seek to use and protect from time to time in the ordinary course of business.

ACT is a trademark of ACT, Inc.

All other trademarks referenced are the property of their respective owners.

ISBN: 978-0-578-16045-0

# CONTENTS

# PRE-ALGEBRA

# ELEMENTARY ALGEBRA

## INTERMEDIATE ALGEBRA

## COORDINATE GEOMETRY

## PLANE GEOMETRY

# Preface

Since 1988, when two Yale University graduates started Summit Educational Group, tens of thousands of students have benefited from Summit's innovative, comprehensive, and highly effective test preparation. You will, too.

Successful test-takers not only possess the necessary academic skills but also understand how to take the ACT. Through your ACT program, you'll learn both. You'll review and develop the academic skills you need, and you'll learn practical, powerful, and up-to-date test-taking strategies.

The *Summit ACT Course Book* provides the skills, strategies, and practice necessary for success on the ACT. The result of much research and revision, this book is the most effective, innovative, and comprehensive preparation tool available.

This book's first chapter – Test-Taking Fundamentals – gives students a solid foundation of ACT information and general test-taking strategies. The following chapters cover the Math and Science content strands of the ACT. Each chapter is divided into manageable topic modules. Modules consist of the skills, strategies, and common question types for particular topics, *Try It Out* questions, and *Put It Together* questions. At the end of each chapter, homework questions provide additional practice.

Some Math modules include frequencies and difficulty ranges for specific question types. These are not absolute, but are general trends based on research of many official ACTs. Difficulty is labeled as "E" (Easy), "M" (Medium), and "H" (Hard). These ratings translate to questions 1-25, 20-45, and 40-60, respectively, in an ACT Math Test.

We are confident that you will not find a more complete or effective ACT program anywhere.

We value your feedback and are always striving to improve our materials. Please write to us with comments, questions, or suggestions for future editions at:

> edits@mytutor.com

Your program will give you the skills, knowledge, and confidence you need to score your best.

Good luck, and have fun!

# Chapter Summaries

We've reproduced the Chapter Summaries below to give you a preview of what you'll be covering. The Summaries are meant to serve as quick, condensed reference guides to the most important concepts. Obviously, you can't bring them into the test with you, but from now up until the night before the test, use them to preview and review the material covered in this book. Of course, Chapter Summaries also reside at the end of each chapter.

# General Test-Taking Summary

❑ Know your limits. Remember: Most students don't need to answer every question to reach their goals.

❑ Pace yourself through each section, and don't get stuck on any one question for too long. You can always skip the question and come back to it.

❑ Don't leave answers blank.

❑ Be aware of attractors.

❑ Carefully read and think about each question. Make sure you know what the question is asking.

❑ Focus on one question at a time. Resist the temptation to think about the 10 questions ahead or the question you did a minute ago.

❑ Use Process of Elimination (POE), and make educated guesses.

# Pre-Algebra Summary

Multiples, Factors, and Divisibility

❏ A multiple of an integer is any integer that is divisible by that integer.

❏ A number is a factor of an integer if it divides evenly into that integer.

❏ A number is divisible by another number if it can be divided evenly by that number.

❏ A remainder is the integer left over when you divide two numbers.


Fractions

❏ To add or subtract fractions, first adjust the fractions so they have a common denominator. Then add or subtract the numerators only.

❏ To multiply fractions, multiply straight across (numerator by numerator and denominator by denominator).

❏ To divide fractions, multiply by the reciprocal of the divisor (the number you're dividing by).


Ratios

❏ Know how to find the ratio between a part and a whole when given a ratio between parts.


Proportions

❏ Solve proportions by cross-multiplying. If $\frac{a}{b} = \frac{c}{d}$, then $a \times d = b \times c$.


Exponents

❏ Know your rules and use your calculator to help compute numerical exponents.


Roots

❏ Know your rules and use your calculator to help compute numerical roots.

❏ If a root has a perfect-square factor, rewrite as a multiplication and simplify.


Digits and Scientific Notation

❏ The position of each digit in a number determines the digit's place value.

❏ In "scientific notation," a number is written so that the largest digit is in the units place, and it is multiplied by a power of 10.

## Percent

❑ Percents, decimals, and fractions can all be used interchangeably.

❑ Find what percent one number is of another by dividing the part by the whole and then converting the resulting decimal to a percent.

## Absolute Value

❑ To simplify an expression within an absolute value sign, simplify just as you would simplify an expression in parentheses. Then take the absolute value of the result.

## Sequences

❑ Often, you'll be able to solve a sequence question by "brute force" – that is, by writing out the terms. If you can't write out the entire sequence, write out enough so you can see what's happening.

## Averages (Arithmetic Mean)

❑ Average = $\dfrac{\text{sum of parts}}{\text{number of parts}}$

❑ Sum of parts = (number of parts) × (average)

## Median and Mode

❑ The median of a set of numbers is the middle number when the numbers are arranged in order. If there is an even number of terms in a set, the median is the mean of the two middle numbers.

❑ The mode of a set of numbers is the number that appears most frequently. Note that it is possible to have more than one mode in a list of numbers.

## Combinations

❑ Calculate combinations using the Fundamental Principle of Counting: the number of possible outcomes can be found by multiplying the number of ways each event can occur.

❑ In combinations where choices cannot be repeated or where order matters, there will be a decreasing number of options available.

## Probability

❑ Probability of an event happening = $\dfrac{\text{\# of ways the event can happen}}{\text{\# of possible outcomes}}$

# Elementary Algebra Summary

Algebraic Expressions

❑ Simplify an expression by combining like terms.

❑ Use the distributive property to multiply a single term by an expression inside parentheses.

❑ When multiplying two binomials, each term should be multiplied by each term in the other binomial.

❑ Factoring is expanding in reverse. Find common factors among the terms in an expression and rewrite using a multiplication.

Equations

❑ To solve for a variable, isolate the variable on one side of the equal sign.

Inequalities

❑ Inequalities can be solved like equations, with one important difference: if you multiply or divide both sides by a negative number, you must switch the direction of the inequality sign.

Translation

❑ Translate math problems word-by-word to create equations.

Word Problems

❑ Follow these broad steps to solve ACT word problems:

1. Determine what information is needed in order to solve the word problem.

2. Break down the problem into manageable parts. Consider what you can do with the information provided.

3. Pick variables to represent unknown values, and translate the word problem into algebraic expressions and equations.

4. Solve for one value at a time until you find your final answer.

5. Check your answer! Is it what the question asked for? Does it make sense with the given information?

# Intermediate Algebra Summary

## Simultaneous Equations

❑ Elimination method: add or subtract equations to cancel one of the variables and solve for the other. You may have to multiply an equation through by some number to eliminate a variable when the equations are added or subtracted.

## Quadratic Equations and Expressions

❑ If you can factor it, factor it! Most quadratics questions require factoring as one of the steps in the solution. Before factoring a quadratic equation, make sure that the equation is set equal to zero.

## Radical Equations

❑ To solve for a variable in a radical, isolate the radical on one side of the equation, and then raise both sides of the equation to the appropriate exponent.

## Functions

❑ To evaluate a function for a particular value of $x$, simply substitute that value everywhere you see an $x$.

## Logarithms

❑ A logarithm represents the exponent to which a base number is raised to produce a given number. $\log_b y = x$ means that $b^x = y$.

## Matrices

❑ To add or subtract matrices, simply perform the operation on the corresponding terms.

❑ To multiply two matrices, multiply each row in the first matrix by each column in the second matrix.

## Complex Numbers

❑ Imaginary numbers are expressed using $i$, which is defined as the square root of $-1$.

# Coordinate Geometry Summary

### Coordinate Geometry Basics

❏ The coordinate plane is a grid made up of two number lines – a horizontal number line called the x-axis, and a vertical number line called the y-axis. These two lines meet at a point called the origin, with coordinates (0,0).

❏ Every point in the coordinate plane can be represented by a pair of coordinates $(x, y)$.

### Midpoint and Distance

❏ The midpoint of a segment is given by: $\left( \dfrac{x_1 + x_2}{2}, \dfrac{y_1 + y_2}{2} \right)$

❏ The distance between two points is given by: $\sqrt{(x_2 - x_1)^2 + (y_2 - y_1)^2}$

### Slope

❏ The slope of a line is given by: $\dfrac{(y_2 - y_1)}{(x_2 - x_1)}$ or $\dfrac{\text{rise}}{\text{run}}$

❏ Parallel lines have equal slopes.

❏ Perpendicular lines have slopes that are negative reciprocals of each other.

❏ Vertical lines have undefined slope.

❏ Horizontal lines have a slope of 0.

### Linear Equations and Inequalities

❏ The standard form of a linear equation is $Ax + By = C$.

❏ The slope-intercept form of a linear equation is $y = mx + b$, where $m$ is the slope of the line and $b$ is the y-intercept. The y-intercept is where the line crosses the y-axis.

## Conic Sections

❑ Equation of a circle: $(x - a)^2 + (y - b)^2 = r^2$

❑ Equation of a parabola: $y = ax^2 + bx + c$

❑ Equation of an ellipse: $\dfrac{(x - h)^2}{a^2} + \dfrac{(y - k)^2}{b^2} = 1$

## Transformations

❑ Translation is the process of moving a point or figure a specified distance in a certain direction.

❑ Reflection is the process of moving a point or figure by mirroring it over a line.

❑ Rotation is the process of moving a point or figure by rotating it around a point – often the origin.

❑ Shapes have symmetry when they can be transformed to be exactly like one another. An axis of symmetry is a line that divides a figure into symmetrical images.

# Plane Geometry Summary

### Angles

☐ Right angle = 90°

☐ Straight line angle = 180°

☐ Sum of interior angles of triangle = 180°

☐ The sum of the interior angles of any polygon = $(n-2) \times 180°$, where $n$ is the number of sides.

### Parallel Lines

☐ When a line crosses through parallel lines, it creates several sets of equal angles and supplementary angles.

### Isosceles and Equilateral Triangles

☐ In an isosceles triangle, two sides are equal, and the two angles opposite those sides are equal.

☐ In an equilateral triangle, all three sides are equal and each of the angles is 60°.

☐ In any triangle, the side opposite the largest angle is the longest side. The side opposite the smallest angle is the shortest side.

☐ In any triangle, the sum of the lengths of any two sides is always greater than the length of the third side.

### Perimeter and Area of Triangles

☐ Area of triangle = $\frac{1}{2}(\text{base} \times \text{height})$

### Right Triangles

☐ Pythagorean Theorem: $a^2 + b^2 = c^2$

### Similar and Congruent Triangles

☐ Similar triangles have corresponding angles that are equal and corresponding sides that are proportional. Similar triangles have the same shape but not necessarily the same size.

☐ Congruent triangles are equal in size and shape. Corresponding sides and angles are equal.

## Quadrilaterals

❏ A trapezoid is a quadrilateral with only one pair of parallel sides. The parallel sides are the bases. In an isosceles trapezoid, the non-parallel sides are equal.

❏ A parallelogram is a quadrilateral in which opposite sides are equal and opposite angles are equal. Its diagonals bisect each other.

❏ A rhombus is a parallelogram with sides of equal length. Its diagonals are perpendicular bisectors of each other.

❏ A rectangle is a parallelogram with four right angles.

❏ A square is a rhombus with four right angles. All sides are congruent.

## Circles

❏ Area of circle = $\pi r^2$

❏ Circumference = $2\pi r$

❏ The area of a sector is a fraction of the area of the circle. Similarly, an arc length is a fraction of the circumference. In both cases, the fraction is determined by the central angle.

## Volume and Surface Area

❏ Cube

Volume = $s^3$

Surface Area = $6s^2$

❏ Rectangle

Volume = $l \times w \times h$

Surface Area = $2lw + 2lh + 2wh$

❏ Cylinder

Volume = $\pi r^2 h$

Surface Area = $2\pi rh + 2\pi r^2$

# Trigonometry Summary

SOH CAH TOA

❑  $\sin \theta = \dfrac{\text{opposite}}{\text{hypotenuse}}$

❑  $\cos \theta = \dfrac{\text{adjacent}}{\text{hypotenuse}}$

❑  $\tan \theta = \dfrac{\text{opposite}}{\text{adjacent}}$

❑  $\sin^{-1} \dfrac{\text{opposite}}{\text{hypotenuse}} = \theta$

❑  $\cos^{-1} \dfrac{\text{adjacent}}{\text{hypotenuse}} = \theta$

❑  $\tan^{-1} \dfrac{\text{opposite}}{\text{adjacent}} = \theta$

Trig Identities

❑  Tangent:  $\tan \theta = \dfrac{\sin \theta}{\cos \theta}$

❑  Cotangent:  $\cot \theta = \dfrac{\cos \theta}{\sin \theta} = \dfrac{1}{\tan \theta}$

❑  Secant:  $\sec \theta = \dfrac{1}{\cos \theta}$

❑  Cosecant:  $\csc \theta = \dfrac{1}{\sin \theta}$

❑  $\sin^2 \theta + \cos^2 \theta = 1$

## Unit Circle

❑ Angles can be measured in both degrees and radians. 180 degrees is equal to $\pi$ radians

❑ The value of the $x$ and $y$ coordinates where the terminal side of the angle intersects the unit circle equals the cosine and sine of the angle, respectively.

❑ Angles can be bigger than 360 degrees, and they can be negative.

## Graphs of Sine and Cosine

❑ The amplitude shows how "tall" the graph is. The amplitude is governed by the coefficient in front of the function. In the function $y = A \sin Bx$, $A$ is the amplitude.

❑ The period is how long it takes for the graph to go through one complete cycle.

In the function $y = A \sin Bx$, $\dfrac{2\pi}{B}$ is the period.

## Laws of Sines and Cosines

❑ Law of Sines: $\dfrac{a}{\sin A} = \dfrac{b}{\sin B} = \dfrac{c}{\sin C}$

❑ Law of Cosines: $c^2 = a^2 + b^2 - 2ab \cos c$

# Science Summary

The Scientific Method

❑ Understand what each step of the scientific method is supposed to achieve.

    Step 1: Ask a Question
    Step 2: Conduct Experiments
    Step 3: Interpret Data
    Step 4: Draw Conclusions

❑ Learn to apply the scientific method to different types of passages. Each type of Science passage focuses on different steps of the scientific method:

Data Representation passages focus on step 3. They look at data presented in tables and graphs and ask questions about trends, patterns, and specific data points.

Research Summary passages focus on steps 2, 3, and 4. They ask you to consider the experimental design and the resulting data collected.

Conflicting Viewpoint passages focus on steps 1 and 4. They look at a scientific question and ask you to compare different conclusions.

Data Representation

❑ Data Representation passages may look intimidating, because they often include large, complicated charts and graphs. However, they are typically the simplest passages.

❑ These passages are your opportunity to move quickly. This is important because you will need more time to work through the more complicated Research Summary and Conflicting Viewpoints passages.

Research Summary

❑ Research Summary passages are often the most challenging passages in the Science Test.

❑ These passages usually take more time than typical Data Representation passages. They also require more careful consideration to solve questions, and there is a greater likelihood of questions that depend on your own understanding of scientific concepts.

Conflicting Viewpoints

❑ Conflicting Viewpoints passages typically resemble the paired passages from the Reading Test. In these cases, you can work through the passages in much the same way as you would a Reading paired passage.

# Assessment and Objectives Worksheet

Complete this worksheet after the first session and refer back to it often. Amend it as necessary. It should act as a guide for how you and your tutor approach the program as a whole and how your sessions are structured.

The assessment will come from information that you and your parent(s) provide and from your initial diagnostic test. Keep in mind that you know yourself better than anyone else. Please be honest and open when answering the questions.

**Student's Self-Assessment and Parent Assessment**

- How do you feel about taking standardized tests? Consider your confidence and anxiety levels.

- Work through Table of Contents. Are there particular areas that stand out as areas for development?

- Other Concerns

**Diagnostic Test Assessment**

- Pacing

    o Did you run out of time on any or all sections? Did you feel rushed? Look for skipped questions or wrong answers toward the end of sections.

    o How will the concepts of Knowing Your Limits and Setting Your Goal help you?

- Carelessness

    o Do you feel that carelessness is an issue? Look for wrong answers on easy questions.

    o Why do you think you make careless mistakes? Rushing? Not checking? Not reading the question carefully? Knowing "why" will allow you to attack the problem.

- Are certain areas for development evident from the diagnostic? Work through the questions you got wrong to further identify areas that might require attention.

## Initial Score Goals

Note that score goals should be adjusted as necessary through the program.

Composite Goal: _____          English Goal: _____

Math Goal: _____          Reading Goal: _____

Science Goal: _____          Writing Goal: _____

## Program Objectives

Consider your assessment, and define your objectives. Make your objectives concrete and achievable.

| Objective* | How to Achieve the Objective |
| --- | --- |
|  |  |
|  |  |
|  |  |
|  |  |
|  |  |
|  |  |
|  |  |

## *Sample Objectives

| Objective | How to Achieve the Objective |
| --- | --- |
| Reduce carelessness by 75%. | Before starting to work on a question, repeat exactly what the question is asking. |
| Use Choosing Numbers and Plugging In fluently. | Tutor will point out all questions that are susceptible to these strategies. Note when a math question is susceptible to one or the other strategies. |
| Reduce test anxiety. | Build confidence and create a detailed testing plan. Start with easier questions to build confidence and slowly build toward more challenging questions. Take pride in successes and continue to reach for goals. Try to relax. |
| Improve calculator use. | Think about the question before jumping to the calculator. Have tutor hold on to calculator until it is needed. |
| Get excited about the test prep. | Stay positive. Know that score goals can be achieved. Learn tricks to beat the test. Make the test like a game. Focus on progress. |

SUMMIT
EDUCATIONAL
GROUP

# Test-Taking Fundamentals

- ❏ About the ACT
- ❏ Your Commitment
- ❏ ACT Structure
- ❏ Content
- ❏ Scoring
- ❏ Knowing Your Limits
- ❏ General Tactics

# About the ACT

❑ What does the ACT measure? According to the ACT folks, it measures your achievement – not IQ – in English, math, reading, science, and writing (if you choose to take the Writing Test). We feel that, to some extent, it measures how good you are at taking standardized tests. Either way, the ACT is an important element in the college admissions process.

Over the course of this program, you are going to learn to master the ACT by developing your test-taking abilities, working on fundamental ACT skills, and practicing with real ACT questions.

❑ Your performance on the ACT is **not** designed to reflect your scores on typical school exams or grades.

You are not expected to achieve a perfect score on the ACT, unlike on a typical school exam. The ACT is designed so that no student is expected to answer every question correctly.

❑ You might need to review and practice skills in one or more topics that appear on the test. You might just be rusty, or the topic might be unfamiliar to you. Your diagnostic will indicate your weak areas. You and your instructor will work to strengthen these weak areas throughout the program.

❑ Your instructor will emphasize both general test-taking strategies and problem-specific strategies, and you will practice these strategies during homework. Our strategies make the ACT less intimidating and more like a challenging game.

You'll practice on ACT-like questions throughout the book, and you'll take official ACT exams. The ACT, like any standardized test, has its own characteristics – from types of questions to timing. There is no more effective practice than working on real tests and simulated ACT questions.

# Your Commitment

❑ Your commitment to the program will determine how much you get out of it. Your instructor has made a commitment to your success on the ACT, and you need to make a commitment to helping yourself.

Attend all sessions.

Pay attention during sessions.

Ask questions when you don't understand something.

Complete all homework assignments.

# ACT Structure

❏ The ACT is made up of four tests, which appear in the same order on every test: English, Math, Reading, and Science. Some of the tests can be divided into subsections. There is also an optional Writing Test.

| Test | English | Mathematics | Reading | Science | Writing |
|---|---|---|---|---|---|
| Time | 45 min | 60 min | 35 min | 35 min | Optional |
| Questions | 75 | 60 | 40 | 40 | 1 |
| Sub-scores | Usage / Mechanics<br><br>Rhetorical Skills | Pre-Algebra / Elementary Algebra<br><br>Intermediate Algebra / Coordinate Geometry<br><br>Plane Geometry / Trigonometry | Social Studies / Natural Sciences<br><br>Arts / Literature | – | Ideas / Analysis<br><br>Development / Support<br><br>Organization<br><br>Language Use |

❏ Without the optional Writing Test, the ACT takes 2 hours and 55 minutes. You are given one 10-minute break.

You are given another 10-minute break before the Writing Test, if you do choose to take it.

❏ Occasionally, the ACT will have an experimental section.

The experimental section is used to try out new problems, and it doesn't count towards your score. It shows up at the end of the test, and is shorter than the other sections (about 20 minutes). That said, don't ever assume that the last section is experimental. Do your best on every section!

# Content

❑ The English Test requires you to revise and edit pieces of writing, using the rules of Standard Written English.

You don't need to know many grammatical terms, but you do need to understand how they work.

❑ The Math Test covers all topics of high school math: Pre-Algebra, Algebra, Plane Geometry, Coordinate Geometry, and Trigonometry.

❑ The Reading Test evaluates your ability to read, understand, and analyze short reading passages.

The Reading Test is made up of four reading passages of about 750 words each.  The passages are always divided into four categories and appear in the same order: Literary Narrative / Prose Fiction, Social Science, Humanities, and Natural Science.

❑ The Science Test asks you to interpret and analyze data, to understand the parts and significance of an experiment, and to recognize the similarities and differences between the views of two scientists.

You don't need to know any scientific facts to do well on the Science Test.

❑ The Writing Test asks you to create a well-structured, well-written essay on a given topic.

Although taking the Writing Test is officially optional, many colleges require a Writing score. Even if you don't think you'll need it, it's a good idea to sign up for the essay. You don't want to have to take the entire ACT again if you find out later that you need the essay score for a specific school.

# Scoring

❑ On the ACT, you receive one raw point for each correct answer. All questions in a test are worth the same, regardless of difficulty. Your **raw score** is the number of questions you answered correctly.

There is no penalty for an incorrect answer. <u>You should never leave an ACT question blank, even if you have to guess.</u>

❑ Your raw scores are converted to **scaled scores** using a conversion table. The conversion table makes up for the slight differences in difficulty between different ACT tests, and allows you to compare different versions of the test.

Here is part of a typical conversion table:

| Scaled Score | Raw Scores | | | |
|---|---|---|---|---|
| | English | Math | Reading | Science |
| 36 | 75 | 60 | 39-40 | 40 |
| 35 | - | 59 | 38 | 39 |
| 34 | 74 | 58 | 37 | - |
| 33 | 73 | 57 | 36 | 38 |
| 32 | 72 | 54-56 | 35 | 37 |
| 31 | 70-71 | 52-53 | 34 | 36 |
| 30 | 68-69 | 50-51 | 33 | - |
| 29 | 66-67 | 48-49 | 32 | 35 |
| 28 | 64-65 | 46-47 | 31 | 33-34 |
| 27 | 61-63 | 44-45 | 30 | 32 |
| 26 | 58-60 | 42-43 | 29 | 31 |
| 25 | 56-57 | 40-41 | 27-28 | 29-30 |
| 24 | 53-55 | 37-39 | 26 | 28 |
| 23 | 51-52 | 35-36 | 25 | 26-27 |
| 22 | 49-50 | 33-34 | 23-24 | 24-25 |
| 21 | 46-48 | 31-32 | 22 | 23 |
| 20 | 43-45 | 29-30 | 20-21 | 21-22 |
| 19 | 41-42 | 26-28 | 19 | 19-20 |
| 18 | 38-40 | 23-25 | 18 | 17-18 |

❑ Your four scaled scores are averaged to find your **composite score**, which is on a 1-36 scale. This composite score is rounded to the nearest whole number.

Your Writing score does not factor into your composite score. A different conversion table is used to calculate a Combined English/Writing Test score.

❑ Your score report will also give you scaled subscores for every test except Science. For example, your English score will be split into Usage/Mechanics and Rhetorical Skills.

# Knowing Your Limits

❑ During the real test, put your time and energy into the problems you are most capable of answering. If you struggle with difficult problems or with finishing sections in time, spend more of your time on the easy and medium problems and less time on the difficult problems. Here's why:

- You do not need to answer every question correctly to score well.

- You'll minimize mistakes on difficult questions, which often contain "attractor" or trap answers.

- You'll be less hurried, and you'll make fewer careless mistakes.

❑ During your test prep, push your limits.

As you prepare for the ACT, try to learn from the questions that give you trouble. Note your mistakes and make sure that you don't repeat them. Pay attention to the questions that are the most difficult and note what makes them so challenging and how to solve them.

As your skills improve, you will be able to answer more and more of the questions on the ACT. You will learn to recognize tricks and traps and to work with more speed and confidence.

These are the results of three students taking the same 12-question section.

Note: This example is not based on an actual test section; it is only for illustration.

### Cautious
Test-Taker

1 (A) (B) (C) (D)
2 (F) (G) (H) (J)
3 (A) (B) (C) (D)
4 (F) (G) (H) (J)
o 5 (A) (B) (C) (D)
6 (F) (G) (H) (J)
7 (A) (B) (C) (D)
o 8 (F) (G) (H) (J)
x 9 (A) (B) (C) (D)
10 (F) (G) (H) (J)
o 11 (A) (B) (C) (D)
o 12 (F) (G) (H) (J)

Raw Score = **7**

### Completist
Test-Taker

1 (A) (B) (C) (D)
x 2 (F) (G) (H) (J)
3 (A) (B) (C) (D)
x 4 (F) (G) (H) (J)
5 (A) (B) (C) (D)
x 6 (F) (G) (H) (J)
7 (A) (B) (C) (D)
8 (F) (G) (H) (J)
9 (A) (B) (C) (D)
x 10 (F) (G) (H) (J)
11 (A) (B) (C) (D)
12 (F) (G) (H) (J)

Raw Score = **8**

### Skilled
Test-Taker

1 (A) (B) (C) (D)
2 (F) (G) (H) (J)
3 (A) (B) (C) (D)
4 (F) (G) (H) (J)
x 5 (A) (B) (C) (D)
6 (F) (G) (H) (J)
7 (A) (B) (C) (D)
8 (F) (G) (H) (J)
9 (A) (B) (C) (D)
x 10 (F) (G) (H) (J)
11 (A) (B) (C) (D)
12 (F) (G) (H) (J)

Raw Score = **10**

x = wrong answer
o = blank

Cautious test-takers may get most of their answers correct, but they spend too much time checking answers on easy questions and they avoid challenging problems. This approach causes cautious test-takers to run out of time and to miss opportunities for reaching their full potential.

Completist test-takers are so determined to answer every question in time that they rush through the section. This approach causes completist test-takers to make careless mistakes on problems that they could have gotten correct if they had worked at a steadier pace.

Skilled test-takers learn to recognize easy and difficult questions, and they spend their time accordingly. Skilled test-takers finish sections on time without having to rush, and they never leave a question blank, but instead make educated guesses on challenging problems.

# General Tactics

❑ Focus on one question at a time.

The ACT is timed, so it's normal to feel pressure to rush. Resist the temptation to think about the 10 questions ahead of you or the question you did a minute ago. Relax and focus on one question at a time. **Patience** on the ACT is what allows you to work more quickly and accurately.

❑ Carefully read and think about each question.

Before you jump to the answers, start scribbling things down, or do calculations, make sure you understand exactly what the question is asking.

❑ Write in your test booklet.

When you're ready to solve the problem, use the space in your test booklet. Cross out incorrect answers, write down calculations to avoid careless errors, summarize reading passages, etc. Write down whatever will help you solve the problem.

❑ Use process of elimination (POE).

If you can <u>legitimately</u> eliminate at least one answer, you should guess. The more answers you can eliminate, the greater advantage you have. Once you have eliminated an answer, cross it out or put an "X" by it.

❑ Memorize the format and instructions before you take the test. At test time, you can skip the instructions and focus on the problems.

❑ The multiple-choice answer to each individual question is independent of the answers to the other questions. For example, sometimes an answer (A) might be correct 2, 3, or 4 times in a row, and that's okay. Don't be afraid to pick any particular multiple-choice answer just because you saw that answer recently. Choose the answer which is best for that particular question.

SUMMIT
EDUCATIONAL
GROUP

# Mathematics Overview

- ❏ The Mathematics Test
- ❏ Format and Scoring
- ❏ Question Difficulty
- ❏ Attractors
- ❏ Setting Your Goal
- ❏ Working Through the Math Test
- ❏ General Tips

# The Mathematics Test

| Format | 60 questions<br>Multiple-choice<br>5 answer choices |
|---|---|
| Content | Pre-Algebra<br>Elementary Algebra<br>Intermediate Algebra<br>Coordinate Geometry<br>Plane Geometry<br>Trigonometry |
| Scoring | Mathematics Test Score: 1-36<br>Subscores:<br>    Pre-Algebra / Elementary Algebra: 1-18<br>    Intermediate Algebra / Coordinate Geometry: 1-18<br>    Plane Geometry / Trigonometry: 1-18 |
| Time | 60 minutes |

❑ Each Math Test contains a specific number of questions in each of six topics:

| Content Area | Questions | Sample Topics |
|---|---|---|
| Pre-Algebra | 14 | Percentages, averages, ratios, exponents |
| Elementary Algebra | 10 | Simple equations, expressions |
| Intermediate Algebra | 9 | Quadratic equations, functions |
| Coordinate Geometry | 9 | Distance, slope, formula of a circle |
| Plane Geometry | 14 | Angles, area and perimeter, volume |
| Trigonometry | 4 | Trig identities, SOHCAHTOA |

❑ According to the ACT, the questions of the ACT Math Test "are designed to measure your mathematical achievement – the knowledge, skills, and reasoning techniques that are taught in high school mathematics courses and needed for college mathematics courses. Therefore, the questions cover a wide variety of concepts, techniques, and procedures." Most students have completed all of the math covered on the ACT by the time they finish 11th grade.

# Format and Scoring

❑ You receive 1 raw point for a correct answer. You lose nothing for incorrect answers. Your **raw score** is calculated by adding up raw points. Your raw score is then scaled to a **scaled score** from 1-36.

❑ The ACT will not provide you with common math formulas or theorems. You must memorize them over the course of your preparation for the test.

❑ The instructions are the same on every ACT. Familiarize yourself with instructions before you take the test. At test time, you can skip the instructions and focus on the problems.

> **DIRECTIONS:** Solve each problem, choose the correct answer, and then fill in the corresponding oval on your answer document.
>
> Do not linger over problems that take too much time. Solve as many as you can, then return to the others in the time you have left for this test.
>
> You are permitted to use a calculator on this test. You may use your calculator for any problems you choose, but some of the problems may best be done without using a calculator.
>
> Note: Unless otherwise stated, all of the following should be assumed.
>
> 1. Illustrative figures are NOT necessarily drawn to scale.
>
> 2. Geometric figures lie in a plane.
>
> 3. The word *line* indicates a straight line.
>
> 4. The word *average* indicates arithmetic mean.

# Question Difficulty

❏ In rough order, the questions in the Math Test progress from easy to difficult.

You may find an easy one late in the test, and you may find a hard one early in the test. Also, what's easy for one student might not be easy for another.

| Mathematics  (60 minutes) | | | | | | | | | | | | | | | | | | | | | | | | | | | | | |
|---|---|---|---|---|---|---|---|---|---|---|---|---|---|---|---|---|---|---|---|---|---|---|---|---|---|---|---|---|---|
| 1 | 2 | 3 | 4 | 5 | 6 | 7 | 8 | 9 | 10 | 11 | 12 | 13 | 14 | 15 | 16 | 17 | 18 | 19 | 20 | 21 | 22 | 23 | 24 | 25 | 26 | 27 | 28 | 29 | 30 |
| EASY | | | | | | | | | | | | → | | | | | | | | MEDIUM | | | | | | | | | |

| 31 | 32 | 33 | 34 | 35 | 36 | 37 | 38 | 39 | 40 | 41 | 42 | 43 | 44 | 45 | 46 | 47 | 48 | 49 | 50 | 51 | 52 | 53 | 54 | 55 | 56 | 57 | 58 | 59 | 60 |
|---|---|---|---|---|---|---|---|---|---|---|---|---|---|---|---|---|---|---|---|---|---|---|---|---|---|---|---|---|---|
| MEDIUM | | | | | | | | | | | | → | | | | | | | | DIFFICULT | | | | | | | | | |

❏ There are three main types of questions: basic problems, word problems, and challenging problems.

Basic problems are typically short and straightforward, and they're usually the easiest.

If 60% of $x$ equals 18, then $x = $ ?

A.  3
B.  30
C.  108
D.  300
E.  1,080

There's no need to be intimidated by word problems. You just need to translate the words into a basic problem, and then solve the basic problem.

A telephone company charges 10 cents per minute for the first 100 minutes used in a month and 7 cents per minute for each additional minute used.  What is the cost for 400 minutes used in one month?

F.  $21.00
G.  $28.00
H.  $31.00
J.  $38.00
K.  $40.00

Challenging problems may require many steps or may be like a difficult riddle. Not all challenging problems are wordy or long. Some are very short and direct-looking.

If $p^2 + q^2 = -2pq$ , what is the value of $p$?

A.  −1
B.  0
C.  1
D.  −$q$
E.  $q$

# Attractors

❑ Be aware of attractor answer choices.

The test writers predict potential mistakes by students and include those mistakes as answer choices. In other words, they set traps for the unsuspecting student. We call these answer choices "attractors." Attractors show up most often on medium and difficult problems.

In the following problem, which answer choices are attractors?

A blouse is originally priced at $40. After one week, its price is reduced 20%. After two more weeks, the sale price is reduced an additional 30%. What does the blouse now sell for?

A. $24.00
B. $22.40
C. $20.00
D. $17.60
E. $12.00

How is answer choice C an attractor?

How is answer choice D an attractor?

# Setting Your Goal

❏ You don't have to get every question right to score well.

To score a 21 on the Math Test – which is above the national average – you need to answer only 31 of the 60 questions correctly. That's only 53%, or just over half of the questions! On your regular school tests, 53% is a failing grade, but on the ACT, it's above average!

❏ Use the table below to set a target for the number of questions you need to answer correctly to hit your goal score for the Math Test.

| Math Scaled Score | Math Raw Score | Percent Correct |
|---|---|---|
| 36 | 60 | 100% |
| 35 | 59 | 98% |
| 34 | 58 | 97% |
| 33 | 57 | 95% |
| 32 | 54-56 | 92% |
| 31 | 52-53 | 88% |
| 30 | 50-51 | 84% |
| 29 | 48-49 | 81% |
| 28 | 46-47 | 78% |
| 27 | 44-45 | 74% |
| 26 | 42-43 | 71% |
| 25 | 40-41 | 68% |
| 24 | 37-39 | 63% |
| 23 | 35-36 | 59% |
| 22 | 33-34 | 56% |
| 21 | 31-32 | 53% |
| 20 | 29-30 | 49% |
| 19 | 26-28 | 45% |
| 18 | 23-25 | 38% |
| 17 | 20-22 | 33% |
| 16 | 17-19 | 28% |
| 15 | 14-16 | 23% |
| 14 | 12-13 | 20% |
| 13 | 10-11 | 17% |
| 12 | 8-9 | 13% |
| 11 | 6-7 | 10% |
| 10 | 5 | 8% |

❑ For most students, attempting every problem on the ACT will prevent them from scoring to their potential. Solving every question means you'll have to rush, which means you're more likely to make careless mistakes.

Having a realistic goal makes the test more manageable. With less pressure to answer every question, you can spend more time on easy and medium problems and less time on the difficult ones.

Remember, you get one raw point for each question, whether it's the simplest basic problem or the most challenging problem. Whether it takes you ten seconds or three minutes, it's still one point.

❑ Create a Plan of Attack for the Math Test.

Using your goal score and the score table, complete the Plan of Attack below. This plan will help you determine your best pace while working through the test.

Most of your time and energy should be spent on the questions needed to achieve your goal score. Assume that you will likely miss some of the questions you attempt, and use educated guessing on the rest.

---

### Mathematics Test Plan of Attack

My overall ACT Goal: _____

My Math Test Goal: _____

How many questions do I need to answer correctly (raw score)? _____

How many questions should I attempt? _____

# Working Through the Math Test

❑ Work through the test in two passes.

❑ On your first pass, answer all of the questions that you can solve quickly.

If you get stuck on a problem, try using one of the techniques in the Math Toolbox. Plugging In, Choosing Numbers, Guesstimating, Bridging the Gap, and Using Your Calculator are helpful with most challenging problems.

If you still cannot solve the problem, circle it and move on.

❑ Make a second pass through the test to work on the problems you skipped and marked, focusing on the ones you think you have the best chance on.

Do as many of these as you can. For some, you might be able to find the right answer. For others, you might be able to eliminate answer choices and make an educated guess.

❑ Guess on the remaining questions.

Since there is no penalty for wrong answers, do not leave any questions blank on your answer sheet! With about 2 minutes to go, you should fill in any remaining bubbles on the answer sheet.

You may temporarily leave questions blank while you're taking the test, but make sure every bubble is filled in when time is called.

# General Tips

❑ Carefully read and think about each question. What is the question asking?

Before you jump to the answers, reach for the calculator, or start scribbling things down, make sure you understand exactly what the question is asking.

❑ Don't erase calculations that you've mangled; just put a slash through them. It's faster.

❑ Use Process of Elimination (POE).

If you can legitimately eliminate at least one answer, you should guess. The more answers you can eliminate, the greater advantage you will have.

❑ Occasionally, an ACT math question will contain information that is not required to solve the question.

If you're fairly certain that you've solved a question without using a particular piece of given information, don't worry – it's very possible that you've done everything right. One or two questions per test contain extraneous information.

❑ Use the available space for scratchwork and figuring.

The right column of each page will be blank except for a heading at the top that says "DO YOUR FIGURING HERE." Use that space to write out your work! Some ACT Math problems can be quite complex, and you should not try to do them in your head.

SUMMIT
EDUCATIONAL
GROUP

# Math Toolbox

- Plugging In
- Choosing Numbers
- Guesstimating
- Bridging the Gap
- Using Your Calculator

# Plugging In

❑ Plugging In is exactly what it sounds like: inserting each multiple choice answer into the math problem and checking one at a time to see which one is correct.

❑ As you progress through your preparation, you want to build your arsenal of skills and strategies. Plugging In is one of the most useful ACT math strategies, because it leverages the multiple-choice format against itself.

❑ Plugging In works regardless of the question's difficulty level, and allows you to solve some very difficult questions even if you can't find the "forward" way to solve.

❑ When plugging in, start with answer choice (C) since numerical answer choices are presented in either ascending or descending order.

## PUT IT TOGETHER

Plug In to solve the following:

1. Which of the following numbers is a solution to $x^2 - 8 = 2x$ ?

    A.  −8
    B.  2
    C.  4
    D.  $4 + \sqrt{2}$
    E.  8

2. Caleb has 65 poker chips that are blue, green, and black. He stacks them on the table and sees that he has 6 fewer green chips than black chips and 11 more blue chips than black chips. How many blue chips does he have?

    F.  14
    G.  19
    H.  20
    J.  25
    K.  31

> You can use Plugging In to solve backwards on some word problems.

# Choosing Numbers

❑ Many ACT Math problems can be solved by Choosing Numbers. Learn to recognize questions that can be solved this way.

❑ Choosing Numbers is most effective on math problems whose answer choices contain variables, rather than constants. By Choosing Numbers, you'll be able to turn the algebraic expressions into hard numbers. Follow these steps:

1. Choose your own easy numbers to replace the variables.  For problems that involve minutes or hours, for instance, you might try 60.

   For problems that involve percents you might try _____.

2. Solve the problem using your numbers.

3. Plug your numbers into **all** the answer choices to see which answer choice(s) matches the solution you found in step 2.

4. If your numbers give you two or more correct answers, go back to step 1 and choose different numbers. You do not need to recalculate the choices you have already eliminated.

❑ Be careful to Choose Numbers that meet any restrictions in the question.

❑ Stay organized by writing down the numbers you choose and the answers you get.

---

Mackenzie is running for class president and she wants to order T-shirts to support her campaign. It costs $25.00 to make the image template for printing the T-shirts, and $5 for each blank T-shirt. Which of the following will be her total materials cost, in dollars, for $s$ campaign t-shirts?

A.  $30s$
B.  $25s + 5$
C.  $125s$
D.  $5s + 25$
E.  $5s - 25$

1. Choose a number for how many shirts Mackenzie will order, $s$: _____

2. Based on the question, what will be the cost for $s$ shirts? _____

3. Substitute the number you chose for $s$ into the answer choices.
   Which gives you the same answer you arrived at in step 2? _____

## PUT IT TOGETHER

Choose Numbers to solve the following:

1.  An online shoe retailer advertises discounts of 20% off the marked
    price of any item for a holiday sale. A coupon discounts an
    additional 10% off the sales price. Which of the following gives
    the sale price, in dollars, of an item with a marked price of $C$
    dollars when bought with a coupon?

    **This is a percent question. What would be a good value to choose for $C$?**

    **A.**  $0.30C$
    **B.**  $C - 0.30$
    **C.**  $C - 0.30C$
    **D.**  $C - 0.33C$
    **E.**  $C - 0.28C$

2.  A right triangle has side lengths one-third the size of the side
    lengths of the right triangle shown below. Which of the following
    gives an expression for the area of the smaller triangle?

    **F.**  $\dfrac{ab}{18}$

    **G.**  $\dfrac{ab}{9}$

    **H.**  $\dfrac{ab}{6}$

    **J.**  $\dfrac{2ab}{9}$

    **K.**  $9ab$

# Guesstimating

❑ Most figures on the ACT are drawn to scale. Therefore, a viable strategy for many geometry questions is to use the figure to guide your reasoning or narrow down answer choices.

Note that the ACT states that you should assume "illustrative figures are NOT necessarily drawn to scale." Usually, figures not drawn to scale will have a disclaimer stating so.

❑ Guesstimate on figures by comparing unknown values to known values. Use your answer sheet or pencil as a "ruler."

In the figure below, ~~if $\overline{AB}$ is a diameter of the circle and the circle has radius 1.5~~, what is the length of $\overline{BC}$?

A.   3
B.   4
C.   5
D.   7
E.   8

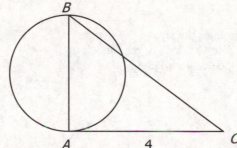

❑ Draw 90° and 45° angles to help you guesstimate angle measures.

Guesstimate the measure of the angle below.

$x =$ _____

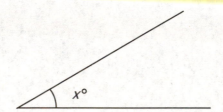

❑ Know the following approximations to help you guesstimate lengths.

$$\sqrt{2} \approx 1.4 \qquad \sqrt{3} \approx 1.7 \qquad \pi \approx 3.1$$

## PUT IT TOGETHER

Guesstimate to solve the following:

1.  In the figure below, the circle has center $O$ and the measure of
    $\overset{\frown}{MN}$ is 120°. What is the measure of $\angle MNO$?

    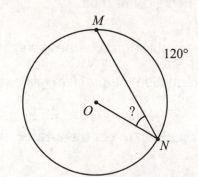

    A.  30°
    B.  40°
    C.  45°
    D.  60°
    E.  80°

# Bridging the Gap

❑ Many challenging ACT math problems require several steps to solve, and it is not always obvious how to move forward to the solutions. You can bridge the gap between what information is provided by a problem and what information is needed for the solution by carefully working from both ends until you find a connection.

❑ To Bridge the Gap on a complicated-looking problem, follow these steps:

1.  Read the problem entirely. Note the information the problem gives you and the information needed for the answer.

2.  Ask yourself: In order to complete the final step to get the answer, what missing pieces do I need?

3.  Go back to the beginning information you identified. Ask yourself: with this information, what else can I calculate?

4.  Start moving systematically through the problem, even if you don't know where it will lead. When you've found the values needed for the sequence of steps you created in Step 2, you'll be able to complete the bridge leading to the solution.

❑ As you move forward through solving a problem, keep your work neat and organized so you can keep track of each step.

❑ Bridging the Gap allows you to solve some of the most intimidating math problems on the ACT by breaking them down into smaller parts and tackling one piece at a time.

A committee of 5 people planned to each contribute equal amounts for a $100 framed painting for an honored guest. One of the committee members decides not to contribute. If the others members then pay equally for the painting, how much more does each have to contribute than they had originally planned?

A. $5.00
B. $16.00
C. $20.00
D. $25.00
E. $100.00

1. What are you looking for? What information is provided?

2. What missing pieces do you need for the final step?

3. With the beginning information, what else can you calculate?

4. Move forward through the problem until you can complete the final step.

5. Check to make sure you've answered what the question is really asking.

## PUT IT TOGETHER

Bridge the Gap to solve the following:

1. A square has a perimeter of 44 inches. What is the area of the square in square inches?

   A. 16
   B. 100
   C. 121
   D. 144
   E. 169

> To calculate the area of a square, what information do you need?
>
> If you know the perimeter of a square, what else can you calculate?

2. Two cars leave on a trip from Goshen to Bernalillo at the same time. The first car travels at an average rate of 75 miles per hour. The second car travels at an average rate of 65 miles per hour. When the first car reaches Bernalillo 12 hours later, how many more miles does the second car have to travel until it reaches Bernalillo?

   F. 110
   G. 120
   H. 130
   J. 150
   K. 210

> What information do you need to find the answer?
>
> What can you calculate?

# Using Your Calculator

❑ Your calculator can help you compute more efficiently, handle fractions more easily, find points of intersection, and more. Make sure you start your program and practice with the same calculator from the beginning of your program to test day. During the test you want your calculator techniques to be so well-practiced that they are automatic.

A warning: **your calculator cannot solve problems for you; it is only a tool.** Your calculator is not always the right tool for the job. As you prepare for the ACT, learn to identify when the calculator is most useful and when it will just slow you down.

❑ We recommend the TI-83 and TI-84 series of graphing calculators, which are widely used in American high schools. Although more advanced models exist, some of them are not permitted for use on the ACT. The following instructions are for those series of calculators.

❑ Calculators follow strict order of operations. Use parentheses when entering a multi-step calculation, key numbers in carefully, and check the display after each entry.

Calculate each of the following, first without and then with a calculator.

$$-5^2 = \underline{\hspace{2cm}} \qquad (-5)^2 = \underline{\hspace{2cm}} \qquad \frac{-6 \times 20}{4 \times 5} = \underline{\hspace{2cm}}$$

❑ Working with Fractions

Use the ▶Frac function to convert decimals or complex fractions into simplified fractions. Press the MATH button; then choose ▶Frac by pressing either 1 or ENTER.

$$\frac{2}{3} - \frac{1}{5} = \underline{\hspace{3cm}} \qquad \qquad \frac{52}{455} = \underline{\hspace{3cm}}$$

❏ Graphing Functions

Use your calculator's graphing function to find zeroes, intercepts, and points of intersection.

Graph the function $f(x) = x^2 - 4$.

Press the ⎡Y =⎤ button and enter your equation using the ⎡X,T,θ,n⎤ button for your independent variable.

Press ⎡GRAPH⎤ to see your function in the coordinate plane or ⎡2nd⎤ + ⎡GRAPH⎤ to see a table.

To change the x- and y-boundaries of the visible graph, press ⎡WINDOW⎤ and adjust accordingly.

Press ⎡TRACE⎤ and use the arrow keys to follow the coordinates on the line.

Press ⎡2nd⎤ and ⎡TRACE⎤ to bring up the CALC menu, and select the VALUE feature. Enter any x-value to see its position and corresponding y-value.

What is the value of y when x = 1.5? _____

What are the coordinates of the function's x-intercepts? _____  _____

Find the intersections of $f(x) = x^2 - 4$ and $g(x) = x - 2$.

Enter both functions and graph them.

Press ⎡2nd⎤ and ⎡TRACE⎤ to bring up the CALC menu, and select the INTERSECT feature.

Use the up/down and ⎡ENTER⎤ keys to choose the two functions whose intercept(s) you wish to calculate, and use the left/right keys to select points near the intersection.

Press ⎡ENTER⎤ one more time to calculate the intersection.

How many times to $g(x)$ and $g(x)$ intersect? _____

What are the coordinates of the intersection(s)? _____

❏ While we can't list all the circumstances in which your calculator's advanced functions might be useful, it's worthwhile to explore its various menus and attempt to use your calculator in creative ways as you practice with ACT Math problems.

## PUT IT TOGETHER

Use your calculator to solve the following:

1. When $y = \dfrac{1}{3}$, what is the value of $\dfrac{1}{y} + 2y$ ?

   A. 1

   B. $3\dfrac{2}{3}$

   C. 5

   D. $6\dfrac{1}{3}$

   E. 9

2. Which of the following is an equation of the line that passes through (8,–3) and (–4,–7) in the standard $(x,y)$ coordinate plane?

   > Use your graphing function to Plug In each equation.

   F. $y = \dfrac{1}{3}x - \dfrac{17}{3}$

   G. $y = \dfrac{1}{3}x - \dfrac{1}{3}$

   H. $y = \dfrac{1}{3}x - 3$

   J. $y = -\dfrac{1}{3}x - \dfrac{1}{3}$

   K. $y = \dfrac{1}{3}x + \dfrac{17}{3}$

3. A rectangular prism has a length of $(x + 3)$ feet, a width of $(x - 3)$ feet, and a height of $(x - 1)$ feet. Which of the following is an expression for the volume, in cubic feet, of the rectangular prism?

   > What's the algebraic expression for the volume of this prism? Use your graphing function to check the multiple choice answers against that expression.

   A. $3x + 9$
   B. $3x - 1$
   C. $x^3 + 9$
   D. $x^3 - 3x^2 - 3x + 9$
   E. $x^3 - x^2 - 9x + 9$

# Pre-Algebra

- ❏ Vocabulary and Foundations
- ❏ Multiples, Factors, and Divisibility
- ❏ Fractions
- ❏ Ratios
- ❏ Proportions
- ❏ Exponents
- ❏ Roots
- ❏ Digits and Scientific Notation
- ❏ Percents
- ❏ Absolute Value
- ❏ Sequences
- ❏ Averages (Arithmetic Mean)
- ❏ Median and Mode
- ❏ Combinations
- ❏ Probability

# Vocabulary and Foundations

❑ An **integer** is any positive or negative whole number or zero.

{..., –3, –2, –1, 0, 1, 2, 3, ...}

❑ A **digit** is any whole number from 0 to 9.

{0, 1, 2, 3, 4, 5, 6, 7, 8, 9} is the set of all digits.

❑ An **odd number** is an integer that is not divisible by 2.

{... –5, –3, –1, 1, 3, 5,...}

An **even number** is an integer that is divisible by 2.

{... –6, –4, –2, 0, 2, 4, 6,...}

Even and odd integers follow certain rules when added, subtracted, or multiplied.

even ± even = even               even × even = even

even ± odd = odd                 even × odd = even

odd ± odd = even                 odd × odd = odd

❑ **Consecutive numbers** are whole numbers that increase or decrease incrementally by 1.

{31, 32, 33, 34} and {–2, –1, 0, 1, 2, 3, 4, 5} are sets of consecutive numbers.

Consecutive numbers can be represented algebraically.

Consecutive integers:              $x, x + 1, x + 2...$
Consecutive odd or even integers:  $x, x + 2, x + 4,...$

❑ A fraction with a denominator equal to 0 is said to be **undefined**.

A fraction with a numerator equal to 0 and a non-zero denominator is always equal to 0.

❑ A **positive number** is any number that is greater than 0.

A **negative number** is any number that is less than 0.

Zero is neither positive nor negative.

Negative numbers follow certain rules when being added, subtracted, multiplied, or divided.

Adding a negative number is the same as subtracting a positive number.

Subtracting a negative number is the same as adding a positive number.

A negative number multiplied or divided by a negative number gives a positive number.

A negative number multiplied by a positive number (or vice versa) gives a negative number.

A negative number divided by a positive number (or vice versa) gives a negative number.

❑ A **sum** is the result of an addition.

❑ A **difference** is the result of a subtraction.

❑ A **product** is the result of a multiplication.

❑ A **quotient** is the result of a division.

A **dividend** is the number being divided in a division.

A **divisor** is the number dividing in a division.

$$\text{divisor} \overline{\smash{)}\text{dividend}}^{\text{quotient}}$$

❑ A **base** is a number being raised to an exponent.

An **exponent** is the number of times you multiply a base by itself.

# Multiples, Factors, and Divisibility    (0-2 per test, Ⓔ Ⓜ H )

Multiples, factors, and divisibility questions rely on knowing the definitions of key terms. These concepts are not often tested directly, but are essential knowledge for basic calculations throughout the ACT Mathematics Test.

❑ A **multiple** of an integer is any integer that is divisible by that integer.

List four multiples of 4: _____ _____ _____ _____

❑ A number is a **factor** of an integer if it divides evenly into that integer.

List two unique pairs of factors of 24: _____ _____

❑ A number is **divisible** by another number if it can be divided evenly by that number.

Is 25 divisible by 4? _____

❑ A **remainder** is the integer left over when you divide two numbers.

What is the remainder when 30 is divided by 7? _____

## PUT IT TOGETHER

1.  What is the least common multiple of 90, 50, and 20?

    A.  $53\frac{1}{3}$
    B.  90
    C.  160
    D.  900
    E.  90,000

    > "Easy" questions that appear toward the beginning of the Math Test can still pose a challenge. Watch out for attractors and avoid making careless mistakes.

2.  What is the largest 2-digit integer that is divisible by 11 and is a multiple of 2?

    F.  22
    G.  44
    H.  88
    J.  99
    K.  110

    > Use process of elimination. Which answer choices match the description?

3.  When a positive number $x$ is divided by 7, the remainder is 3. What is the remainder when $x$ is divided by 3?

    A.  3
    B.  2
    C.  1
    D.  0
    E.  Cannot be determined from the given information

    > Choose Numbers. What are some possible values for $x$?

# Fractions

(1-3 per test, (E)(M) H )

Fractions are used to represent portions of a whole. Fractions also represent divisions, with the numerator divided by the denominator.

Fraction skills are essential throughout all content areas of the ACT Mathematics Test.

❑ To add or subtract fractions, first adjust the fractions so they have a common denominator. Then add or subtract the numerators only.

$$\frac{3}{10}+\frac{5}{6}=$$

$$4\frac{3}{5}-2\frac{1}{2}=$$

❑ To multiply fractions, multiply straight across (numerator by numerator and denominator by denominator).

To cross-simplify before multiplying, look for common factors between the numerators and denominators of each fraction, then reduce.

$$\frac{2}{3}\times\frac{1}{7}=$$

$$\frac{3}{7}\times\frac{14}{15}=$$

❑ To divide fractions, multiply by the reciprocal of the divisor (the number you're dividing by).

$$\frac{1}{2}\div\frac{1}{3}=$$

$$12\div\frac{2}{5}=$$

Use the mnemonic "Keep, Change, Flip" to help remember the steps involved for dividing by a fraction. Keep the dividend the same, Change the operation to a multiplication, and Flip the numerator and denominator of the divisor.

## PUT IT TOGETHER

1. The expression $\dfrac{4+\dfrac{1}{9}}{1+\dfrac{1}{18}}$ is equal to which of the following?

   A. 2
   B. 3
   C. $\dfrac{74}{19}$
   D. 6
   E. $\dfrac{703}{9}$

> Sometimes the key to solving a problem is converting a value to a different form. Try rewriting whole numbers as fractions.

2. Which rational number lies exactly halfway between $\dfrac{1}{7}$ and $\dfrac{1}{5}$?

   F. $\dfrac{1}{2}$
   G. $\dfrac{1}{6}$
   H. $\dfrac{2}{35}$
   J. $\dfrac{6}{35}$
   K. $\dfrac{12}{35}$

3. If $a=\dfrac{2}{3}$, $b=\dfrac{3}{5}$, $c=\dfrac{5}{8}$, and $d=\dfrac{4}{7}$, which of the following lists $a$, $b$, $c$, and $d$ by increasing size?

   A. $a<c<b<d$
   B. $b<d<c<a$
   C. $b<a<c<d$
   D. $d<b<c<a$
   E. $d<c<b<a$

> To compare fractions, convert to a common denominator. You can also use your calculator to convert them to decimals.

SUMMIT
EDUCATIONAL
GROUP

# Ratios

(1 per test, Ⓔ Ⓜ H )

A ratio compares one quantity to another. A ratio is typically set up as a fraction.

Most ACT ratio problems ask you to determine a certain value based on a given ratio.

❑ Know how to find the ratio between a part and a whole when given a ratio between parts.

The ratio of boys to girls in a classroom is 2:3.

What fraction of the students are boys? _____

What fraction of the students are girls? _____

The total number of students in the classroom must be a multiple of _____.

❑ RATIO AND TOTAL questions. If a ratio problem gives you a ratio and a total, solve by setting up an algebraic equation or by setting up a table.

In a fruit basket, the ratio of apples to oranges is 1:2. If there are 45 pieces of fruit, how many oranges are in the basket?

Method 1: Write an algebraic equation to solve for the number of apples and oranges in the basket.

_____

Method 2: Complete the table below.

|  | Part (apples) | Part (oranges) | Whole |
|---|---|---|---|
| Ratio |  |  |  |
| Multiply by |  |  |  |
| Actual numbers |  |  |  |

❑ Ratio questions with numerical answer choices can often be solved by Plugging In.

## PUT IT TOGETHER

1.  For the line segment below, the ratio of the length of *AB* to the length of *BC* is 2:5. If it can be determined, what is the ratio of the length of *AB* to the length of *AC*?

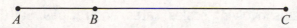

    A.  2:3
    B.  2:7
    C.  5:2
    D.  7:2
    E.  Cannot be determined from the given information

2.  Anna cuts a 50-ft speaker wire into 2 pieces. The ratio of the lengths of the pieces is 3:7. What is the length, to the nearest foot, of the shorter piece?

    F.  10
    G.  15
    H.  21
    J.  25
    K.  35

3.  The interior angles of a triangle are in the ratio of 7:11:12. What is the measure of the smallest interior angle?

    A.  42°
    B.  63°
    C.  77°
    D.  84°
    E.  99°

> What is the sum of the interior angles of a triangle?

# Proportions

A proportion is a statement that two ratios are equivalent.  $\dfrac{a}{b} = \dfrac{c}{d}$  is a proportion.

Proportion questions are typically word problems involving scales, rates, and recipes. Set up a proportion to solve word problems that compare two ratios.

❑ Solve proportions by cross-multiplying.  If $\dfrac{a}{b} = \dfrac{c}{d}$, then $a \times d = b \times c$.

Solve for $n$:

$$\frac{n}{2} = \frac{4}{1}$$

$$\frac{6}{15} = \frac{n}{10}$$

$$\frac{3.1}{1.2} = \frac{n}{3.6}$$

❑ When setting up a proportion, keep the same units in the numerators and the same units in the denominators.

The price of a watermelon is based on its weight. If a watermelon weighing 6 pounds costs $4.50, how much would an 8-pound watermelon cost?

Set up the proportion:  $\dfrac{6}{4.5} = \dfrac{\rule{1cm}{0.4pt}}{\rule{1cm}{0.4pt}}$

Cross multiply and solve: ___ × ___ = ___ × ___

## PUT IT TOGETHER

1.  A building casts a shadow 40 feet long across a level football field. At the same time of day, a student standing on the field casts an 8-foot shadow. The student is 6 feet tall. What is the height, in feet, of the building?

    A.  5

    B.  $10\dfrac{2}{3}$

    C.  30

    D.  48

    E.  $53\dfrac{1}{3}$

2.  On a map, the lengths of three stretches of walking paths are 5, 8, and 11 inches. The shortest path has an actual length of 880 yards. Which of the following is the actual length, in yards, of the longest path?

    F.  80

    G.  110

    H.  176

    J.  1408

    K.  1936

    > Can you use Process of Elimination based on whether the answer should be greater than or less than 880?

3.  A slug travels at a constant rate of 50 yards per hour. At this rate, which of the following is the closest to the number of *feet* the slug travels in 2 *minutes*?

    A.  $\dfrac{5}{3}$

    B.  5

    C.  25

    D.  100

    E.  300

    > Occasionally, you will have to convert units so they match.

# Exponents

(1-2 per test, (E)(M) H )

An exponent shows the number of times that a value is multiplied by itself.

Most exponent questions are straightforward tests of whether you know the exponent rules.

❑ Memorize the following exponent rules.

$$x^a \cdot x^b = x^{a+b} \qquad\qquad \frac{x^a}{x^b} = x^{a-b} \qquad\qquad \left(x^a\right)^b = x^{ab}$$

$$\left(\frac{x}{y}\right)^a = \frac{x^a}{y^a} \qquad\qquad x^{-a} = \frac{1}{x^a} \qquad\qquad \left(xy\right)^a = x^a \cdot y^a$$

$$x^0 = 1 \qquad\qquad x^1 = x$$

Solve:

$$2^3 \times 2^2 = \qquad\qquad \frac{x}{x^3} = \qquad\qquad \left(x^3\right)^4 =$$

$$\left(\frac{1}{2}\right)^3 = \qquad\qquad 5^{-2} = \qquad\qquad \left(6xy^3\right)^2 =$$

$$7^0 = \qquad\qquad 10^1 =$$

❑ EXPONENT IS A VARIABLE questions. To solve an equation with a variable as an exponent, first make sure that each exponent has the same base. Then set the exponents equal to each other and solve.

If $2^{x+4} = 2^{2x}$, what is the value of $x$?

## PUT IT TOGETHER

1. For nonzero real numbers $x$, $y$, and $z$, the expression $\dfrac{x^7 y^2 z^3}{3x^4 y^5 z}$ is equivalent to:

   A.  $\dfrac{x^3 z^2}{3y^3}$

   B.  $\dfrac{x^3 z^3}{3y^3}$

   C.  $\dfrac{x^3 yz^3}{3y^3 z}$

   D.  $\dfrac{(xyz)^{12}}{(3xyz)^9}$

   E.  $3x^{11} y^7 z^4$

2. If $x$, $y$, and $z$ are positive integers such that $x^y = j$ and $z^y = k$, then $jk = ?$

   F.  $xz^y$

   G.  $xz^{2y}$

   H.  $(xz)^y$

   J.  $(xz)^{2y}$

   K.  $(xz)^{y^2}$

> Make sure you know all of your exponent rules.

3. $(-ab)(ab^9)^7$ is equivalent to:

   A.  $a^7 b^{63}$
   B.  $-a^7 b^{63}$
   C.  $-a^8 b^{64}$
   D.  $-a^6 b^{70}$
   E.  $-a^{64} b^{64}$

4. If $(x^{a-2})^5 = x^{15}$, what is the value of $a$?

   F.  0
   G.  1
   H.  3
   J.  5
   K.  6

# Roots

The root of a number is a value that, when multiplied by itself a certain number of times, gives the number. Think of roots as the inverse of exponents.

Roots skills are not often tested directly on the ACT, but they are important throughout the test. The key to solving ACT roots questions is knowing the roots rules and how to simplify roots.

❑ A root can be expressed using a radical sign or a fractional exponent.

$$x^{\frac{a}{b}} = \sqrt[b]{x^a}$$

$25^{\frac{1}{2}} =$ _____          $(-8)^{\frac{1}{3}} =$ _____

❑ Memorize the following rules for multiplying and dividing roots.

$$\sqrt{x} \cdot \sqrt{y} = \sqrt{xy}$$          $$\sqrt{\frac{x}{y}} = \frac{\sqrt{x}}{\sqrt{y}}$$

$\sqrt{8} \times \sqrt{16} =$ _____          $\sqrt{\frac{16}{49}} =$ _____

❑ Watch out for expressions that look equal, but aren't. Stick to your rules.

Does $\sqrt{64 + 36} = \sqrt{64} + \sqrt{36}$ ? _____

❑ Know how to simplify roots.

If a root has a perfect-square factor, rewrite as a multiplication and simplify.

Eliminate roots in denominators by multiplying both the numerator and denominator by the root.

Simplify:

$\sqrt{18} =$ _____          $\dfrac{1}{\sqrt{2}} =$ _____

$\sqrt{12x^2} =$ _____          $\dfrac{x}{\sqrt{8}} =$ _____

**PUT IT TOGETHER**

1.  What is the smallest integer greater than $\sqrt{68}$ ?

    A.  5
    B.  6
    C.  9
    D.  11
    E.  34

    > Do you need to know the exact value of $\sqrt{68}$ to solve this problem?

2.  If $\dfrac{2\sqrt{5}}{x\sqrt{5}} = \dfrac{2\sqrt{5}}{5}$, then $x = ?$

    F.  1
    G.  $\sqrt{5}$
    H.  5
    J.  $\sqrt{10}$
    K.  10

3.  $\sqrt{32} + \sqrt{98} = ?$

    A.  $11\sqrt{2}$
    B.  $12\sqrt{2}$
    C.  $2\sqrt{7} + 2\sqrt{4}$
    D.  $65\sqrt{2}$
    E.  $\sqrt{130}$

    > Can you use your calculator to solve?

4.  For positive real numbers $a$, $b$, and $c$, which of the following expressions is equivalent to $a^{\frac{1}{3}}b^{\frac{3}{4}}c^{\frac{7}{12}}$ ?

    F.  $\sqrt[4]{ab^3c^4}$
    G.  $\sqrt[12]{ab^3c^7}$
    H.  $\sqrt[12]{a^4b^3c^7}$
    J.  $\sqrt[12]{a^4b^9c^7}$
    K.  $\sqrt[19]{ab^3c^7}$

    > Find a common denominator for rational exponents.

# Digits and Scientific Notation

(0-1 per test, Ⓔ Ⓜ Ⓗ)

Digits questions and Scientific Notation questions require careful, accurate work to avoid careless mistakes. Take notes as you solve these questions and check your answers.

❏ The position of each digit in a number determines the digit's place value.

ones (or "units")

tens   tenths

hundreds   hundredths

thousands   thousandths

$$6,328.541$$

❏ In "scientific notation," a number is written so that the largest digit is in the units place, and it is multiplied by a power of 10.

$$3,642,000,000,000 = 3.642 \times 10^{12} \qquad 0.0000000146 = 10^{-9}$$

❏ To convert a number written in scientific notation to regular decimal format, simply move the decimal point according to the exponent on the 10.

If the exponent is positive, move the decimal to the right by that many places. If the exponent is negative, move the decimal to the left by that many places.

Write 0.000000000000678 in scientific notation:

Write $8.63 \times 10^6$ in decimal format:

## PUT IT TOGETHER

1.  Which of the following numbers is greatest in value?

    A.  $2.8 \times 10^{-9}$
    B.  $280 \times 10^4$
    C.  $0.28 \times 10^9$
    D.  280,000
    E.  $0.0028 \times 10^7$

2.  What percentage of the integers from 1 to 50, inclusive, have a units digit that is three times the tens digit?

    F.  3
    G.  6
    H.  12
    J.  16
    K.  24

3.  If there are $6 \times 10^7$ oxygen molecules in a volume of $3 \times 10^2$ cubic centimeters, what is the average number of oxygen molecules per cubic centimeter?

    A.  $5 \times 10^{-6}$
    B.  $2 \times 10^5$
    C.  $2 \times 10^9$
    D.  $18 \times 10^9$
    E.  $18 \times 10^{14}$

# Percents

(1-2 per test, Ⓔ Ⓜ H )

A percent is a ratio that compares a number to 100.

Most percent questions on the ACT are word problems involving changes to a certain value. Some questions can be simplified by converting percents to familiar fractions or decimals.

❑ Percents, decimals, and fractions can all be used interchangeably. Memorize common percent-fraction-decimal equivalents.

Complete the table below.

| Fraction | | | $\frac{1}{3}$ | $\frac{1}{2}$ | |
|----------|----|----|----|----|----|
| Percent | 10% | | | | 80% |
| Decimal | | 0.20 | | | |

❑ Find what percent one number is of another by dividing the part by the whole and then converting the resulting decimal to a percent.

Remember the "is over of" rule. The number next to the "is" should go in the numerator (the part). The number next to the "of" should go in the denominator (the whole).

9 is what percent of 12?

❑ PERCENT INCREASE/DECREASE questions. To find the percent increase or decrease from one number to another, divide the difference between the numbers by the original number, then convert the resulting decimal to a percent.

$$\% \text{ increase/decrease} = \frac{\text{change}}{\text{original \#}}$$

The price of a printer is marked down from $200 to $150. What is the percent markdown in price?

❑ MULTIPLE PERCENT CHANGE questions. On percentage questions that ask you to make two or more percentage changes to a number, attack one change at a time. Don't just add or subtract the percentages.

> During winter, an elk that weighed 500 lbs lost weight over a period of 2 months. In the first month, the elk lost 10% of its body weight. In the second month, it lost 10% of its body weight. By what percent did the elk's body weight decrease over the two months?
>
> What was the elk's weight after the first month? _____
>
> How much weight did the elk lose in the second month? _____
>
> How much weight did the elk lose during the two months? What percent of its original weight did it lose?

❑ If a percentage question does not give you a number to start with, you can Choose Numbers. Usually, 100 is the simplest number to use.

> The population of Smithville increased by 20% between 2001 and 2002 and by 30% between 2002 and 2003. By what percent did the population increase between 2001 and 2003?

## PUT IT TOGETHER

1.  A sweater originally priced at $60 is discounted to $48. What is the percent of discount on this sweater?

    A.  10%
    B.  12%
    C.  20%
    D.  24%
    E.  80%

2.  Art starts filling an empty tank at 6 pm. At 6:10 pm, the water level, measured from the bottom of the tank, is 50 cm. At 6:20 pm, the water level is 70 cm. By what percent did the water level rise between 6:10 pm and 6:20 pm?

    F.  25%
    G.  33%
    H.  40%
    J.  45%
    K.  70%

3.  In 2004, the price of hot dogs at a local ballpark increased 20% from the 2003 price. In 2005, hot dog prices rose 10% from the 2004 price. By what percent did the price of hot dogs increase between 2003 and 2005?

    **Since no specific price is given, try Choosing Numbers.**

    A.  22%
    B.  28%
    C.  30%
    D.  32%
    E.  33%

4.  If $x$ is 20% of $y$, then 145% of $y$ is what percent of $x$?

    **Remember the "is over of" rule.**

    F.  165%
    G.  205%
    H.  362.5%
    J.  725%
    K.  900%

# Checkpoint Review

1.  A recipe that makes 48 chocolate chip cookies requires 3 cups of
    flour, 1 cup of white sugar, 1 cup of brown sugar, and 1 cup of
    butter. If the recipe were increased to make 72 cookies, how many
    total cups of white and brown sugar would the recipe require?

    A.  $\dfrac{5}{32}$

    B.  $1\dfrac{1}{3}$

    C.  $1\dfrac{1}{2}$

    D.  2

    E.  3

2.  What is the least common denominator for the fractions $\dfrac{2}{15}$, $\dfrac{17}{80}$,

    and $\dfrac{5}{32}$?

    F.  96
    G.  480
    H.  1,200
    J.  7,680
    K.  38,400

3.  Ty must read *The Iliad* before classes start in the fall, and he puts
    off his assignment until he has only two weeks left. He reads 1/24
    of the book for each of the first 3 days, and then reads nothing for
    the next 4 days. Over the remaining days until class begins, what
    fraction of the book, on average, must Ty read per day?

    A.  $\dfrac{1}{24}$

    B.  $\dfrac{1}{12}$

    C.  $\dfrac{1}{8}$

    D.  $\dfrac{1}{7}$

    E.  $\dfrac{1}{5}$

# Checkpoint Review

4. $2x^3 \cdot 5x^7$ is equivalent to:

   F. $7x^4$
   G. $7x^{10}$
   H. $7x^{21}$
   J. $10x^{10}$
   K. $10x^{21}$

5. If $\dfrac{x}{\sqrt{5}} = \sqrt{5}$ is true, then $x =$

   A. $\sqrt{5}$
   B. 5
   C. 10
   D. $5\sqrt{5}$
   E. 25

6. 33 is what percent of 132?

   F. 400%
   G. 25%
   H. 4%
   J. 2.5%
   K. 0.4%

# Absolute Value

(1-2 per test, Ⓔ Ⓜ Ⓗ)

The absolute value of a number is the distance between the number and zero on the number line. Think of the absolute value of a number as the "positive value" of that number.

Most absolute value questions can be solved with basic algebra skills. When solving absolute value problems, be very careful with positive and negative signs.

❑ To simplify an expression within an absolute value sign, simplify just as you would simplify an expression in parentheses. Then take the absolute value of the result.

$|7(-3) + 4(5)| = $ _____

$|5 - 3| - |6 - 9| = $ _____

**PUT IT TOGETHER**

1. $-3|-6 + 7| = ?$

   A. $-39$
   B. $-3$
   C. $-2$
   D. $3$
   E. $39$

2. If $|x| = x + 2$, then $x = ?$

   F. $-4$
   G. $-2$
   H. $-1$
   J. $1$
   K. $2$

3. For one of the following values of $a$, the equation $a + |b| = 7$ has no solution for $b$. Which one?

   A. $-3$
   B. $0$
   C. $4$
   D. $5$
   E. $8$

   > Can you solve by Plugging In?

4. If $x < y$, then $|x - y|$ is equivalent to which of the following?

   F. $x + y$
   G. $-(x + y)$
   H. $\sqrt{x - y}$
   J. $x - y$
   K. $-(x - y)$

   > Choose Numbers for $x$ and $y$.

# Sequences

(1 per test, Ⓔ Ⓜ Ⓗ)

Sequence questions will usually ask you to identify a term in a sequence of numbers. It is often easy to make careless mistakes while solving sequence questions, so be careful and methodical.

Arithmetic sequences add or subtract the same number between terms. Geometric sequences multiply or divide by the same number between terms.

❑ Often, you'll be able to solve a sequence question by "brute force" – that is, by writing out the terms. If you can't write out the entire sequence, write out enough so you can see what's happening.

What is the 8th term in the arithmetic sequence whose first three terms are –1, 3, 7?

If the 2nd, 3rd, and 4th terms in a geometric sequence are –6, 12, and –24, respectively, what is the 1st term in the sequence?

❑ REPEATING SET questions. Solve repeating sets by noting the number of terms (or letters or objects) that are in the repeating set. Then use multiples of that number to help you find the term you're looking for.

The fraction 2345/9999 is equivalent to the repeating decimal $0.\overline{2345}$ . What is the 101st digit to the right of the decimal point?

Which digit is in the 4th position? _____

Which digit is in the 8th position? _____

Which digit is in any position that is a multiple of 4? _____

Which digit is in the 101st position? _____

## PUT IT TOGETHER

1.  The sixth term of an arithmetic sequence is 8, and the fifth term is
    −17. What is the first term?

    A.  −142
    B.  −117
    C.  −17
    D.  8
    E.  17

2.  The decimal representation of $\frac{1}{14}$ repeats and can be written as
    $0.0\overline{714285}$. What is the 50th digit to the right of the decimal point
    in this decimal representation?

    F.  0
    G.  1
    H.  5
    J.  7
    K.  8

3.  The first two terms in a geometric sequence are $x$ and $\frac{x}{p}$. What is
    the 500th term of this sequence?

    A.  $\dfrac{x}{p^{501}}$

    B.  $\dfrac{x}{p^{500}}$

    C.  $\dfrac{x}{p^{499}}$

    D.  $xp^{499}$
    E.  $xp^{500}$

> Try Choosing Numbers.
> Test the first few terms in the
> sequence until you recognize
> a pattern.

# Averages (Arithmetic Mean)

(1-2 per test, Ⓔ Ⓜ H )

There are three important numbers in averages questions: the number of parts, the sum of those parts, and the average itself. You will typically be given two of these numbers. You should solve for the third using one of the two formulas below.

❑ Average = $\dfrac{\text{sum of parts}}{\text{number of parts}}$

Tiffany took 5 quizzes this semester and scored 87, 93, 74, 78, and 83. What is her average quiz score?

❑ Sum of parts = (number of parts) × (average)

The average of 8 numbers is 40. What is their sum?

**PUT IT TOGETHER**

1.  A data set contains 6 elements and has a mean of 8. Five of the elements are 1, 7, 12, 13, and 15. Which of the following is the $6^{th}$ element?

    A.  0
    B.  6
    C.  7
    D.  8
    E.  12

    > If there are 6 numbers with an average of 8, what must be the sum of the numbers?

2.  Ms. Watson calculates each student's overall test score by deleting the lowest score and finding the average of the remaining scores. Blake took 5 tests this semester, earning the following scores: 83, 73, 79, 72, and 84. What overall test score did Blake earn in Ms. Watson's class?

    F.  78.0
    G.  78.2
    H.  79.5
    J.  79.75
    K.  80.0

3.  A student is taking an English class that has four tests during the semester. The student's scores on the first three tests were 76, 92, and 83. Assuming the highest possible score on a test is 100, what grade must the student get on the fourth test in order to achieve an average test grade of exactly 85 for the semester?

    > If the average of four scores is 85, what is the sum of those four scores?

    A.  85
    B.  87
    C.  89
    D.  90
    E.  The student cannot achieve an average of 85.

# Median and Mode

Median questions and mode questions appear rarely on the ACT. The key to solving these questions is staying organized and sticking to the definitions of the terms.

❑ The **median** of a set of numbers is the middle number when the numbers are arranged in order. If there is an even number of terms in a set, the median is the mean of the two middle numbers.

List A consists of the numbers 12, 15, 17, 19, and 20.

List B consists of List A as well as the numbers 24, 25, and 27.

What is the median of List A? _____

What is the median of List B? _____

❑ The **mode** of a set of numbers is the number that appears most frequently. Note that it is possible to have more than one mode in a list of numbers.

What is the mode of the set {2, 35, 23, 37, 18, 37, 49, 8, 60, 1, 38, 17, 38}? _____

❑ When you are given a number set, organize by arranging numbers from smallest to largest.

{44, 47, 19, 18, 6, 24, 12, 24, 21}

Rewrite in ascending order:

Median: _____

Mode: _____

## PUT IT TOGETHER

1.  A data set contains 9 elements and has a mode of 6. Eight of the elements are 2, 3, 3, 4, 6, 6, 7, and 9. Which of the following must be the ninth element?

    A.  3
    B.  4
    C.  6
    D.  8
    E.  14

2.  List $k$ consists of all the integers in List $j$ below and also 3 integers $x$, $y$, and $z$, where $x \leq -3$, $y = x$, and $z \geq 27$. What is the median of the integers in List $k$ ?

    List $j$: 3, 5, 8, 12, 14, 20, 23, 35, 45

    F.  8
    G.  9
    H.  12
    J.  13
    K.  14

    > Rearrange the list in ascending order, including values for $x$, $y$, and $z$.

3.  A data set has 7 elements. The 7 elements in a second data set are obtained by multiplying each element in the first data set by 8. The 7 elements in a third data set are obtained by decreasing each element of the second data set by 3. The median of the third data set is 77. What is the median of the first data set?

    A.  7
    B.  8
    C.  10
    D.  80
    E.  539

# Combinations

(0-1 per test, Ⓔ Ⓜ Ⓗ)

Combinations are used to determine the number of different possibilities that can occur in a given situation.

Most combinations questions are word problems that describe a situation involving several choices. The key to solving these questions is determining how many options are available for each choice.

❑ Calculate combinations using the Fundamental Principle of Counting: the number of possible outcomes can be found by multiplying the number of ways each event can occur.

If there are 2 candidates for class president and 3 candidates for vice president, how many different combinations of president/vice president are possible? _____

❑ In combinations where choices cannot be repeated or where order matters, there will be a decreasing number of options available.

At a movie theatre, there are 4 friends who are going to sit in a row of 6 seats. How many different ways can the friends arrange themselves in the row?

How many options does the first friend have? _____

How many options does the second friend have? _____

Multiply the numbers of options each friend would have: ____ × ____ × ____ × ____

What is the total number of arrangements? _____

❑ GEOMETRY COMBINATION questions. If a geometry question asks how many different lines can be created in a certain situation, draw the possibilities until you recognize a pattern, then find the sum.

What is the maximum number of distinct chords that can be drawn connecting the points on the circle shown below?

How many chords can be drawn from point *A*? _____

How many more chords can be drawn from point *B*? _____

Sum of different chords originating at each point:

____ + ____ + ____ + ____ + ____ = _____

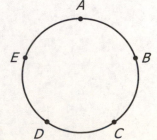

**PUT IT TOGETHER**

1.  A vehicle manufacturer produces 7 models of cars. Each model is offered with 1 of 3 levels of interior trim and 1 of 5 standard colors. How many possible combinations of vehicles are available when choosing 1 model of car, 1 level of trim, and 1 color?

    > **Remember the Fundamental Principle of Counting.**

    A.  3
    B.  15
    C.  21
    D.  26
    E.  105

2.  How many unique line segments have endpoints that are the points labeled in the figure below?

    (Note: $\overline{OP}$ and $\overline{PO}$ are the same line segment.)

    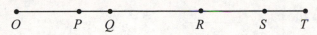

    F.  5
    G.  10
    H.  15
    J.  20
    K.  Infinitely many

3.  Eight unique paintings are to be arranged in a gallery's 8 spots. If each spot must have a painting, how many possible arrangements are there for the paintings?

    A.  8
    B.  36
    C.  56
    D.  64
    E.  40,320

# Probability

Probability is the likelihood of a certain event occurring.

Most probability questions are solved by finding two of the values in the formula below and then solving for the third value. Challenging probability questions require more calculation and consideration to find the values needed for this formula.

❑ Probability of an event happening $= \dfrac{\text{\# of ways the event can happen}}{\text{\# of possible outcomes}}$

In a pack of marbles, 9 of the marbles are white, 7 are yellow, and 4 are blue.  If a marble is picked randomly from the bag, what is the probability that the marble is NOT blue?

What is the total number of marbles in the pack?  _____

How many marbles are not blue?  _____

Create a fraction to represent the probability:

❑ Some difficult probability questions require combinations skills to calculate numbers of outcomes.

A coin is flipped 3 times, and every flip results in "heads" or "tails." What are the odds that every flip results in "tails"?

Find the number of possible outcomes:

How many outcomes satisfy the description in the question?  _____

Create a fraction to represent the probability:

## PUT IT TOGETHER

1.  A bag of jelly beans contains 5 red jelly beans, 7 orange jelly beans, and 6 yellow jelly beans. How many more yellow jelly beans must be added to the pack so that the probability of randomly picking a yellow jelly bean is $\frac{3}{5}$?

    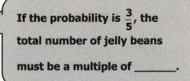

    If the probability is $\frac{3}{5}$, the total number of jelly beans must be a multiple of _____.

    A.  6
    B.  12
    C.  18
    D.  20
    E.  24

2.  An elementary-school classroom of 20 students puts names in a hat to select two class leaders for the month. There are 11 girls and 9 boys in the class. The teacher will draw one name and then, without replacement, draw a second name. Which of the following expressions gives the probability that the teacher will draw two girls' names?

    F.  $\frac{11}{20} \times \frac{10}{19}$

    G.  $\frac{10}{20} \times \frac{10}{19}$

    H.  $\frac{11}{20} \times \frac{10}{20}$

    J.  $\frac{11}{20} \times \frac{11}{19}$

    K.  $\frac{11}{19} \times \frac{10}{19}$

# Pre-Algebra Summary

Multiples, Factors, and Divisibility

❑ A multiple of an integer is any integer that is divisible by that integer.

❑ A number is a factor of an integer if it divides evenly into that integer.

❑ A number is divisible by another number if it can be divided evenly by that number.

❑ A remainder is the integer left over when you divide two numbers.

Fractions

❑ To add or subtract fractions, first adjust the fractions so they have a common denominator. Then add or subtract the numerators only.

❑ To multiply fractions, multiply straight across (numerator by numerator and denominator by denominator).

❑ To divide fractions, multiply by the reciprocal of the divisor (the number you're dividing by).

Ratios

❑ Know how to find the ratio between a part and a whole when given a ratio between parts.

Proportions

❑ Solve proportions by cross-multiplying.  If $\dfrac{a}{b} = \dfrac{c}{d}$, then $a \times d = b \times c$.

Exponents

❑ Know your rules and use your calculator to help compute numerical exponents.

Roots

❑ Know your rules and use your calculator to help compute numerical roots.

❑ If a root has a perfect-square factor, rewrite as a multiplication and simplify.

Digits and Scientific Notation

❑ The position of each digit in a number determines the digit's place value.

❑ In "scientific notation," a number is written so that the largest digit is in the units place, and it is multiplied by a power of 10.

## Percent

❑ Percents, decimals, and fractions can all be used interchangeably.

❑ Find what percent one number is of another by dividing the part by the whole and then converting the resulting decimal to a percent.

## Absolute Value

❑ To simplify an expression within an absolute value sign, simplify just as you would simplify an expression in parentheses. Then take the absolute value of the result.

## Sequences

❑ Often, you'll be able to solve a sequence question by "brute force" – that is, by writing out the terms. If you can't write out the entire sequence, write out enough so you can see what's happening.

## Averages (Arithmetic Mean)

❑ $\text{Average} = \dfrac{\text{sum of parts}}{\text{number of parts}}$

❑ Sum of parts = (number of parts) × (average)

## Median and Mode

❑ The median of a set of numbers is the middle number when the numbers are arranged in order. If there is an even number of terms in a set, the median is the mean of the two middle numbers.

❑ The mode of a set of numbers is the number that appears most frequently. Note that it is possible to have more than one mode in a list of numbers.

## Combinations

❑ Calculate combinations using the Fundamental Principle of Counting: the number of possible outcomes can be found by multiplying the number of ways each event can occur.

❑ In combinations where choices cannot be repeated or where order matters, there will be a decreasing number of options available.

## Probability

❑ $\text{Probability of an event happening} = \dfrac{\text{\# of ways the event can happen}}{\text{\# of possible outcomes}}$

SUMMIT
EDUCATIONAL
GROUP

# Pre-Algebra Practice

## Multiples, Factors, and Divisibility

Questions 1-2:     E

1.  Which of the following is an odd, positive integer?

    A.  $11(-7)$
    B.  $4^3$
    C.  $\dfrac{-6\times5}{-2}$
    D.  $\dfrac{36}{9}$
    E.  $38 - 14$

2.  What is the sum of the prime factors of 105?

    F.  8
    G.  10
    H.  15
    J.  22
    K.  29

## Fractions

Questions 3-4:     E
Questions 5-10:    M

3.  Which of the following lies between 3 and 4?

    A.  $\dfrac{8}{2}\times\dfrac{5}{3}$
    B.  $\dfrac{8}{3}\times\dfrac{5}{2}$
    C.  $\dfrac{8}{3}\times\dfrac{7}{5}$
    D.  $\dfrac{8}{5}\times\dfrac{3}{2}$
    E.  $\dfrac{8}{7}\times\dfrac{5}{3}$

4.  What is the correct ordering of $\sqrt{2}$, $\dfrac{9}{7}$, and $\dfrac{3}{2}$ from least to greatest?

   F.  $\dfrac{3}{2} < \dfrac{9}{7} < \sqrt{2}$

   G.  $\dfrac{3}{2} < \sqrt{2} < \dfrac{9}{7}$

   H.  $\dfrac{9}{7} < \sqrt{2} < \dfrac{3}{2}$

   J.  $\sqrt{2} < \dfrac{3}{2} < \dfrac{9}{7}$

   K.  $\sqrt{2} < \dfrac{9}{7} < \dfrac{3}{2}$

5.  If $q - \dfrac{2}{3} = 17 + \dfrac{4}{3}$, then $q =$

   A.  $6\dfrac{1}{3}$

   B.  $17\dfrac{2}{3}$

   C.  18

   D.  19

   E.  $19\dfrac{2}{3}$

6.  When $a + b + c = 4$, what is the value of
    $3(a+b+c) + (a+b+c)^2 - \dfrac{a+b+c}{2(a+b+c)}$?

   F.  $15\dfrac{1}{2}$

   G.  26

   H.  $27\dfrac{1}{2}$

   J.  $28\dfrac{1}{2}$

   K.  32

7. If $\dfrac{1}{y} - \dfrac{3}{4} = \dfrac{1}{2}$, what is the value of $y$?

   A. $\dfrac{1}{3}$

   B. $\dfrac{1}{2}$

   C. $\dfrac{4}{5}$

   D. $\dfrac{5}{6}$

   E. $\dfrac{4}{3}$

8. When $x = \dfrac{1}{3}$, what is the value of $\dfrac{3x^2 - 9}{3x}$?

   F. $-8\dfrac{8}{9}$

   G. $-8\dfrac{2}{3}$

   H. $\dfrac{1}{9}$

   J. $8\dfrac{8}{9}$

   K. $9\dfrac{1}{9}$

9. For what value(s) of $x$ is the expression $\dfrac{1}{(x-2)(x-3)}$ undefined?

   A. 2
   B. −3
   C. −2, −3
   D. 2, −3
   E. 2, 3

10. $\dfrac{2a}{4} + \dfrac{3a}{7} + \dfrac{4a}{14} = ?$

    **F.** $\dfrac{9a}{28}$

    **G.** $\dfrac{17a}{14}$

    **H.** $\dfrac{17a}{7}$

    **J.** $\dfrac{29a}{28}$

    **K.** $\dfrac{17a}{9}$

## Ratios

Question 11:      E
Question 12:      M

11. Three friends found $45 in the street and decide to split it in the ratio of 5:3:1. What is the amount of the largest share?

    **A.** $1
    **B.** $3
    **C.** $5
    **D.** $15
    **E.** $25

12. If the ratio of $x$ to $y$ is 5:6, and the ratio of $y$ to $z$ is 1:2, what is the ratio of $x$ to $z$?

    **F.** 1:3
    **G.** 5:12
    **H.** 3:5
    **J.** 5:3
    **K.** 5:2

## Proportions

Question 13:      E
Question 14:      M

13. Cory presented a scale drawing of the tree house he was working on to his class. In the drawing, the tree house is 15 inches wide and 12 inches tall. Cory told the class that he planned for the tree house to be 8 feet tall. Given this information, how wide did he plan for the tree house to be?

    **A.** 6 feet
    **B.** 7.5 feet
    **C.** 9 feet
    **D.** 10 feet
    **E.** 12 feet

**14.** Jen and her friends decide to sell lemonade on their street corner. They use 5 scoops of lemonade mix to make 3 pitchers of lemonade. Later, Jen decides that she and her friends will be able to sell eleven more pitchers of lemonade before it is time for supper. How many scoops of lemonade mix will be needed to make the additional eleven pitchers?

F. 5

G. $6\frac{2}{3}$

H. 7

J. $11\frac{1}{3}$

K. $18\frac{1}{3}$

## Exponents

Questions 15-16:   E
Questions 17-19:   M

**15.** $6m^3$ is the product of $3m$ and

A. 2
B. $2m$
C. $3m$
D. $2m^2$
E. $3m^2$

**16.** Which of the following expressions is equivalent to $\left(-5x^3y^4\right)^2$?

F. $-25x^6y^8$
G. $-25x^5y^6$
H. $-5x^6y^8$
J. $25x^5y^6$
K. $25x^6y^8$

**17.** If $x \neq 0$ and $\dfrac{x^{a-b}}{x^3} = x^5$ for all values of $x$, what is the value of $a - b$?

A. 7
B. 8
C. 9
D. 10
E. 15

18. If $x$ and $y$ are real numbers and $\dfrac{x^2}{y^3}$ is negative, which of the

following *must* be true about the value of $y$?

    F.   $y$ is negative.
    G.   $y$ is positive.
    H.   $y$ is a fraction.
    J.   $y$ equals $-1$.
    K.   $y$ is a prime number.

19. $\left(\dfrac{1}{3}x + y^2\right)^2 = ?$

    A.   $\dfrac{1}{3}x^2 + y^4$

    B.   $\dfrac{1}{9}x^2 + y^4$

    C.   $\dfrac{1}{3}x^2 + \dfrac{2}{3}xy^2 + y^4$

    D.   $\dfrac{1}{9}x^2 + \dfrac{1}{3}xy + y^4$

    E.   $\dfrac{1}{9}x^2 + \dfrac{2}{3}xy^2 + y^4$

## Roots

Questions 20-21:   M
Question 22:      H

20. Which of the following expressions are equivalent to $x$ for all positive real numbers $x$?

    I.    $|-x|$

    II.   $\sqrt{(-x)^2}$

    III.   $\sqrt{-(x)^2}$

    F.   I only
    G.   II only
    H.   I and II only
    J.   I and III only
    K.   I, II, and III

21. If $x$ is a real number, and $\sqrt[3]{x} = 5$, then $x - 2\sqrt{x} = ?$

    A.   15
    B.   $25 - 5\sqrt{5}$
    C.   100
    D.   $125 - 10\sqrt{5}$
    E.   $125 - 5\sqrt{5}$

**22.** If $a^2b = 12$, and $ab^3 = 54$, what is the value of $b\sqrt{a}$ ?

    **F.** $2\sqrt{3}$

    **G.** $3\sqrt{2}$

    **H.** $3\sqrt{3}$

    **J.** $4\sqrt{2}$

    **K.** $4\sqrt{3}$

## Digits & Scientific Notation

Question 23:     M

**23.** A micrometer is one millionth of a meter, or $10^{-6}$ meters. A nanometer is 1,000 times smaller than a micrometer. Which of the following expressions gives the length of a nanometer?

    **A.** $10^{-3}$ meters

    **B.** $10^{-7}$ meters

    **C.** $10^{-8}$ meters

    **D.** $10^{-9}$ meters

    **E.** $10^{-18}$ meters

## Percents

Questions 24-27:    E
Questions 25-31:    M

**24.** If $60\%$ of $x = 90$, then $x = ?$

    **F.** 54

    **G.** 108

    **H.** 126

    **J.** 150

    **K.** 540

**25.** Sally bought two shirts at a local department store for a total of $19.99, not including taxes. If there is an 8% sales tax on the shirts, to the nearest cent, how much tax did Sally have to pay on her shirts?

    **A.** $1.45

    **B.** $1.52

    **C.** $1.60

    **D.** $1.76

    **E.** $1.95

**26.** The regular price of a table is $225. If the table is on sale at 40% off, what is the sale price, in dollars, of the table?

    **F.** $90

    **G.** $125

    **H.** $135

    **J.** $150

    **K.** $185

27. If there are 2,000 ducks in a wildlife sanctuary, and 1.5% of them are mallards, how many mallards are in the sanctuary?

    A. 1.5
    B. 3
    C. 15
    D. 30
    E. 300

28. Usually, Blue Jeans Co. sells their jeans for $25 a pair. This week, however, the store is offering a deal of 5 pairs of jeans for $75. What is the percent decrease in price per pair of jeans?

    F. 10%
    G. 20%
    H. 25%
    J. 35%
    K. 40%

29. On the first day of a two-day school telethon to collect money for the Senior Class graduation party, the seniors received 250 donations. The next day, they received 30% more donations than they had on the previous day. What is the total number of donations the telethon received in the two days?

    A. 325
    B. 333
    C. 575
    D. 600
    E. 683

30. Of the 698 seniors in a certain high school, approximately 20% are in the art club. Of the seniors who are in the art club, approximately 30% paint with acrylics. Which of the following is closest to the number of seniors who paint with acrylics?

    F. 42
    G. 56
    H. 105
    J. 140
    K. 210

31. Randy's batting average increased by 20% from 1995 to 1996, and increased by 25% from 1996 to 1997. By what percent did Randy's batting average increase from 1995 to 1997?

    A. 5%
    B. 45%
    C. 48%
    D. 50%
    E. 55%

## Absolute Value

Questions 32-33:    E
Question 34:        M

**32.** $|8 - 6| - |6 - 8| = ?$

    **F.** −12
    **G.** −4
    **H.** −6
    **J.** 0
    **K.** 12

**33.** What is the value of $|-13| - |2 - 39|$?

    **A.** −50
    **B.** −24
    **C.** 24
    **D.** 50
    **E.** 58

**34.** $|-3|^3 + |(-3)^3| =$

    **F.** 0
    **G.** 9
    **H.** 18
    **J.** 27
    **K.** 54

## Sequences

Questions 35-37:    M
Question 38:        H

**35.** The first term in a sequence is 1, and the second term in the sequence is 3. Each term thereafter is the square of the difference of the two terms immediately preceding it. What is the fifth term in the sequence?

    **A.** 1
    **B.** 4
    **C.** 6
    **D.** 8
    **E.** 9

**36.** Which of the following statements is NOT true about the arithmetic sequence 4, 1, −2, −5,…?

    **F.**   The fifth term is −8.
    **G.**   The square of the seventh term is 121.
    **H.**   The ninth term is −20.
    **J.**   The positive difference between the first and fifth term is 12.
    **K.**   The common difference between adjacent terms is −3.

$A, B, C, D, E, A, B, C, D, E, \ldots$

**37.** If the above pattern continues, which letter will fall in the 89th position?

   **A.** $A$
   **B.** $B$
   **C.** $C$
   **D.** $D$
   **E.** $E$

**38.** A scientist studying a rabbit population saw the number of rabbits start at 2, and increase to 10 after 1 year, 50 after 2 years, and 250 after three years. If this pattern continues, what would the population of rabbits be after 8 years?

   **F.** $8 \times 50$
   **G.** $5^8$
   **H.** $2 \times 5^7$
   **J.** $2 \times 5^8$
   **K.** $2 \times 5^9$

## Average, Median, & Mode

Questions 39-44:    M

**39.** Molly's scores for her first four rounds of golf were 76, 79, 81, and 88. Her goal was for her average to be an 80 after her fifth round. If Molly met her goal exactly, then what score did she earn in her final round?

   **A.** 70
   **B.** 74
   **C.** 75
   **D.** 76
   **E.** 78

**40.** During an average week, Steve's Sporting Goods rents 15 bikes each weekday and 22 bikes each Saturday and Sunday. What is the average number of bikes that Steve's rents each day?

   **F.** 15
   **G.** 16
   **H.** 17
   **J.** 20
   **K.** 22

**41.** The average of four numbers is 15. After three new numbers are added, the average of the seven numbers is 12. What is the sum of the three new numbers?

    **A.** 24
    **B.** 26
    **C.** 27
    **D.** 32
    **E.** 35

**42.** In a set of seven different numbers, which of the following CANNOT affect the value of the median?

    **F.** Increasing the two smallest numbers
    **G.** Dividing each number by three
    **H.** Increasing the two largest numbers
    **J.** Multiplying each number by two
    **K.** Decreasing the largest number by 2

Questions 43 and 44 refer to following table.

### MATH LEAGUE FINAL EXAM

| Student | Right | Wrong | Unfinished | Score |
|---------|-------|-------|------------|-------|
| Chris | 6 | 2 | 2 | |
| Melanie | 6 | 4 | 0 | |
| Erik | 5 | 1 | 4 | |
| Fiona | 2 | 4 | 4 | |
| Pat | 1 | 1 | 8 | |

**43.** The table above shows the final exam standings for each of the students in the Math League. Each student's score is calculated as follows: 4 points are awarded for each right answer, 2 points are subtracted for each wrong answer, and 0 points are awarded for questions left unfinished. Who received the median score?

    **A.** Chris
    **B.** Melanie
    **C.** Erik
    **D.** Fiona
    **E.** Pat

**44.** What is the average of the five scores in the table above?

    **F.** 11.2
    **G.** 12
    **H.** 12.2
    **J.** 12.4
    **K.** 13

## Combinations

Questions 45-46: E
Question 47: M

45. At a cafeteria, there are 3 choices for lunch on Monday, 2 choices on Tuesday, and 5 choices on Wednesday. How many different combinations of lunches are possible during these three days?

    A. 10
    B. 11
    C. 13
    D. 30
    E. 36

46. Two friends use a secret code that involves 5 letters, 7 numbers, and 3 shapes. Each code word has one letter, one number, and one shape. The letter must be in the first spot, the number must be in the second spot, and the shape must be in the third spot. How many combinations of letters, numbers, and shapes are possible?

    F. 15
    G. 17
    H. 38
    J. 77
    K. 105

47. There are twenty people running for three senior class offices: president, vice president, and treasurer. Assuming that one person can hold only one office, how many different combinations of president, vice president, and treasurer are possible?

    A. $20^2$
    B. $19 \times 18 \times 17$
    C. $19^3$
    D. $20 \times 19 \times 18$
    E. $20^3$

## Probability

Question 48:        E
Questions 49-50:    M

**48.** A roulette wheel has 38 slots numbered 1 through 36, 0, and 00. What is the probability of a ball rolled on the roulette wheel stopping in a slot numbered between 1 and 19, inclusive?

F. $\dfrac{1}{38}$

G. $\dfrac{1}{4}$

H. $\dfrac{1}{3}$

J. $\dfrac{1}{2}$

K. $\dfrac{2}{3}$

**49.** A circle is divided into three portions. One portion has a central angle of 60°, one has a central angle of 90°, and the third has a central angle of 210°. If a point is picked at random from within the circle, what is the probability that it will be in the largest portion of the circle?

A. $\dfrac{1}{6}$

B. $\dfrac{1}{4}$

C. $\dfrac{5}{12}$

D. $\dfrac{1}{2}$

E. $\dfrac{7}{12}$

**50.** An integer from 500 through 999, inclusive, is chosen at random. What is the probability that the number chosen will have 0 as at least 1 digit?

F. $\dfrac{19}{500}$

G. $\dfrac{20}{500}$

H. $\dfrac{95}{500}$

J. $\dfrac{100}{500}$

**K.** $\dfrac{195}{500}$

## Miscellaneous

Questions 51-56: E
Questions 57-70: M
Questions 71-75: H

**51.** If $a = 6$, what is the positive difference between $3 - a$ and $|3 - a|$?

    **A.** $-6$
    **B.** $-3$
    **C.** $0$
    **D.** $3$
    **E.** $6$

**52.** What is the least common multiple of 50, 80, and 90?

    **F.** $50$
    **G.** $220$
    **H.** $360$
    **J.** $3600$
    **K.** $360,000$

**53.** The expression $\left(10 + \dfrac{1}{3}\right) \div \left(1 + \dfrac{1}{6}\right)$ is equal to which of the

following?

    **A.** $5$
    **B.** $6$
    **C.** $\dfrac{62}{7}$
    **D.** $12$
    **E.** $\dfrac{217}{3}$

**54.** $5x^4 \cdot 7x^2$ is equivalent to:

    **F.** $12x^2$
    **G.** $12x^6$
    **H.** $12x^8$
    **J.** $35x^6$
    **K.** $35x^8$

**55.** A bowl contains 7 red marbles, 3 green marbles, and 5 blue marbles, all of the same shape and size. When 1 marble is randomly picked from the bowl, what is the probability that it is blue?

A. $\dfrac{1}{15}$

B. $\dfrac{1}{5}$

C. $\dfrac{1}{3}$

D. $\dfrac{8}{15}$

E. $\dfrac{2}{3}$

**56.** What is 150% of 264?

F. 39.6
G. 176
H. 396
J. 3,960
K. 39,600

**57.** What is the next term after $\dfrac{1}{9}$ in the geometric sequence

$-81, 9, -1, \dfrac{1}{9} \ldots$ ?

A. $-\dfrac{1}{27}$

B. $-\dfrac{1}{81}$

C. 0

D. $\dfrac{1}{27}$

E. $\dfrac{1}{3}$

**58.** Shelby's cookie recipe calls for $2\frac{3}{4}$ cups of flour and $1\frac{2}{3}$ cups of sugar. In cups, what is the total dry volume of these ingredients?

    **F.** $1\frac{1}{12}$

    **G.** $2\frac{6}{7}$

    **H.** $3\frac{3}{4}$

    **J.** $4\frac{5}{12}$

    **K.** $4\frac{1}{2}$

**59.** Which of the following is the least common denominator for the expression below?

$$\frac{1}{19\times29\times59^2}+\frac{1}{19^2\times29}+\frac{1}{19\times29^3}$$

    **A.** $19\times29$
    **B.** $19\times29\times59$
    **C.** $19\times29\times59^2$
    **D.** $19^2\times29^3\times59^2$
    **E.** $19^4\times29^5\times59^2$

**60.** An architect is designing a city block that will contain plots for six buildings, constructed side by side, as shown in the figure below. Each building will measure a different height. City zoning laws dictate that the three shortest buildings must be built on the southernmost half of the block, and the three tallest buildings must be built on the northernmost half of the block. How many different building configurations are possible if the architect is to design the city block to comply with this zoning law?

    **F.** 8
    **G.** 12
    **H.** 24
    **J.** 36
    **K.** 720

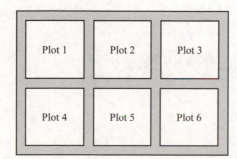

**61.** Eric is taking inventory of batteries. There are 30 batteries in a pack, and Eric has 5 partially-filled packs. 1 pack is $\frac{1}{2}$ full, 1 pack is $\frac{3}{5}$ full, and 3 packs are $\frac{4}{5}$ full. How many batteries are in the 5 partially-filled packs?

 A. 57
 B. 93
 C. 105
 D. 120
 E. 150

**62.** The domain of the function $f(x) = \frac{2}{17-|x|}$ contains all real values of $x$ EXCEPT:

 F. 0
 G. 0 and 17
 H. 0 and $\frac{1}{17}$
 J. $-\frac{1}{17}$ and $\frac{1}{17}$
 K. $-17$ and 17

**63.** The positive integer $x!$ is defined as the product of all the positive integers less than or equal to $x$. For example, $4! = (1)(2)(3)(4) = 24$. What is the value of the expression $\frac{8!}{4!2!}$?

 A. 1
 B. 4
 C. 8
 D. 840
 E. 40,320

**64.** The first 3 terms of a geometric sequence are 18, 30, and 50. What is the next term of the sequence?

 F. 62
 G. 70
 H. 78
 J. 80
 K. $83\frac{1}{3}$

65. A pair of sneakers has a regular price of $89.95 before taxes. It goes on sale at 40% below the regular price. Before taxes are added, what is the sale price of the pair of sneakers?

   A. $87.45
   B. $53.97
   C. $49.95
   D. $44.98
   E. $35.98

66. For all $x \neq 0$, the expression $\dfrac{4x^4}{4x^7}$ equals:

   F. $\dfrac{1}{3}$
   G. $-x^3$
   H. $x^3$
   J. $-\dfrac{1}{x^3}$
   K. $\dfrac{1}{x^3}$

| | Parallel Bars Score |
|---|---|
| Wanda | 5 |
| Shauna | 3.5 |
| Lynn | 3 |
| Mariah | 2 |
| Anne | 2.5 |

67. The table above shows the Parallel Bars scores of the 5 Varsity gymnasts. 4 members of the Junior Varsity team also competed in the Parallel Bars event. If the Junior Varsity team average was 2.75, what was the average score for all 9 gymnasts?

   A. 2.95
   B. 3
   C. 3.2
   D. 3.25
   E. 3.5

68. Rosalind is trying to find a drill bit to match a previously-drilled hole. The $\frac{7}{8}$-inch drill bit is too large, and the $\frac{13}{16}$-inch drill bit is too small. Which of the following could be the size of the drill bit that will recreate the previously-drilled hole's diameter?

F. $\frac{3}{4}$-inch

G. $\frac{25}{32}$-inch

H. $\frac{27}{32}$-inch

J. $\frac{29}{64}$-inch

K. $\frac{57}{64}$-inch

69. Which of the following is a rational number?

A. $\sqrt{3}$

B. $\left(\sqrt{\pi}\right)^2$

C. $\sqrt{8}$

D. $\sqrt{\frac{7}{49}}$

E. $\sqrt{\frac{81}{25}}$

70. Georgia bought a pair of boots that had an original price of $110.00. The store offered at 30% discount on the original price of the boots, and Georgia paid 8% sales tax on the discounted price of the boots. How much did Georgia pay for the boots, including tax?

F. $68.20
G. $70.84
H. $83.16
J. $85.80
K. $134.20

**71.** There are 18 cards face down on the table: 6 clubs, 5 diamonds, 4 spades, and 3 hearts. What is the probability that a card chosen at random is NOT a club?

A. $\dfrac{1}{18}$

B. $\dfrac{1}{12}$

C. $\dfrac{1}{9}$

D. $\dfrac{3}{5}$

E. $\dfrac{2}{3}$

**72.** The seven integers below add up to 600:

$x - 3$
$x - 2$
$x - 1$
$x$
$x + 1$
$x + 2$
$x + 8$

What is the value of $x$?

F. 83
G. 84
H. 85
J. 86
K. 87

**73.** In the real numbers, what is the solution of the equation
$27^{3x-1} = 9^{2+x}$ ?

A. $\dfrac{1}{7}$

B. $\dfrac{5}{8}$

C. 1

D. $\dfrac{3}{2}$

E. 7

74. In the equation $j = \dfrac{4}{2-k}$, $k$ represents a positive number such that $k < 2$. As $k$ approaches 2, the value of $j$:

   F.  gets closer and closer to 0.
   G.  gets closer and closer to 2.
   H.  gets closer and closer to 4.
   J.  remains constant.
   K.  gets larger and larger.

75. What is the sum of the first 60 terms of the arithmetic sequence 51, 52, 53, ...?

   A.  220
   B.  1530
   C.  3060
   D.  4830
   E.  5610

# Elementary Algebra

- ❑ Algebraic Expressions

- ❑ Equations

- ❑ Inequalities

- ❑ Translation

- ❑ Word Problems

# Algebraic Expressions

(2-3 per test, Ⓔ M H )

An algebraic expression is a phrase that contains one or more terms and does not contain an equal sign. An expression can include constants, variables, and operating symbols (such as addition signs and exponents).

Most expressions questions are relatively simple and straightforward. However, they may require several steps, so make sure you work carefully and follow the Order of Operations.

❏ Simplify an expression by combining like terms.

Simplify:

$(7k^3 + 3k + 5 + 5k - 5) - (4k + 4k + 4k) =$ _____

❏ Use the **distributive property** to multiply a single term by an expression inside parentheses:

$-2(x^2 - 7x + 1) =$ _____

❏ When multiplying two binomials, each term must be multiplied by each term in the other binomial.

Remember the **FOIL** method for multiplying two binomials: multiply the first terms, outside terms, inside terms, and last terms.

$(3y + 6)(y - 5) =$ _____

❏ Factoring is expanding in reverse. Find common factors among the terms in an expression and rewrite using a multiplication.

Factor:

$(8x^3 - 12x^2 + 20x^4) =$ _____

**PUT IT TOGETHER**

1. For all $x$, $-2(x+4) + x(x+2) = ?$

   A. $x^2 - 8$
   B. $x^2 + 8$
   C. $-4x + 8$
   D. $x^2 + 4x - 8$
   E. $x^2 - 4x - 8$

2. $5y^2 - 2y + 3 - (3y+2)(y-4) = ?$

   F. $2y^2 + 8y + 11$
   G. $2y^2 - 8y + 11$
   H. $2y^2 - 8y - 5$
   J. $8y^2 - 12y - 5$
   K. $8y^2 + 12y + 11$

3. $(a^3 + 3a^2 + 2a)(a-1) = ?$

   A. $a^4 + 2a^3 - a^2 - 2a$
   B. $a^4 + 2a^3 + 5a^2 - 2a$
   C. $a^4 + 3a^3 + 2a^2 - 2a$
   D. $a^4 + 3a^3 + 2a^2 + 2a$
   E. $a^4 + 3a^3 - 2a$

4. $(2x - 3) - (-4x + 9)$ is equivalent to:

   F. $3(2x + 6)$
   G. $3(2x + 2)$
   H. $3(2x - 2)$
   J. $3(2x - 4)$
   K. $3(2x - 12)$

# Equations

(1-2 per test, Ⓔ Ⓜ H )

An equation is a statement that two expressions are equal. An equation must be kept balanced. If you do something to one side, you must do the same thing to the other side.

Equations questions can often be solved by Plugging In or Choosing Numbers. Although these questions are typically not challenging, the skill of balancing equations is very important for other, more difficult questions throughout the test.

❑ To solve for a variable, isolate the variable on one side of the equal sign.

If $2x + 1 = 5$, what is the value of $x$?

❑ If an equation contains fractions, clear them by multiplying both sides of the equation by a common denominator.

If $\frac{3}{4}x - 1 = 2$, what is the value of $x$?

Multiply both sides by 4: _____

Isolate $3x$ on one side of the equation: _____

Solve for $x$: _____

❑ Some equation problems can be quickly solved by Plugging In.

**PUT IT TOGETHER**

1.  For which of the following values of $a$ does $\dfrac{a+2}{10-a} - 2 = a$?

    Can you solve by Plugging In?

    Can you also solve this the old-fashioned way?

    A.  $-9$
    B.  $-1$
    C.  $0$
    D.  $1$
    E.  $9$

2.  Given the equation $\dfrac{x}{6} - \dfrac{1}{9} = -\dfrac{4}{3}$, $x$ must lie between which of the following numbers?

    F.  $-7$ and $-9$
    G.  $-4$ and $-7$
    H.  $-1$ and $-2$
    J.  $3$ and $6$
    K.  $7$ and $9$

3.  For the equation $3x - f = g$, which of the following expressions gives $x$ in terms of $g$ and $f$?

    A.  $\dfrac{(g+f)}{3}$

    B.  $\dfrac{(g+3)}{f}$

    C.  $\dfrac{(g-f)}{3}$

    D.  $\dfrac{(f-g)}{3}$

    E.  $g + f + 3$

4.  If $a = \dfrac{4b}{c^3}$, what happens to the value of $a$ when both $b$ and $c$ are doubled?

    Try to solve by Choosing Numbers.

    F.  $a$ is not changed
    G.  $a$ is halved
    H.  $a$ is divided by 4
    J.  $a$ is doubled
    K.  $a$ is multiplied by 6

SUMMIT
EDUCATIONAL
GROUP

# Inequalities

An inequality is a statement that an expression is less than or greater than another expression.

Inequalities can be solved with most of the same skills used for solving equations, but inequalities questions are usually more challenging and abstract. Inequalities questions often connect inequalities to other concepts, such as the number line or absolute values.

❑ Inequalities can be solved like equations, with one important difference: if you multiply or divide both sides by a negative number, you must switch the direction of the inequality sign.

Solve for $x$:

$4 - 3x < -22$

❑ Some inequality problems can be solved by Choosing Numbers to test which values satisfy the inequality.

Which of the following is a solution for the inequality $5x - 1 > 3x + 7$?

A.  $x < -2$
B.  $x < 2$
C.  $x > 2$
D.  $x < 4$
E.  $x > 4$

Does $x = 1$ satisfy the inequality? _____

Does $x = 3$ satisfy the inequality? _____

Does $x = 5$ satisfy the inequality? _____

Which answer choice matches these results? _____

### PUT IT TOGETHER

1.  Which of the following shows the solution set for the inequality $2x - 1 \geq 5$?

    > **Try to use Process of Elimination by testing values for *x*.**

    **A.**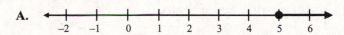

    **B.**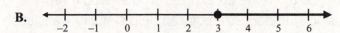

    **C.**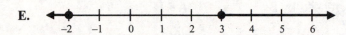

    **D.**

    **E.**

2.  Given real numbers $p, q, r, s,$ and $t$ such that $t < q, p < t, p > s,$ and $s > r$, which of these numbers is the smallest?

    **F.**  $p$
    **G.**  $q$
    **H.**  $r$
    **J.**  $s$
    **K.**  $t$

3.  Let $j$ and $k$ be numbers such that $j < k < 0$. Which of the following inequalities *must* be true for all such $j$ and $k$?

    > **Try to solve by Choosing Numbers for *j* and *k*.**

    **A.**  $j - k > k - 6$

    **B.**  $\dfrac{k}{j} > 1$

    **C.**  $\dfrac{1}{j} < \dfrac{1}{k}$

    **D.**  $j^2 < k^2$

    **E.**  $-j > -k$

4.  If $x \leq 7$, then $|x - 7| = ?$

    **F.**  $0$
    **G.**  $x + 7$
    **H.**  $x - 7$
    **J.**  $-x - 7$
    **K.**  $-x + 7$

# Translation

When math problems are described by words, rather than shown in mathematical terms, you need to know how to translate those words into the language of math.

The most common translation questions ask you to create an expression that would represent a certain real-world situation. Using the Choosing Numbers strategy can help simplify translation questions that might otherwise be very challenging.

❏ Learn to recognize common translations.

| | |
|---|---|
| The sum of X and Y; X increased by Y; X more than Y | X + Y |
| The difference between A and B; A decreased by B | A − B |
| The product of J and K | JK |
| The quotient of M and N | M ÷ N |
| Dave is at most 14 years old. | D ≤ 14 |
| A bus travels at a speed greater than or equal to 50 mph | B ≥ 50 |
| There are 37 people in line at the RMV. | P = 37 |

❏ Translate math problems word-by-word to create equations.

30 is 2 times the sum of 4 and what number?

Assign a variable to the unknown value: _____

Translate into an equation: _____

Solve for the unknown value: _____

❏ CREATE AN EXPRESSION questions.  For word problems that ask for an expression to represent a situation, check your answer by Choosing Numbers for variables.

The cruising speed of a commercial jet exceeds 4 times the top speed of a passenger train by 50 mph. The speed of the train is $n$ mph.

Write an expression to represent the speed of the jet in terms of $n$: _____

Assume $n = 100$. According to the problem, what would be the speed of the jet? _____

Does this match the value of your expression when $n = 100$? _____

## PUT IT TOGETHER

1. Which of the following is an expression for $e$ decreased by the sum of $f$ and 12?

   A. $e - f + 12$
   B. $e - (f + 12)$
   C. $f - 12 + e$
   D. $(f + 12) - e$
   E. $e - 12 + f$

2. To attend a professional training seminar, members pay $100 per session while nonmembers pay $125 per session. What are the total fees, in dollars, for 13 member sessions and $K$ nonmember sessions?

   F. $K + 13$
   G. $(125 + 100)K$
   H. $125(K + 100)$
   J. $125(K + 13)$
   K. $125K + 13(100)$

3. At a bowling alley, one can play five strings of bowling for $12.00. Each additional string costs $3.00. Which of the following expressions, in dollars, gives the cost of bowling $k$ strings, given that $k > 5$?

   A. $12 \times 3(k - 5)$
   B. $12 + 3k$
   C. $12 + 3(k - 5)$
   D. $15k - 12$
   E. $15k$

   > Choose Numbers for $k$.

4. The larger of two numbers is greater than 3 times the smaller number but less than 4 times the smaller number. If the smaller of the two numbers is 60, then the larger number must be

   F. 5
   G. between 15 and 20
   H. less than 180
   J. between 180 and 240
   K. 240

# Word Problems

(4-5 per test, Ⓔ Ⓜ Ⓗ)

❑ Word problems appear frequently throughout the Mathematics test. Most ACT math skills are occasionally tested as word problems. The key to solving most ACT word problems is working systematically to determine your objective, find relevant information, and translate.

❑ Follow these broad steps to solve ACT word problems:

1. Determine what information is needed in order to solve the word problem.

2. Break down the problem into manageable parts. Consider what you can do with the information provided.

3. Pick variables to represent unknown values, and translate the word problem into algebraic expressions and equations.

4. Solve for one value at a time until you find your final answer.

5. Check your answer! Is it what the question asked for? Does it make sense with the given information?

Jeb's pickup truck travels an average of 12 miles per gallon of gasoline, and Edith's hybrid vehicle travels an average of 50 miles per gallon of gasoline. Both of them drive 600 miles from Indianapolis to Minneapolis. During their trips, how many more gallons will Jeb's pickup truck consume than Edith's hybrid vehicle?

1. In order to calculate the final answer, what values do you need?


2. What information provided in the problem can be used to find the answer?


3. Translate the word problem into algebraic equations that will help you find the needed values.


4. Solve for unknown values.


5. Are you done? Solve for the final answer.

❑ DISTANCE = RATE × TIME questions. Most word problems involving "miles per hour" can be solved using this formula.

> Michelle completes a 240-mile drive in 4 hours. If she continues at this rate, how many miles will she travel in the next 3 hours?

❑ FORMULA questions. Word problems that provide complex formulas can be solved by simply plugging in values for variables, which are provided in the problem.

> Given the formula $C = \dfrac{5}{9}(F - 32)$, where $C$ is the temperature in degrees Celsius and $F$ is the temperature in degrees Fahrenheit, what is the corresponding temperature in degrees Celsius for a temperature of 50 degrees Fahrenheit?

❑ For some word problems, you can use the answer choices to work backward. This method is really just Plugging In for word problems.

**PUT IT TOGETHER**

1. Mark's 5-hour bike ride was 64 miles long. For the first two hours, he averaged 14 miles per hour. Which of the following was his average speed, in miles per hour, for the remainder of his bike ride?

   A. 10
   B. 12
   C. 13
   D. 15
   E. 18

2. Mary made a batch of brownies for her family. On the first evening, they ate $\frac{1}{2}$ of the brownies. The second evening, they ate $\frac{1}{2}$ of the brownies that were left. On the third evening, they ate $\frac{1}{4}$ of what was left. If there were 6 brownies left after the third evening, how many brownies were there initially?

   > Many word problems can be solved by Plugging In.

   F. 18
   G. 24
   H. 32
   J. 48
   K. 96

3. A moving company charges truck rental fees of $69.45 per day, including 50 miles of driving per day. Any mileage above 50 miles per day incurs a fee of $0.29/mile. What is the cost of renting a truck for 3 days and moving 600 miles? (note: no sales tax is involved.)

   A. $382.35
   B. $367.85
   C. $338.85
   D. $243.45
   E. $228.95

4.  A university surveyed its students about their modes of
    transportation. Of the 350 students who responded to the survey,
    232 wrote that they used public transportation, 113 wrote that they
    used personal vehicles, and 57 said that they used both. How many
    of the 350 students used public transportation, personal vehicles, or
    both?

    F.  57
    G.  176
    H.  233
    J.  288
    K.  293

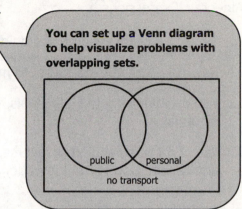

You can set up a Venn diagram
to help visualize problems with
overlapping sets.

public    personal

no transport

5.  Compound interest is calculated using the formula $T = d(1 + i)^c$,
    where $T$ is the total value of an investment account, $d$ is the value
    of the deposit, $i$ is the rate of interest each compounding period,
    and $c$ is the number of compounding periods. Which of the
    following values is closest to the calculated value of an investment
    account with an initial deposit of $50,000, after 18 years of 2.5%
    yearly interest compounded annually?

    A.  $51,250
    B.  $77,983
    C.  $872,500
    D.  $922,500
    E.  $2,775,558

# Elementary Algebra Summary

## Algebraic Expressions

❑ Simplify an expression by combining like terms.

❑ Use the distributive property to multiply a single term by an expression inside parentheses:

❑ When multiplying two binomials, each term must be multiplied be each term in the other binomial.

❑ Factoring is expanding in reverse.  Find common factors among the terms in an expression and rewrite using a multiplication.

## Equations

❑ To solve for a variable, isolate the variable on one side of the equal sign.

## Inequalities

❑ Inequalities can be solved like equations, with one important difference: if you multiply or divide both sides by a negative number, you must switch the direction of the inequality sign.

## Translation

❑ Translate math problems word-by-word to create equations.

## Word Problems

❑ Follow these broad steps to solve ACT word problems:

1. Determine what information is needed in order to solve the word problem.

2. Break down the problem into manageable parts. Consider what you can do with the information provided.

3. Pick variables to represent unknown values, and translate the word problem into algebraic expressions and equations.

4. Solve for one value at a time until you find your final answer.

5. Check your answer! Is it what the question asked for? Does it make sense with the given information?

# Elementary Algebra Practice

## Expressions

Questions 1-7:    E

1.  What is the value of $x^2 + 3x - 3$ if $x = -2$ ?

    A.  $-13$
    B.  $-5$
    C.  $-1$
    D.  $7$
    E.  $13$

2.  The expression $xa + 2xb$ is equivalent to which of the following?

    F.  $-x(a + 2b)$
    G.  $x(a + 2b)$
    H.  $2(a + xb)$
    J.  $2(xa + xb)$
    K.  $2x(a + b)$

3.  $-(x^2 + 3x - 4) + 3(x^2 - x) + 4$ is equivalent to:

    A.  $2x^2$
    B.  $2x^2 + 8$
    C.  $2(x^2 - 3x)$
    D.  $2x^2 - 6x + 8$
    E.  $4x^2 + 3x$

4.  For all $x$, $(3x - 1)^2 = ?$

    F.  $9x^2 - 1$
    G.  $9x^2 + 1$
    H.  $9x^2 - 6x + 1$
    J.  $9x^2 + 6x + 1$
    K.  $9x^2 + 9x + 1$

5.  $k^2 + 23k + 17 - 36k^2 - 22k$ is equivalent to:

    A.  $-17k^2$
    B.  $-17k^6$
    C.  $-35k^4 + k^2 + 17$
    D.  $-35k^2 + k + 17$
    E.  $-36k^2 + k + 17$

6.  The expression $(11s + 3t)(3s - t)$ is equivalent to:

    F.  $33s^2 - 3t^2$
    G.  $33s^2 + 20st - 3t^2$
    H.  $33s^2 + 20st + 3t^2$
    J.  $33s^2 - 2st - 3t^2$
    K.  $33s^2 - 2st + 3t^2$

7.  For all nonzero $a$ and $b$, $\dfrac{(5ab^2)(3a^3b)^2}{15a^6b^3} = ?$

    A.  $ab$
    B.  $3ab$
    C.  $3b^2$
    D.  $3ab^2$
    E.  $9ab$

## Equations

Questions 8-10:     E
Questions 11-17:    M

8.  If $x = 9y + 7$, then $y = ?$

    F.  $\dfrac{x}{9} - 7$

    G.  $\dfrac{x - 7}{9}$

    H.  $\dfrac{x + 7}{9}$

    J.  $\dfrac{x}{9} + 7$

    K.  $9x + 7$

9.  If $(10 - x)^2 = 49$, what is one possible value of $x$?

    A.  $-3$
    B.  $3$
    C.  $5$
    D.  $7$
    E.  $10$

10. Three sodas and two candy bars cost $4.30. If one soda costs
    $0.90, what is the cost of one candy bar?

    F.  $.75
    G.  $.80
    H.  $.85
    J.  $.90
    K.  $1.10

**11.** Which value of $x$ satisfies the equation $(3^3)(9) = 3^x$ ?

    **A.**  3
    **B.**  4
    **C.**  5
    **D.**  6
    **E.**  7

**12.** What is one possible solution to the equation $x^2 - 15x = 0$ ?

    **F.**  −5
    **G.**  −3
    **H.**  3
    **J.**  5
    **K.**  15

**13.** If $y = \dfrac{x^3}{z^2}$ , what happens to the value of $y$ when both $x$ and $z$ are doubled?

    **A.**  $y$ does not change
    **B.**  $y$ is halved
    **C.**  $y$ is doubled
    **D.**  $y$ is multiplied by 4
    **E.**  $y$ is multiplied by 8

**14.** If $c \neq a$ and $c \neq b$ , what are the values of $x$ that satisfy the equation $\dfrac{(x-a)(x-b)}{(x-c)} = 0$ ?

    **F.**  $-a$ and $-b$
    **G.**  $-a$, $-b$, and $-c$
    **H.**  $a$ and $b$
    **J.**  $b$ and $c$
    **K.**  $a$, $b$, and $c$

**15.** If $x = 7a - 3$ and $y = 15 - a$ , which of the following expresses $x$ in terms of $y$?

    **A.**  $6y - 12$
    **B.**  $6y + 12$
    **C.**  $102 - 7y$
    **D.**  $102 - y$
    **E.**  $102 + 7y$

**16.** If one gallon of paint will cover a wall that is $x$ feet high and $y$ feet long, how many gallons of paint will cover a wall that is 250 square feet?

F. $\dfrac{250x}{y}$

G. $\dfrac{x}{250y}$

H. $\dfrac{250}{xy}$

J. $250x$

K. $250 + x + y$

**17.** Which of the following is the solution set of the equation $|6x - 3| = 15$?

A. $x = -3$ or $x = 2$
B. $x = -3$ or $x = -2$
C. $x = -3$
D. $x = 3$ or $x = -2$
E. $x = 3$ or $x = 2$

## Inequalities

Questions 18-23:    M

**18.** If $5x - 8 \geq 12$, then which of the following MUST be true?

F. $x < 0$
G. $x \neq 6$
H. $x > 5$
J. $x \geq 4$
K. $-5 < x < 8$

**19.** The temperature in a meat freezer, in degrees Fahrenheit, must be kept cold enough to keep the meat from going bad, but not so cold that the meat freezes completely. The butcher devises an inequality, $|t - 6| \leq 10$, that the temperature must satisfy in order to keep the meat in the right temperature range. Which of the following temperatures does NOT satisfy this inequality?

A. $-3°$
B. $-1°$
C. $7°$
D. $13°$
E. $18°$

**20.** How many integers are in the solution set of $|p - 4| < 3$?

    **F.** 2
    **G.** 4
    **H.** 5
    **J.** 6
    **K.** 7

**21.** If $|2x - 3| > 5$, what are the possible values of $x$?

    **A.** $x < -4$ or $x > 1$
    **B.** $-4 < x < 1$
    **C.** $-1 < x < 4$
    **D.** $1 < x < 4$
    **E.** $x < -1$ or $x > 4$

**22.** Which of the following graphs given below represents the equation $x \geq 4$?

    **F.**

    **G.**

    **H.**

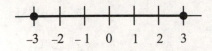

    **J.**

    **K.**

**23.** The graph on the number line below represents which of the following equations?

    **A.** $x = 3$ or $x = -3$
    **B.** $x \leq -3$ or $x \geq 3$
    **C.** $x < -3$ or $x > 3$
    **D.** $-3 < x < 3$
    **E.** $-3 \leq x \leq 3$

## Translation

Question 24:       E
Questions 25-26:    M

24. Which of the following is an expression for the sum of $a$ and $b$ decreased by 12?

    F.  $a - b + 12$
    G.  $a + b - 12$
    H.  $a(b - 12)$
    J.  $ab - 12$
    K.  $12 - (a + b)$

25. When he does his math homework each night, Mike spends 5 minutes organizing all of his materials, and then spends an average of 7 minutes on each level 1 problem, and 9 minutes on each level 2 problem. Suppose that one evening Mike finished $x$ level 1 problems and $y$ level 2 problems. Which of the following expressions gives the total amount of time, in minutes, that Mike spent on his math homework on this evening?

    A.  $5 + 7x + 9y$
    B.  $5 + 9x + 7y$
    C.  $5 + 7xy + 9xy$
    D.  $5 + 8(x + y)$
    E.  $5 + 63xy$

26. If Perry eats doughnuts at an average rate of $n$ dozen per hour, how many dozen does he eat in $h$ hours, in terms of $n$ and $h$?

    F.  $n - h$
    G.  $n + h$
    H.  $\dfrac{n}{h}$
    J.  $\dfrac{h}{n}$
    K.  $nh$

## Word Problems

Questions 27-30:    M

27. Every day, Wendy leaves for work at 9 a.m. She always travels at the speed limit of 30 miles per hour, and arrives for work at exactly 10 a.m. One day, Wendy decides she wants to bike to work instead. Assuming she travels at an average rate of 18 miles per hour, at exactly what time should Wendy leave if she wants to get to work at 10 a.m.?

   A.  8:00 a.m.
   B.  8:12 a.m.
   C.  8:15 a.m.
   D.  8:20 a.m.
   E.  8:40 a.m.

28. An interior decorator charges a one-time advising fee of $60, plus $75 for each hour spent decorating. If she bills a client $585, how many hours of decoration does the bill include?

   F.  $4\dfrac{1}{3}$
   G.  7
   H.  7.8
   J.  8.5
   K.  9.75

29. Bill and his father decide to build a fence around their rectangular lawn. Their lawn is 5 times as long as it is wide, and has a perimeter of 96 yards. In square yards, what is the area of Bill's lawn?

   A.  84
   B.  96
   C.  144
   D.  192
   E.  320

30. Ali decides he needs a better Internet service plan to keep up with his increasing Internet research for school. His Internet Service Provider offers two service plans:

   Plan 1:    Unlimited Internet usage for one month at a cost of $24.95 per month.

   Plan 2:    Basic charge of $9.95 per month for 10 hours of Internet usage, and additional hours of Internet usage can be purchased at a cost of $0.15 per hour.

   For how many hours of Internet usage is the cost of Service Plan 1 equal to the cost of Service Plan 2?

   F.  20
   G.  100
   H.  110
   J.  120
   K.  166

## Miscellaneous

Questions 31-40:   E
Questions 41-47:   M
Questions 48-50:   H

**31.** The expression $7(x-3)$ is equivalent to:

   **A.** $7x-21$
   **B.** $7x-4$
   **C.** $7x-3$
   **D.** $x-21$
   **E.** $-21x$

**32.** If $x^3+3x+1=y$ and $x=4$, what is the value of $y$?

   **F.** 64
   **G.** 77
   **H.** 113
   **J.** 161
   **K.** 209

**33.** If $a^2 = 121$ and $b^2 = 64$, what is the least possible value for $a + b$?

   **A.** $-21$
   **B.** $-19$
   **C.** $-3$
   **D.** 3
   **E.** 19

**34.** The relationship between degrees Fahrenheit and degrees Celsius is given by the formula $F = \dfrac{9}{5}C + 32$. A thermometer reads 72° Fahrenheit. To the nearest degree, what is the corresponding thermometer reading for degrees Celsius?

   **F.** 18°
   **G.** 22°
   **H.** 47°
   **J.** 73°
   **K.** 162°

**35.** If $x^4 = 27x$, and $x \neq 0$, what is the value of $x$?

   **A.** $-3$
   **B.** $-\dfrac{1}{3}$
   **C.** $\dfrac{1}{3}$
   **D.** 3
   **E.** 9

36. What is the value of $|2x - 6|$ if $x = -4$ ?

    F.  $-14$
    G.  2
    H.  12
    J.  14
    K.  24

37. If $(x + 3)(2x - 1) = 2x^2 + kx - 3$, what is the value of $k$?

    A.  $-5$
    B.  $-3$
    C.  0
    D.  3
    E.  5

38. The expression $(5q - 7)(6q + 8)$ is equivalent to:

    F.  $11q^2 - 56$
    G.  $11q^2 + 2q - 56$
    H.  $30q^2 - 56$
    J.  $30q^2 - 27q - 56$
    K.  $30q^2 - 2q - 56$

39. If $17q - 6(q + 3) = 17q - 3q$, what is the value of $q$?

    A.  $-10$
    B.  $-6$
    C.  $-2$
    D.  2
    E.  6

40. If $1\frac{2}{3} + x = 5\frac{5}{9}$, then what is the value of $x$?

    F.  $3\frac{1}{2}$

    G.  $3\frac{5}{6}$

    H.  $3\frac{8}{9}$

    J.  $4\frac{1}{9}$

    K.  $4\frac{2}{9}$

**41.** What is the value of $k$ when $-\dfrac{5}{3}k + 15 = 5$ ?

    **A.**  −25
    **B.**  −6
    **C.**  6
    **D.**  12
    **E.**  25

**42.** For all real numbers $a$, $b$, and $c$, if $a + b = -c$ and $c \neq 0$, then

$$\left(\frac{a+b}{-c}\right)^3 = ?$$

    **F.**  $-c^2$
    **G.**  $(-c)^2$
    **H.**  $-1$
    **J.**  $1$
    **K.**  $(a+b)^3$

**43.** If $x = \dfrac{1}{3}$, what is the value of $\dfrac{-2\left(x - \dfrac{2}{3}\right)}{3x^2}$ ?

    **A.**  $-2$
    **B.**  $-\dfrac{2}{3}$
    **C.**  $\dfrac{2}{3}$
    **D.**  $2$
    **E.**  $3$

**44.** The variables $a$, $b$, $c$, and $d$ are all integers, $a + b < 0$, and $a + b + c + d = 100$. If $c = 1$, which of the following *must* be true of $d$?

    **F.**  $d < 0$
    **G.**  $0 < d < 100$
    **H.**  $d = 100$
    **J.**  $d \geq 100$
    **K.**  $d \geq 150$

**45.** When $x = \dfrac{1}{3}$, what is the value of $\dfrac{x^2}{1-x}$?

    **A.** $-\dfrac{1}{6}$

    **B.** $\dfrac{1}{9}$

    **C.** $\dfrac{1}{6}$

    **D.** $\dfrac{2}{3}$

    **E.** $\dfrac{27}{2}$

**46.** If $3j - 15 = 27$, then $4j = ?$

    **F.** 4

    **G.** 14

    **H.** 16

    **J.** 36

    **K.** 56

**47.** Which of the following is equivalent to the inequality
$x + 3 < 7x + 21$?

    **A.** $x > -4$

    **D.** $x > 3$

    **C.** $x < -3$

    **D.** $x > 3$

    **E.** $x < 4$

**48.** If $b + c \neq 0$, which of the following values of $a$ make the equation
$\dfrac{a^2 b + a^2 c}{2b + 2c} = \dfrac{9}{2}$ true?

    **F.** $\dfrac{3}{2}$

    **G.** 3

    **H.** $\dfrac{9}{2}$

    **J.** 9

    **K.** All positive numbers

49. The compound interest formula is given by the equation

$A = P\left(1+\dfrac{r}{n}\right)^{nt}$, where $P$ is the initial amount of money, $r$ is the

interest rate, $n$ is the number of times interest is compounded per year, $t$ is the time since the initial investment in years, and $A$ is the final amount. If an initial investment of $1100 is made, compounded four times a year at 5% interest ($r = 0.05$), approximately how much money will there be after two years?

   A.  1198
   B.  1206
   C.  1215
   D.  1222
   E.  1247

50. The harbormaster made the true statement below:

   If the incoming storm is upgraded to a hurricane, vessels above 500 gross tons must depart the port.

   Which of the following statements is logically equivalent to the ruling?

   F.  If the incoming storm is not upgraded to a hurricane, then vessels above 500 gross tons must not depart the port.
   G.  Vessels above 500 gross tons must depart the port if and only if the incoming storm is upgraded to a hurricane.
   H.  If the incoming storm is not upgraded to a hurricane, then vessels above 500 gross tons must depart the port.
   J.  If vessels above 500 gross tons must depart the port, then the incoming storm has been upgraded to a hurricane.
   K.  If vessels above 500 gross tons must not depart the port, then the incoming storm has not been upgraded to a hurricane.

# Intermediate Algebra

- ❑ Simultaneous Equations

- ❑ Quadratic Equations and Expressions

- ❑ Radical Equations

- ❑ Functions

- ❑ Logarithms

- ❑ Matrices

- ❑ Complex Numbers

# Simultaneous Equations

(0-2 per test, Ⓔ Ⓜ H )

On the ACT, simultaneous equation questions ask you to find a mutual solution for two linear equations. When simultaneous equations are graphed, the mutual solution is the point of intersection.

Some simultaneous equation questions will give the two equations and ask you to solve. Other times, the equations are hidden in a word problem, requiring you to set up the equations first and then solve.

❑ Elimination method: add or subtract equations to cancel one of the variables and solve for the other. You may have to multiply an equation through by some number to eliminate a variable when the equations are added or subtracted.

If $2x + y = 16$ and $x - 2y = 3$, what is the value of $x$?

Stack the equations:  $2x + y = 16$
$x - 2y = 3$

What do you need to multiply the top equation by to make the $y$ disappear when you add the two equations? _____

Rewrite the equations and add them. Solve for $x$.

❑ Word problems that require you to define two variables are often simultaneous equation questions. Learn to recognize them and translate to set up the equations.

1000 tickets were sold to the Seaport Aquarium's Dolphin Show. Adult tickets cost $10, children's tickets cost $2, and a total of $5200 was collected. How many adult tickets were sold?

What are your two variables?  Define them.

A = number of Adult tickets sold

C = _____

Write an equation for the total number of tickets:  A + C = 1000

Write an equation for the total cost of the tickets:  _____

Solve the simultaneous equations for A.

## PUT IT TOGETHER

1.  If $2m + 5n = 6$ and $m + 4n = -6$, what is the value of $n$?

    A.  –6
    B.  –4
    C.  0
    D.  2
    E.  5

2.  At a clothing store, 6 shirts and 3 pants cost $201, and 2 shirts and 3 pants cost $117. What is the cost of 1 shirt?

    F.  $18
    G.  $20
    H.  $21
    J.  $21.50
    K.  $22.50

    > Write two equations. One for "6 shirts and 3 pants cost $210" and another for "2 shirts and 3 pants cost $117."

3.  An airplane at an altitude of 31,000 feet is ascending at a constant rate of 1,000 feet per minute. Another airplane at an altitude of 39,000 feet is descending at a constant rate of 400 feet per minute. After how many minutes, to the nearest tenth of a minute, will the two planes be at the same altitude?

    A.  1.3
    B.  5.0
    C.  5.7
    D.  13.3
    E.  20.0

4.  For the system of equations below, what is the value of $x$?

    $$x - y = -a$$
    $$x + 2y = b$$

    F.  $-\dfrac{a-b}{3}$

    G.  $3b - a$

    H.  $\dfrac{b-2a}{3}$

    J.  $a + 2b$

    K.  $\dfrac{1}{2}$

# Quadratic Equations and Expressions (0-2 per test, Ⓔ Ⓜ Ⓗ)

A quadratic equation or expression has a term with a variable that is squared.

If you can factor it, factor it! Most quadratics questions require factoring as one of the steps in the solution. Before factoring a quadratic equation, make sure that the equation is set equal to zero.

❑ Most quadratic equations on the ACT can be solved by factoring with easy-to-spot factors.

　1.　Set the equation equal to zero.

　2.　Factor the equation.

　3.　Set each factor equal to zero.

　4.　Solve each of the resulting equations.

　　　Solve for $x$: $x^2 + 8x = -7$

　　　1.　Set the equation equal to 0.


　　　2.　Factor the equation, looking for factors of 7 that have a sum of 8.


　　　3.　Set each expression equal to 0 and solve.


❑ Memorize these common quadratics:

　　$(a + b)^2 =$　　$(a + b)(a + b) = a^2 + ab + ba + b^2$　　$= a^2 + 2ab + b^2$

　　$(a - b)^2 =$　　$(a - b)(a - b) = a^2 - ab - ba + (-b)^2$　　$= a^2 - 2ab + b^2$

　　$(a + b)(a - b) =$　　$a^2 - ab + ba - b^2$　　$= a^2 - b^2$

　　Factor:

　　$x^2 - 16 = ($ _____ $)($ _____ $)$

❑ Occasionally, you'll need the **quadratic formula** to solve a quadratic equation.

　　$x = \dfrac{-b \pm \sqrt{b^2 - 4ac}}{2a}$, where $a$, $b$, and $c$ are coefficients in the equation $ax^2 + bx + c = 0$.

## PUT IT TOGETHER

1.  What is the product of the 2 solutions to the equation
    $x^2 - 4x - 12 = 0$ ?

    A.  −12
    B.  −8
    C.  4
    D.  8
    E.  12

2.  Which of the following is the least common denominator for
    $\dfrac{1}{x^2 - 9} + \dfrac{1}{3x - 9}$ ?

    > If you can factor it, factor it!

    F.  $(x-3)$
    G.  $3(x+3)$
    H.  $(x-3)(x+3)$
    J.  $3(x-3)(x+3)$
    K.  $3(x-3)^2(x+3)$

3.  When solved for $x$, the equation $x^2 - 16x + k = 0$ will have exactly
    one real solution for which of the following values of $k$?

    > What does it mean for a
    > quadratic equation to have
    > only one solution?

    A.  2
    B.  4
    C.  8
    D.  16
    E.  64

4.  Which of the following equations correctly solves $3x^2 + x - 8 = 0$
    using the quadratic formula?

    F.  $x = \dfrac{1 \pm \sqrt{1 - 4(3)(8)}}{2(3)}$

    G.  $x = \dfrac{1 \pm \sqrt{1 - 4(3)(-8)}}{2(3)}$

    H.  $x = \dfrac{-1 \pm \sqrt{1 - 4(3)(8)}}{2(3)}$

    J.  $x = \dfrac{-1 \pm \sqrt{1 - 4(3)(-8)}}{2(3)}$

    K.  $x = \dfrac{-1 \pm \sqrt{1 + 4(3)(-8)}}{2(3)}$

# Radical Equations

Radical equation questions rarely appear on the ACT. Once you square both sides of the equation to eliminate the radical, these questions can usually be solved like familiar, straightforward equations questions.

❑ To solve for a variable in a radical, isolate the radical on one side of the equation, and then raise both sides of the equation to the appropriate exponent.

If $6\sqrt{2x} + 11 = 41$, what is the value of $x$?

Isolate $\sqrt{2x}$ on one side of the equation.

Square both sides of the equation.

Solve for $x$.

## PUT IT TOGETHER

1.  If $\sqrt{x^2 + 36} = 10$, what is one possible value of $x$?

    A.  $-6$
    B.  $\sqrt{26}$
    C.  $\sqrt{46}$
    D.  8
    E.  64

    > Can you also solve this problem by Plugging In?

2.  If $\sqrt{x + 8} = 3y$, then $x = $?

    F.  $3y - 8$
    G.  $9y - 8$
    H.  $3y^2 - 8$
    J.  $9y^2 - 8$
    K.  $9y^2 + 8$

# Functions

A function is an "instruction" or "process" that will give you a single value of $f(x)$ as a result for any value of $x$ you put in.

The main challenge to most function questions is understanding their notation. Though they might look intimidating, most function questions can be solved by simply plugging given values into an equation. Difficult function questions usually involve composite functions.

❑ To evaluate a function for a particular value of $x$, simply substitute that value everywhere you see an $x$.

Consider the following function: $f(x) = x^2 + 6x + 3$

$f(1) = $ _____

$f(a) = $ _____

If $f(a) = 19$, what is one value of $a$? _____

❑ ACT FUNCTION questions. Some function problems use symbols to define a set of operations. Solve by simply using the function as a set of instructions.

A new operation, Ш, is defined as follows: $a \text{ Ш } b = ab + 2b$. What is the value of $7 \text{ Ш } 3$?

❑ COMPOSITE FUNCTION questions. Most of the difficult function problems involve composition of functions, in which one function is expressed in terms of the other.

Order-of-operations rules apply here. Evaluate the function inside parentheses first.

Given $f(x) = x + 2$ and $g(x) = x^2$, solve for the following:

$f(g(3)) = $ _____

$g(f(1)) = $ _____

**PUT IT TOGETHER**

1.  If $f(x) = x - \sqrt{x}$ and $g(x) = x^3 - 9$, what is the value of $\dfrac{f(16)}{g(3)}$?

    A.  $\dfrac{2}{3}$

    B.  $\dfrac{5}{6}$

    C.  $\dfrac{8}{9}$

    D.  $\dfrac{19}{18}$

    E.  $\dfrac{10}{9}$

2.  For non-zero integers $m$ and $n$, an operation @ can be defined by

    $m @ n = \dfrac{m}{n} + \dfrac{n}{m}$. If the sum of $m$ and $n$ is 11 and the product of $m$

    and $n$ is 30, which of the following is a possible value of $m @ n$?

    F.  $\dfrac{11}{5}$

    G.  $\dfrac{11}{6}$

    H.  $\dfrac{11}{30}$

    J.  $\dfrac{61}{30}$

    K.  $\dfrac{61}{11}$

3.  Given $f(x) = 2x - 3$ and $g(x) = x^2 - 1$, which of the following is
    an expression for $g(f(x))$?

    A.  $x^2 + 6x + 5$
    B.  $x^2 + 12x + 5$
    C.  $4x^2 + 6x + 5$
    D.  $4x^2 + 8$
    E.  $4x^2 - 12x + 8$

# Logarithms

A logarithm represents the exponent to which a base number is raised to produce a given number. $\log_b y = x$ means that $b^x = y$.

About half of the logarithm questions on the ACT will only require you to have a basic understanding of the logarithm notation. The other, more difficult questions will require you to know the logarithm rules shown below.

❑ Most ACT logarithm problems can be solved by rewriting the equation using an exponent.

What is the value of $a$ if $\log_a 32 = 5$ ?

❑ Memorize the following logarithm rules:

$$\log_b x + \log_b y = \log_b(xy)$$

$$\log_b x - \log_b y = \log_b\left(\frac{x}{y}\right)$$

$$y \log_b x = \log_b(x^y)$$

## PUT IT TOGETHER

1.  If $\log_b a = 5$, which of the following could be values of $a$ and $b$?

    I.   $a = 32, b = 2$
    II.  $a = 100{,}000, b = 10$
    III. $a = 25, b = 5$

    A.  I only
    B.  II only
    C.  I and II only
    D.  II and III only
    E.  I, II, and III

2.  If $b$ is a positive number such that $\log_b \dfrac{1}{16} = -4$, then $b = ?$

    F.  2
    G.  4
    H.  64
    J.  $\dfrac{1}{2}$
    K.  $\dfrac{1}{4}$

    > **Rewrite the logarithm using an exponent.**

3.  If $\log_3 27 - \log_3 3 = x$, what is the real value of $x$?

    A.  4
    B.  3
    C.  2.5
    D.  2
    E.  1.5

# Matrices

Matrices questions do not often appear on the ACT, and they usually do not require any matrix skills to solve. About half of matrices questions ask you to find a "determinant," for which they provide a formula; these can be treated like ACT function questions. Other questions might ask you to add or multiply matrices.

❑ To add or subtract matrices, simply perform the operation on the corresponding terms.

$$\begin{bmatrix} 1 & 2 \\ 3 & 4 \end{bmatrix} + \begin{bmatrix} w & x \\ y & z \end{bmatrix} = \begin{bmatrix} 1+w & 2+x \\ 3+y & 4+z \end{bmatrix}$$

❑ To multiply two matrices, multiply each row in the first matrix by each column in the second matrix.

$$\begin{bmatrix} 1 & 2 \\ 3 & 4 \end{bmatrix} \times \begin{bmatrix} w & x \\ y & z \end{bmatrix} = \begin{bmatrix} 1w+2y & 1x+2z \\ 3w+4y & 3x+4z \end{bmatrix}$$

Note that the top left result in the answer combines the top row of the 1st matrix with the left column of the 2nd matrix. Similarly, the bottom right combines the bottom row of the 1st matrix and right column of the 2nd matrix.

**PUT IT TOGETHER**

1.  If $A = \begin{bmatrix} 2 & -1 \\ 0 & 1 \end{bmatrix}$ and $B = \begin{bmatrix} 0 & 1 \\ 1 & 0 \end{bmatrix}$, what is the sum of $A$ and $B$?

    A.  $\begin{bmatrix} 1 & 3 \\ 0 & -1 \end{bmatrix}$

    B.  $\begin{bmatrix} 2 & 0 \\ 1 & 1 \end{bmatrix}$

    C.  $\begin{bmatrix} 20 & 0 \\ 1 & 0 \end{bmatrix}$

    D.  $\begin{bmatrix} 3 & -1 \\ 0 & 2 \end{bmatrix}$

    E.  $\begin{bmatrix} 2 & 0 \\ 3 & 0 \end{bmatrix}$

2.  If $\det \begin{bmatrix} a & b \\ c & d \end{bmatrix} = ad - bc$, then $\det \begin{bmatrix} -a & d \\ b & -c \end{bmatrix} = ?$

    F.  $-ac - bd$

    G.  $ac - bd$

    H.  $-ad - bc$

    J.  $-ad + bc$

    K.  $ad + bc$

# Complex Numbers

(0-1 per test, E (M)(H))

An **imaginary number** has a square that is a negative number. A complex number is the sum of a real and an imaginary number.

Complex number questions might require you to simplify a root with a negative number or, for more challenging questions, to multiply two complex numbers.

❏ Imaginary numbers are expressed using *i*, which is defined as the square root of −1.

$$i = \sqrt{-1}$$

$$i^2 = -1$$

$$i^3 = \left(i^2 \cdot i\right) = (-1 \cdot i) = -i$$

$$i^4 = \left(i^2 \cdot i^2\right) = (-1 \cdot -1) = 1$$

$$i^5 = \underline{\hspace{2cm}} \qquad\qquad i^6 = \underline{\hspace{2cm}}$$

❏ Simplify roots of negative numbers by using *i*.

Simplify:

$$\sqrt{-12} = \underline{\hspace{2cm}} \qquad\qquad \sqrt{-50} = \underline{\hspace{2cm}}$$

❏ When using FOIL to multiply two expressions containing *i*, be meticulous about your positive and negative signs.

$$(1 + i)(1 - i) =$$

$$i(2 + i)(3 - i) =$$

**PUT IT TOGETHER**

1. Which of the following equals the complex number $(1-i)^2$ ?

   A. $-2-2i$
   B. $2-2i$
   C. $-2i$
   D. $2$
   E. $0$

2. Which of the following complex numbers is equal to the sum of $\sqrt{-80}$ and $\sqrt{-125}$ ?

   F. $-20i\sqrt{5}$
   G. $-9i\sqrt{5}$
   H. $i\sqrt{5}$
   J. $9i\sqrt{5}$
   K. $20i\sqrt{5}$

3. Which of the following complex numbers is equal to $(4+5i)(x-4i)$ ?

   FOIL, and be very careful with your signs.

   A. $4x-20i$
   B. $(4-x)-20i$
   C. $(4-x)+20i$
   D. $(4x-20)+(5x-16)i$
   E. $(4x+20)+(5x-16)i$

# Intermediate Algebra Summary

### Simultaneous Equations

❏ Elimination method: add or subtract equations to cancel one of the variables and solve for the other. You may have to multiply an equation through by some number to eliminate a variable when the equations are added or subtracted.

### Quadratic Equations

❏ If you can factor it, factor it! Most quadratics questions require factoring as one of the steps in the solution. Before factoring a quadratic equation, make sure that the equation is set equal to zero.

### Radical Equations and Expressions

❏ To solve for a variable in a radical, isolate the radical on one side of the equation, and then raise both sides of the equation to the appropriate exponent.

### Functions

❏ To evaluate a function for a particular value of $x$, simply substitute that value everywhere you see an $x$.

### Logarithms

❏ A logarithm represents the exponent to which a base number is raised to produce a given number. $\log_b y = x$ means that $b^x = y$.

### Matrices

❏ To add or subtract matrices, simply perform the operation on the corresponding terms.

❏ To multiply two matrices, multiply each row in the first matrix by each column in the second matrix.

### Complex Numbers

❏ Imaginary numbers are expressed using $i$, which is defined as the square root of $-1$.

SUMMIT
EDUCATIONAL
GROUP

# Intermediate Algebra Practice

## Simultaneous Equations

Question 1:        E
Question 2:        M

1.  At a restaurant, the cost of one appetizer and two entrées is $22.30.
    The cost of three appetizers and one entrée is $22.40. If all
    appetizers are the same price, and all entrées are the same price,
    what is the cost of one appetizer?

    A.  $4.50
    B.  $5.10
    C.  $5.50
    D.  $8.10
    E.  $8.90

2.  For what value of $a$ would the following system of equations have
    an infinite number of solutions?

    $x + 3y = 2a$
    $3x + 9y = 12$

    F.  1
    G.  2
    H.  4
    J.  16
    K.  48

## Quadratic Equations and Expression

Questions 3-5:      E
Questions 6-8:      M
Questions 9-10:     H

3.  What is the sum of the two solutions to the equation
    $x^2 - 4x + 3 = 0$?

    A.  −4
    B.  −2
    C.  1
    D.  3
    E.  4

4.  $x = -2$ and $x = 4$ are the two solutions to which of the following
    quadratic equations?

    F.  $(x-4)(x-2) = 0$
    G.  $(x-4)(x+2) = 0$
    H.  $(x+4)(x-2) = 0$
    J.  $(x+4)(x+2) = 0$
    K.  $(x+4)^2 = 0$

5.  Which of the following gives all of the solutions to the equation
    $x^2 + 3x = 10$?

    A.  −2 and −5
    B.  −2  and 5
    C.  2 and −5
    D.  3 and −7
    E.  3 and 7

6.  If $x^2 - y^2 + 16xy = 16xy$, then which of the following could be the
    value of $x$?

    F.  $-2y$
    G.  $-y$
    H.  $2y$
    J.  $4y$
    K.  $8y$

7.  For a certain quadratic equation, the factors are $(4x + 1)$ and
    $(3x + 4)$. What are the two solutions to this quadratic equation?

    A.  $-\dfrac{1}{4}$ and $-\dfrac{4}{3}$

    B.  $-\dfrac{1}{3}$ and $-\dfrac{3}{4}$

    C.  $-\dfrac{1}{3}$ and $\dfrac{3}{4}$

    D.  $\dfrac{1}{3}$ and $-\dfrac{3}{4}$

    E.  $\dfrac{1}{4}$ and $\dfrac{4}{3}$

8.  Which of the following numbers is the average of the two solutions
    to the equation $x^2 + 15 = 8x$?

    F.  3
    G.  4
    H.  5
    J.  8
    K.  15

9.  If $(x-1)^2 = 3x + 1$, and $x \neq 0$, what is the value of $x$?

    A.  1
    B.  2
    C.  3
    D.  4
    E.  5

10. What are the solutions for $x$ for the quadratic equation
    $x^2 - x(2y - 5z) - 10yz = 0$ ?

    **F.**  $-2y$ and $5z$
    **G.**  $-y$ and $-10z$
    **H.**  $-y$ and $10z$
    **J.**  $2y$ and $-5z$
    **K.**  $2y$ and $5z$

## Radical Equations

Questions 11-12:   M

11. If $7 - \sqrt{t} = 2$ , then $t$ equals

    **A.**  $-5$
    **B.**  $5$
    **C.**  $25$
    **D.**  $\sqrt{5}$
    **E.**  $-\sqrt{5}$

12. What is the value of $x$ in the equation $3\sqrt{x - 3} = 27$ ?

    **F.**  9
    **G.**  12
    **H.**  78
    **J.**  84
    **K.**  144

## Functions

Questions 13-14:   E
Questions 15-16:   H

13. A group of high school students is going to sell t-shirts to raise
    money.  The amount raised by selling $x$ t-shirts is given by the
    function $M(x) = 2(x) - 75$, where $M$ is the net amount raised, in
    dollars.  If the students sell 100 t-shirts, how much money, in
    dollars, will they raise?

    **A.**  25
    **B.**  50
    **C.**  100
    **D.**  125
    **E.**  200

**14.** The table below shows some values for the function $f$. If $f$ is a linear function, what is the value of $b - a$?

| $x$ | $f(x)$ |
|-----|--------|
| 3 | 8 |
| 4 | $a$ |
| 5 | 14 |
| 6 | $b$ |

F. 6
G. 11
H. 27
J. 28
K. It cannot be determined from the information given.

**15.** Let a function be defined by $f(x\,|\,y) = -xy - (x - y)$. What is the value of $f(2\,|\,-5)$ ?

A. −17
B. −3
C. 3
D. 7
E. 17

**16.** If $f(x) = \dfrac{x+6}{2}$ and $g(x) = x^2 - 9$, what is the value of $g(f(4))$ ?

F. 11
G. 16
H. 55
J. 116
K. 991

## Logarithms

Questions 17-18:    H

**17.** What value of $x$ satisfies the equation $\log_4 256 = x$?

A. 2
B. 4
C. 8
D. 16
E. 64

**18.** If $\log_b 2 = 0.3869$ and $\log_b 5 = 0.8982$, what is the value of $\log_b 10$?

F. 0.3475
G. 0.5113
H. 1.2851
J. 1.8774
K. 2.4792

SUMMIT
EDUCATIONAL
GROUP

## Matrices

Question 19:     M
Question 20:     H

19. $\begin{bmatrix} 3 & -5 \\ 17 & 8 \end{bmatrix} + \begin{bmatrix} -1 & 4 \\ 3 & -5 \end{bmatrix} =$

   A. 22
   B. 24
   C. $\begin{bmatrix} 25 & 1 \end{bmatrix}$
   D. $\begin{bmatrix} 2 & -1 \\ 20 & 3 \end{bmatrix}$
   E. $\begin{bmatrix} 4 & 1 \\ 14 & 3 \end{bmatrix}$

20. $\begin{bmatrix} 5 \\ 3 \\ 1 \end{bmatrix} \times \begin{bmatrix} -2 & -1 & 0 \end{bmatrix} = ?$

   F. $\begin{bmatrix} -10 & -3 & 0 \end{bmatrix}$
   G. $\begin{bmatrix} -2 & -3 & 0 \end{bmatrix}$
   H. 0
   J. $\begin{bmatrix} -10 & -5 & 0 \\ -6 & -3 & 0 \\ -2 & -1 & 0 \end{bmatrix}$
   K. $\begin{bmatrix} -10 & -6 & -2 \\ -5 & -3 & -1 \\ 0 & 0 & 0 \end{bmatrix}$

## Miscellaneous

Questions 21-24:   E
Questions 25-26:   M
Questions 27-30:   H

**21.** For the function $f(x) = -2x^2 - 3x$, what is the value of $f(-2)$?

   A.  $-14$
   B.  $-10$
   C.  $-2$
   D.  $2$
   E.  $10$

**22.** Which of the following are the solutions of the equation $x^2 - x = 6$?

   F.  $x = -3$ and $x = -2$
   G.  $x = -3$ and $x = 2$
   H.  $x = -3$
   J.  $x = 3$ and $x = -2$
   K.  $x = 3$ and $x = 2$

**23.** For which of the following equations is $x = -3$ a solution?

   A.  $x^2 + 3x - 6 = 0$
   B.  $x^2 + 3x + 6 = 0$
   C.  $x^2 - 6x - 9 = 0$
   D.  $x^2 + 6x + 9 = 0$
   E.  $x^2 - 6x + 9 = 0$

**24.** What is the sum of the 2 solutions of the equation $x^2 - x - 12 = 0$?

   F.  $13$
   G.  $8$
   H.  $7$
   J.  $1$
   K.  $-1$

**25.** For $x^2 \neq 1$, $\dfrac{(x-1)^2}{x^2 - 1} = ?$

   A.  $\dfrac{x-1}{x+1}$

   B.  $x - 1$

   C.  $\dfrac{1}{x+1}$

   D.  $x + 1$

   E.  $\dfrac{1}{x-1}$

**26.** If $|x^2 + 5x| < 6$, what are the possible values of $x$?

    **F.** $x < -2$ or $x > 1$
    **G.** $x < -1$ or $x > 4$
    **H.** $-1 < x < 4$
    **J.** $-1 < x < 2$
    **K.** $-6 < x < 1$

**27.** Which of the following values of $x$ satisfies the equation
$\log_x 64 = 3$ ?

    **A.** 2
    **B.** 3
    **C.** 4
    **D.** 6
    **E.** 8

**28.** Given the matrix equation shown below, what is the value of
$\dfrac{x}{z} - y$ ?

$$\begin{bmatrix} 3! \\ 2! \\ 1 \end{bmatrix} + \begin{bmatrix} 4! \\ 3! \\ 2! \end{bmatrix} = \begin{bmatrix} x \\ y \\ z \end{bmatrix}$$

(Note: for positive integer $a$, the notation $a!$ represents the product of the integers from $a$ to 1. For example, $4! = 4 \times 3 \times 2 \times 1$.)

    **F.** 2
    **G.** 3
    **H.** 4
    **J.** 5
    **K.** 6

**29.** For the functions $f(x)$ and $g(x)$, tables of values are shown below. What is the value of $g(f(1))$?

| $x$ | $f(x)$ | $g(x)$ |
| --- | --- | --- |
| -3 | 7 | -3 |
| -2 | 5 | -3 |
| -1 | 3 | -2 |
| 0 | 2 | 0 |
| 1 | -2 | 1 |
| 2 | -3 | 3 |
| 3 | -3 | 6 |

    **A.** -3
    **B.** -2
    **C.** 2
    **D.** 3
    **E.** 7

**30.** What is the value of $a$ if $x+3$ is a factor of $2x^3+9x^2+ax+3$?

    **F.** $-4$
    **G.** $-1$
    **H.** $0$
    **J.** $8$
    **K.** $10$

SUMMIT
EDUCATIONAL
GROUP

# Coordinate Geometry

---

- ❏ Coordinate Geometry Basics

- ❏ Midpoint and Distance

- ❏ Slope

- ❏ Linear Equations and Inequalities

- ❏ Conic Sections

- ❏ Transformations

# Coordinate Geometry Basics

(0-1 per test, Ⓔ M H )

❑ The **coordinate plane** is a grid made up of two number lines – a horizontal number line called the **x-axis**, and a vertical number line called the **y-axis**. These two lines meet at a point called the **origin**, with coordinates (0,0).

❑ Every point in the coordinate plane can be represented by a pair of coordinates $(x,y)$.

Points on the $x$-axis have a $y$-coordinate of 0.

Points on the $y$-axis have an $x$-coordinate of 0.

Plot the following points on the graph:

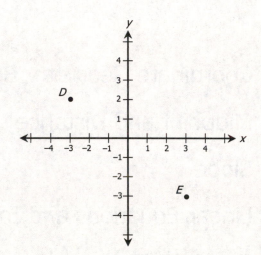

A:  (2,2)

B:  (–4,–3)

C:  (0,0)

What are the coordinates of point D?  _____

What are the coordinates of point E?  _____

❑ Draw coordinate axes and plot points when a question doesn't provide a graph.

## PUT IT TOGETHER

1.  A point at $(2,5)$ in the standard $(x,y)$ coordinate plane is shifted down 2 units and left 7 units. What are the new coordinates of the point?

    Draw coordinate axes and plot points.

    A.  $(-5,3)$
    B.  $(-2,2)$
    C.  $(0,-2)$
    D.  $(4,12)$
    E.  $(9,7)$

2.  Each side of a square is 4 cm long. One vertex of the square is at $(3,2)$ on a square coordinate grid marked in centimeter units. Which of the following points on the grid could be another vertex of the square?

    F.  $(7,2)$
    G.  $(3,4)$
    H.  $(1,0)$
    J.  $(1,-2)$
    K.  $(-2,4)$

3.  If point Q does not lie on the $x$-axis or the $y$-axis and its $x$ and $y$ coordinates have opposite signs, then point Q *must* be located in which of the 4 quadrants, as shown below?

    A.  I only
    B.  III only
    C.  I or III only
    D.  I or IV only
    E.  II or IV only

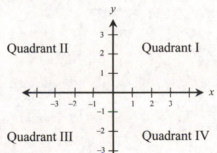

4.  If the rectangle in the figure below is rotated 180° counter-clockwise about the origin, what are the new coordinates of $C$?

    F.  $(5,-4)$
    G.  $(5,4)$
    H.  $(-4,-5)$
    J.  $(4,5)$
    K.  $(-5,-4)$

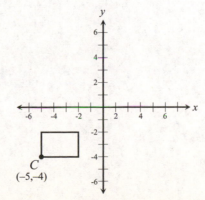

# Midpoint and Distance

(1-2 per test, Ⓔ Ⓜ H )

There is almost always one midpoint question, and it usually requires a direct application of the formula. More difficult questions might have variables as coordinates and require that you solve algebraically. Distance questions that require the distance formula are rare, and can be solved by setting up a right triangle.

❑ The midpoint of a segment is given by:

$$\text{midpoint} = \left( \frac{x_1 + x_2}{2}, \frac{y_1 + y_2}{2} \right)$$

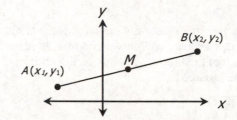

❑ The distance between two points is given by:

$$\text{distance} = \sqrt{(x_2 - x_1)^2 + (y_2 - y_1)^2}$$

❑ Instead of using the distance formula, try calculating the distance between two points by creating a right triangle, with the two endpoints as the hypotenuse. Then, solve using the Pythagorean Theorem or special right triangles.

What is the distance between (2,2) and (−2, −1)?

Use the distance formula to solve:

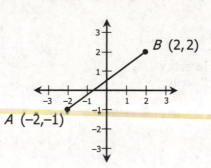

Now solve by plotting points and drawing a right triangle:

**PUT IT TOGETHER**

1.  In the standard $(x,y)$ coordinate plane, the coordinates of the endpoints of $\overline{AB}$ are $(2,-1)$ and $(12,9)$. What is the $x$-coordinate of the midpoint of $\overline{AB}$?

    A.  4
    B.  5
    C.  6
    D.  7
    E.  8

2.  In the standard $(x,y)$ coordinate plane, the point $(-1,9)$ is the midpoint of the line segment with endpoints $(-7,13)$ and $(a,b)$. What is $(a,b)$?

    F.  $(-4,2)$
    G.  $(-3,2)$
    H.  $(5,5)$
    J.  $(3,-2)$
    K.  $(4,-11)$

3.  What is the distance, in coordinate units, between the points $J(-4,3)$ and $K(8,-2)$?

    A.  $\sqrt{13}$
    B.  $\sqrt{17}$
    C.  5
    D.  13
    E.  17

    Solve this in two ways:
    - use the distance formula
    - draw a right triangle

# Slope

Slope questions that require a direct application of the slope formula occur on about half of ACT tests. More challenging questions ask about perpendicular or parallel lines.

❑ Slope is the amount a line moves vertically for every unit the line moves horizontally.

Lines that slant up to the right have positive slope. Lines that slant down to the right have negative slope.

❑ The slope of a line is given by:

$$\text{slope} = \frac{(y_2 - y_1)}{(x_2 - x_1)} = \frac{\text{rise}}{\text{run}}$$

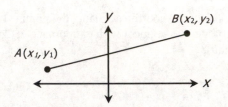

❑ **Parallel lines** have equal slopes.

❑ **Perpendicular lines** have slopes that are negative reciprocals of each other.

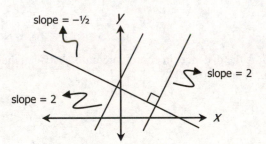

❑ **Vertical lines** have undefined slope.

❑ **Horizontal lines** have a slope of 0.

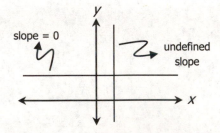

Find the slopes of the following:

$\overline{PR}$  _____

$\overline{QS}$  _____

Any line parallel to $\overline{PR}$ _____

Any line perpendicular to $\overline{PR}$ _____

Any line perpendicular to $\overline{QS}$ _____

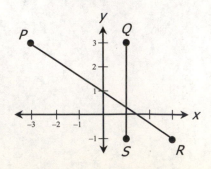

### PUT IT TOGETHER

1. In the standard $(x,y)$ coordinate plane, what is the slope of the line containing the points $(1,8)$ and $(-2,-4)$?

   A. $\dfrac{1}{8}$

   B. $\dfrac{1}{4}$

   C. $\dfrac{1}{2}$

   D. $4$

   E. $8$

2. In the standard $(x,y)$ coordinate plane, line $l$ is perpendicular to line $m$. If line $l$ has a $y$-intercept of $(0,3)$ and an $x$-intercept of $(2,0)$, what is the slope of line $m$?

   F. $-\dfrac{3}{2}$

   G. $-\dfrac{2}{3}$

   H. $0$

   J. $\dfrac{2}{3}$

   K. $\dfrac{3}{2}$

3. A six-sided figure $ABCDEF$ lies in the $(x,y)$ coordinate plane as shown below with the lengths of the sides marked in units. Point $G$ is located exactly halfway between points $B$ and $F$. If a line segment were drawn from point $G$ to point $C$, which of the following gives the slope of $\overline{GC}$?

   > What are the coordinates of *F*? Of *C*? Of *G*?

   A. $-\dfrac{5}{10.5}$

   B. $\dfrac{1}{2}$

   C. $-\dfrac{2}{1}$

   D. $-\dfrac{10.5}{5}$

   E. $\dfrac{15}{10.5}$

   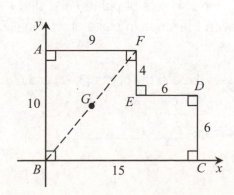

# Linear Equations and Inequalities

(3-4 per test, Ⓔ Ⓜ Ⓗ)

Linear equations and inequalities constitute one of the most frequently tested topics on the ACT Mathematics Test. Converting an equation in standard form to one in slope-intercept form is a typical first step in easy and medium questions. Common questions test your ability to identify the slope of parallel and perpendicular lines and to move comfortably between equations and inequalities and their graphs. Other questions in this category test your ability to recognize a linear function in a real-world setting.

❑ A linear equation is an equation whose graph is a straight line.

❑ The **standard form** of a linear equation is $Ax + By = C$.

❑ The **slope-intercept form** of a linear equation is $y = mx + b$, where $m$ is the slope of the line and $b$ is the **y-intercept**. The y-intercept is where the line crosses the y-axis ($x = 0$ at the y-intercept).

❑ When you see a line in standard form, convert it to slope-intercept form.

A line is given by the equation $6x - 2y = 7$.

What form is the equation in? _____

Write in slope-intercept form: _____

What is the slope? _____

What is the y-intercept? _____

Write an equation of a line that is parallel to the line: _____

Write an equation of a line that is perpendicular to the line: _____

❑ To find the equation of a line when given two sets of points, first find the slope of the line. Next, write an equation $y = mx + b$ with the slope in place of $m$. Finally, plug in one of the points to the equation and solve for $b$.

Find the equations for a line that passes through the points $(3, -1)$ and $(-5, 3)$.

What is the slope? _____

Write the equation in slope-intercept form: _____

Plug in one of the points to solve for $b$.

❑ To graph an inequality, first rewrite as an equation and graph the resulting line. The graph of the inequality will be the area above or below this line.

If the solution to the inequality does not include the points on the line, use a dashed line.

Graph $y > x + 1$

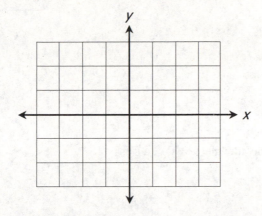

❑ Common linear equation question types:

- Given a line in standard form, draw conclusions about slope

- Determine the equation of a line, given two points or given one point and the slope

- Identify the graph of a linear inequality, given the equation

- Identify the equation of a linear inequality, given the graph

- Identify the graph of a given linear equation

- Identify the equation of a given linear graph

- Identify a linear function from a word problem

**PUT IT TOGETHER**

1. In the standard $(x, y)$ coordinate plane, a line passes through the origin and the point $(3, a)$. If the slope of the line is 2, what is the value of $a$?

> Draw a graph to visualize coordinate geometry word problems.

    **A.** $-\dfrac{3}{2}$

    **B.** $\dfrac{3}{2}$

    **C.** 2

    **D.** 3

    **E.** 6

2. In the standard $(x, y)$ coordinate plane, the line $y = -\dfrac{1}{2}x + 8$ is perpendicular to the line:

    **F.** $y = 2x + 8$

    **G.** $y = -2x + 8$

    **H.** $y = \dfrac{1}{2}x + 8$

    **J.** $y = \dfrac{1}{2}x$

    **K.** $y = -\dfrac{1}{2}x - 8$

3. Johnny took a plane trip from Chicago to Boston, traveling 860 miles at a constant speed. He constructed a graph of his trip, plotting time elapsed along the $x$-axis and distance to Boston along the $y$-axis. The shape of the graph can best be described as a:

    **A.** vertical line segment.

    **B.** horizontal line segment.

    **C.** circle.

    **D.** line segment with positive slope.

    **E.** line segment with negative slope.

4. The graphs of the equations $f(x) = -x + 3$ and $g(x) = (x - 1)^2$ are shown in the standard $(x, y)$ coordinate plane below. What real values of $x$, if any, satisfy the inequality $-x + 3 > (x - 1)^2$?

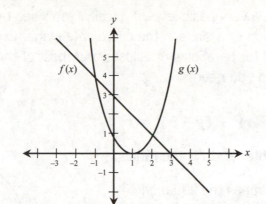

F. $x < 0$ and $x > 1$
G. $x < 1$ and $x > 2$
H. $0 < x < 1$
J. $-1 < x < 2$
K. No real values

5. Which of the following best represents the graph of $y \geq ax + b$ for some negative $a$ and negative $b$?

A.

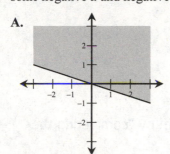

B.

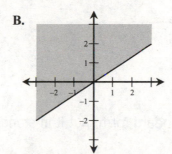

C.

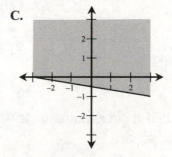

D.

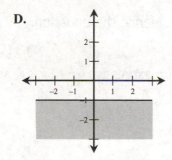

E.

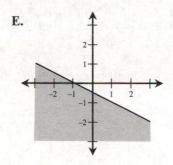

Eliminate answers based on slope, y-intercept, and direction of the inequality.

# Conic Sections

(1-2 per test,  E Ⓜ Ⓗ)

The ACT tests conic sections on a very basic level. Typically, you'll see one question that requires you to know the equation of a circle in the coordinate plane. On rare occasions, you will need to know the equations for parabolas or ellipses, but most of these questions will provide you with the information you need.

❑ **Equation of a circle:** $(x - a)^2 + (y - b)^2 = r^2$

In this form, $(a, b)$ is the center and $r$ is the radius.

A circle centered at the origin has the equation $x^2 + y^2 = r^2$.

What is the equation of a circle with a radius of 4 and a center at point (0,3)

_____

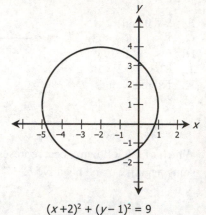

$(x + 2)^2 + (y - 1)^2 = 9$

center: $(-2, 1)$

radius: 3

❑ If a circle equation is not in standard form, put it in standard form by "completing the square."

For an expression $x^2 + bx$, rewrite as $\left(x + \dfrac{b}{2}\right)^2$, then FOIL and rebalance the equation.

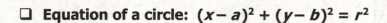

If $x^2 + 6x + y^2 = 0$, put in standard form by completing the square for expression $x^2 + 6x$.

Rewrite $x^2 + 6x$ as a squared binomial:  $(x + 3)^2$

FOIL: _____

$x^2 + 6x +$ _____ $+ y^2 = 0 +$ _____

Standard form: _____

## ❑ Equation of a parabola:  $y = ax^2 + bx + c$

Note that, when $y = 0$, this is the standard form of a quadratic equation. The $x$-intercepts of the parabola are the zeroes or solutions to the quadratic when $y = 0$. The parabola's axis of symmetry is the $x$ value of the midpoint of these $x$-intercepts.

In this form, $x = -\dfrac{b}{2a}$ is the axis of symmetry.

A parabola centered at the origin has the equation $y = ax^2$.

If $a$ is positive, the parabola points up.

If $a$ is negative, the parabola points down.

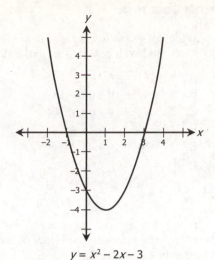

$$y = x^2 - 2x - 3$$

axis of symmetry: $x = 1$

vertex: $(1, -4)$

## ❑ Equation of an ellipse:  $\dfrac{(x-h)^2}{a^2} + \dfrac{(y-k)^2}{b^2} = 1$

In this form, $(h, k)$ is the center.

$2a$ = length of the horizontal axis of the ellipse.

$2b$ = length of the vertical axis of the ellipse.

An ellipse centered at the origin has the equation $\dfrac{x^2}{a^2} + \dfrac{y^2}{b^2} = 1$.

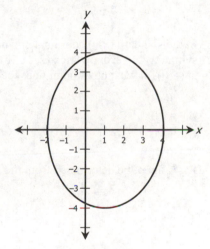

$$\dfrac{(x-1)^2}{9} + \dfrac{y^2}{16} = 1$$

center: $(1, 0)$

horizontal axis: 6

vertical axis: 8

## PUT IT TOGETHER

1.  Which of the following is an equation of a circle tangent to the
    $y$-axis and with center $(4,6)$ in the standard $(x,y)$ coordinate plane?

    > Draw the circle on a coordinate plane to visualize.

    A.  $(x-4)^2 + (y-6)^2 = 2$
    B.  $(x-4)^2 + (y-6)^2 = 16$
    C.  $(x-4)^2 + (y-6)^2 = 36$
    D.  $(x-6)^2 + (y-4)^2 = 16$
    E.  $(x+6)^2 + (y+4)^2 = 36$

2.  In the standard $(x,y)$ coordinate plane, which of the following
    coordinate points is the center of the circle with equation
    $x^2 + 4x + y^2 - 2y = 21$?

    F.  $(2,1)$
    G.  $(-2,1)$
    H.  $(2,-1)$
    J.  $(1,2)$
    K.  $(-1,2)$

3.  In the standard $(x,y)$ coordinate plane, a parabola has axis of
    symmetry $x = 2$ and vertex $(2,4)$. If the parabola crosses the $x$-axis
    at $(5,0)$, at what other point does the parabola cross the $x$-axis?

    A.  $(8,0)$
    B.  $(1,0)$
    C.  $(-1,0)$
    D.  $(-3,0)$
    E.  Cannot be determined from the given information

# Transformations

A transformation is an alteration to a figure.

Most questions in this category require carefully mapping changes to coordinate points or figures. These questions can often be solved by visualizing the transformations. Occasionally, questions require you to know function graph transformation rules.

❑ The result of a transformation is called the **image** of the original figure. The image is often labeled with a small mark (called a "prime").

 The transformed image of *XYZ* is *X'Y'Z'*.

❑ **Translation** is the process of moving a point or figure a specified distance in a certain direction.

 If *P*(−1,1) is shifted down 3 units, what will be the coordinates of *P'*? _____

❑ **Reflection** is the process of moving a point or figure by mirroring it over a line.

 A helpful way to visualize a reflection is to imagine the ink on the figure is wet, then fold the paper along the reflecting line. The imprint of the figure on the other side of the line is the reflection.

 If *P*(−1,1) is reflected over the *y*-axis, what will be the coordinates of *P'*? _____

❑ **Rotation** is the process of moving a point or figure by rotating it around a point – often the origin.

 The best way to visualize rotation is to draw a line segment from a point on the figure to the origin (or whatever point the figure is rotated around). Then, keeping the end on the origin fixed, rotate the line by the specified amount (like the minute hand on a clock). The endpoint of the rotated line is the new rotated point.

 If *P*(−1,1) is rotated 180° about the origin, what will be the coordinates of *P'*? _____

❑ Shapes have **symmetry** when they can be transformed to be exactly like one another. An axis of symmetry is a line that divides a figure into symmetrical images.

❑ FUNCTION TRANSFORMATION Questions. These questions ask you to identify how changes to a function affect the graph of the function. You should memorize the following rules:

$f(x) + n$ shifts the graph UP by $n$ units.

$f(x) - n$ shifts the graph DOWN by $n$ units.

$f(x + n)$ shifts the graph to the LEFT by $n$ units.

$f(x - n)$ shifts the graph to the RIGHT by $n$ units.

$-f(x)$ reflects the graph over the $x$-axis.

$f(-x)$ reflects the graph over the $y$-axis.

The graph of $y = f(x)$ is shown below.  Draw the graph of $y = f(x - 2) - 3$.

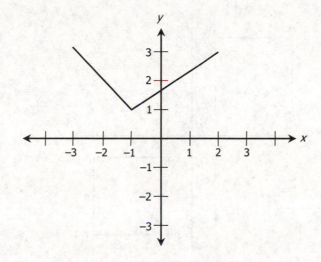

❑ To transform a figure, focus on one corner point (vertex) of the figure at a time. Then redraw the figure.

**PUT IT TOGETHER**

1. In the standard $(x, y)$ coordinate plane, $P(-1, 2)$ will be rotated clockwise (↻) by 90° about the origin. What will be the coordinates of the image of $P$?

   A. $(-1, 2)$
   B. $(1, 2)$
   C. $(2, 1)$
   D. $(2, -1)$
   E. $(-2, -1)$

2. Figure $PQRST$ has been reflected across a line to figure $P'Q'R'S'T'$, as shown in the standard $(x, y)$ plane below. Which of the following is the line of reflection?

   F. $y = 0$

   G. $y = x$

   H. $y = -x$

   J. $y = \dfrac{1}{2}x$

   K. $y = -\dfrac{1}{2}x$

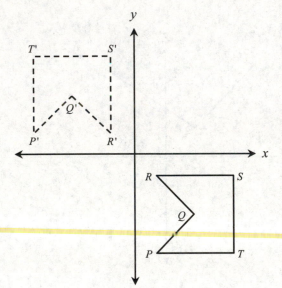

**3.** The graph of $y = f(x)$ is shown in the standard $(x, y)$ coordinate
plane below. Which of the following is the graph of
$y = f(x + 1) - 3$?

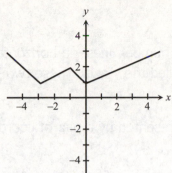

**A.**

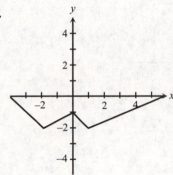

**D.**

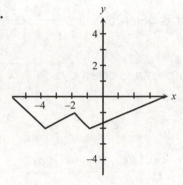

**B.**

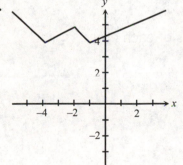

**E.**

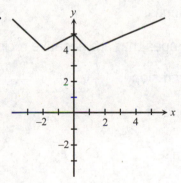

**C.**

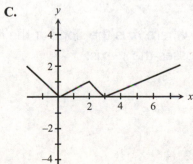

# Coordinate Geometry Summary

Coordinate Geometry Basics

❑ The coordinate plane is a grid made up of two number lines – a horizontal number line called the x-axis, and a vertical number line called the y-axis. These two lines meet at a point called the origin, with coordinates (0,0).

❑ Every point in the coordinate plane can be represented by a pair of coordinates $(x,y)$.

Midpoint and Distance

❑ The midpoint of a segment is given by: $\left( \dfrac{x_1 + x_2}{2}, \dfrac{y_1 + y_2}{2} \right)$

❑ The distance between two points is given by: $\sqrt{(x_2 - x_1)^2 + (y_2 - y_1)^2}$

Slope

❑ The slope of a line is given by: $\dfrac{(y_2 - y_1)}{(x_2 - x_1)}$ or $\dfrac{\text{rise}}{\text{run}}$

❑ Parallel lines have equal slopes.

❑ Perpendicular lines have slopes that are negative reciprocals of each other.

❑ Vertical lines have undefined slope.

❑ Horizontal lines have a slope of 0.

Linear Equations and Inequalities

❑ The standard form of a linear equation is $Ax + By = C$.

❑ The slope-intercept form of a linear equation is $y = mx + b$, where $m$ is the slope of the line and $b$ is the $y$-intercept. The y-intercept is where the line crosses the $y$-axis.

## Conic Sections

❑ Equation of a circle:  $(x - a)^2 + (y - b)^2 = r^2$

❑ Equation of a parabola:  $y = ax^2 + bx + c$

❑ Equation of an ellipse:  $\dfrac{(x - h)^2}{a^2} + \dfrac{(y - k)^2}{b^2} = 1$

## Transformations

❑ Translation is the process of moving a point or figure a specified distance in a certain direction.

❑ Reflection is the process of moving a point or figure by mirroring it over a line.

❑ Rotation is the process of moving a point or figure by rotating it around a point – often the origin.

❑ Shapes have symmetry when they can be transformed to be exactly like one another. An axis of symmetry is a line that divides a figure into symmetrical images.

SUMMIT
EDUCATIONAL
GROUP

# Coordinate Geometry Practice

## Coordinate Geometry Basics

Question 1:        E

1.  The right triangle shown in the figure below lies in the standard
    $(x, y)$ coordinate plane, and is to be rotated 180° around the origin.
    Which of the following coordinate pairs represents the coordinates
    of the vertex of the right angle after the rotation?

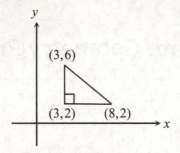

A.  (−8, 2)
B.  (−8, −2)
C.  (3, −2)
D.  (−3, 2)
E.  (−3, −2)

## Midpoint and Distance

Questions 2-5:        E
Questions 6-8:        M

2.  On a number line, a line segment is drawn from −18 to 15. What is
    the midpoint of the line segment?

F.  −6
G.  −1.5
H.  1.5
J.  3
K.  17.5

3.  In the standard $(x, y)$ coordinate plane, what is the distance between
    the points (−4, 3) and (2, 2)?

A.  $\sqrt{17}$
B.  5
C.  $\sqrt{37}$
D.  $\sqrt{65}$
E.  12

4.  A line segment runs from the origin to the point (7,6) in the standard $(x,y)$ coordinate plane. What is the midpoint of the line segment?

    F.  (−3.5, 3)
    G.  (3, 3.5)
    H.  (3, 4)
    J.  (3.5, 3)
    K.  (3.5, 3.5)

5.  In the standard $(x,y)$ coordinate plane, what is the midpoint of a line segment that has endpoints (−2,−6) and (5,8)?

    A.  (−1.5, −1)
    B.  (1.5, −1)
    C.  (1.5, 1)
    D.  (3, 2)
    E.  (2, 3)

6.  The two points (7,−4) and $(x,8)$ have a distance between them of 13 coordinate units. Which of the following could be a value of $x$?

    F.  −2
    G.  0
    H.  5
    J.  7
    K.  12

7.  A line segment in the standard $(x,y)$ coordinate plane has an endpoint at (10,2) and a midpoint at (14,−4). What are the coordinates of the other endpoint of the line segment?

    A.  (12,−1)
    B.  (12,1)
    C.  (18,−10)
    D.  (18,−1)
    E.  (28,−1)

8.  In the standard $(x,y)$ coordinate plane, the midpoint of the line between $(a,b)$ and (12,20) is (4,−10). Which of the following is the value of the sum of $a + b$?

    F.  −44
    G.  −36
    H.  −26
    J.  13
    K.  29

## Slope

Questions 9-11:    E
Questions 12-14:   M

9.  What is the slope of a line segment in the standard $(x,y)$ coordinate plane with endpoints at $(5,8)$ and $(13,12)$?

    A.  $-\dfrac{1}{2}$

    B.  $\dfrac{1}{2}$

    C.  $1$

    D.  $2$

    E.  $\dfrac{16}{7}$

10. A right triangle in the standard $(x,y)$ coordinate plane has vertices at $(2,2)$, $(6,2)$, and $(6,5)$. What is the slope of the hypotenuse?

    F.  $-\dfrac{3}{4}$

    G.  $\dfrac{3}{4}$

    H.  $\dfrac{4}{3}$

    J.  $3$

    K.  $5$

11. Which of the following lines is parallel to the line given by the equation $y = -2x + 7$?

    A.  $y = -2x - 7$

    B.  $y = \dfrac{1}{2}x + 7$

    C.  $y = x + 7$

    D.  $y = 2x - 4$

    E.  $y = 4x + 14$

12. Which of the following is NOT true about the graph of the line $y = 8$?

    F.  It is perpendicular to the line $x = 3$.
    G.  It has a slope of $0$.
    H.  Its slope is undefined.
    J.  It is parallel to the $x$-axis.
    K.  It contains the point $(0,8)$.

**13.** Shown below is the graph of the equation $y = 4x + 1$. Suppose a second line is drawn that passes through the origin and is perpendicular to the given line. What are the coordinates of the point of intersection of the two lines?

A. $\left(-\dfrac{4}{17}, \dfrac{1}{17}\right)$

B. $(1, -4)$

C. $\left(1, \dfrac{1}{4}\right)$

D. $\left(\dfrac{17}{4}, -17\right)$

E. $\left(\dfrac{17}{4}, 17\right)$

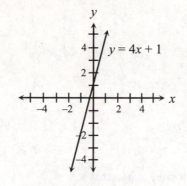

**14.** Points $A$ and $B$ lie in the standard $(x, y)$ coordinate plane. If point $A$ has coordinates $(4, -3)$ and point $B$ has coordinates $(-4, 3)$, then which of the following *must* be true about $\overline{AB}$?

F. It passes through Quadrant III.
G. It has a negative slope.
H. It is perpendicular to the line $y = -2x + b$.
J. It is parallel to the $x$-axis.
K. Its slope is undefined.

## Linear Equations and Inequalities

Questions 15-16:    E
Questions 17-18:    M

**15.** Which of the following equations is written in slope-intercept form?

A. $-2x = y + 5$
B. $x + 5y = 88$
C. $y - 7 = 3x$
D. $y - x = 0$
E. $y = x + 2$

16. If the $y$-intercept of a line is at the point $(0,4)$, and the line also passes through the point $(3,13)$, then what is the equation of the line in slope-intercept form?

    F.  $y = \dfrac{1}{3}x + 4$

    G.  $y = 2x + 2$

    H.  $y = 3x + 4$

    J.  $y = 9x - 3$

    K.  $y = 9x + 4$

17. Shown below is the graph of the equation $y = -\dfrac{1}{2}x + \dfrac{7}{2}$ for all

    values of $y$ such that $-2 \le y \le 3$. Which of the following statements is true?

    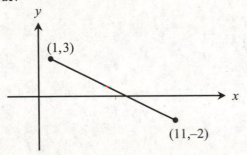

    I.   The line segment has slope $= -\dfrac{1}{2}$.

    II.  The domain of the graph consists of all values of $x$ such that $1 \le x \le 11$.

    III. The $x$-intercept is $(7,0)$.

    A.  I only
    B.  I and II
    C.  I and III
    D.  I, II, and III
    E.  None of the statements are true.

18. If a line has an equation of $y = \dfrac{1}{4}x + b$ and passes through the

    points $(4,0)$ and $(24,5)$, what is the value of $b$?

    F.  −25
    G.  −4
    H.  −1
    J.  4
    K.  5

## Conic Sections

Question 19:    M
Question 20:    H

19. In the $(x, y)$ coordinate plane, a circle is given by the equation $(x - 3)^2 + (y + 2)^2 = 9$.  What are the coordinates of the center of the circle?

    A.  $(2, 9)$
    B.  $(3, 2)$
    C.  $(-3, 2)$
    D.  $(3, -2)$
    E.  $(3, 9)$

20. A circle is tangent to the $y$-axis and has a center with coordinates $(4, 8)$. Which of the following is the equation for this circle?

    F.  $x^2 + y^2 = 8$
    G.  $(x - 4)(y - 8) = 8$
    H.  $(x - 4)^2 + (y - 8)^2 = 4$
    J.  $(x - 4)^2 + (y - 8)^2 = 16$
    K.  $(x + 4)^2 + (y + 8)^2 = 16$

## Transformations

Question 21:    M

21. A rectangle in Quadrant I is to be reflected over the $y$-axis in the standard $(x, y)$ coordinate plane. Which of the following *must* be true about the new graph of this rectangle?

    A.  It is in Quadrant II.
    B.  It is in Quadrant III.
    C.  It is in Quadrant IV.
    D.  Its vertices all have negative $y$-coordinates.
    E.  It is now a square.

## Miscellaneous

Questions 22-24:    E
Questions 25-28:    M
Questions 29-33:    H

22. The midpoint of a line segment has coordinates $(h, 4)$. If $(7, 4)$ and $(1, 4)$ are the coordinates of the two endpoints, then $h = ?$

    F.  1
    G.  2
    H.  3
    J.  4
    K.  7

23. What is the slope of the line through the points $(-4, 1)$ and $(-6, -3)$ in the standard $(x, y)$ coordinate plane?

    A.  $-7$

    B.  $-\dfrac{1}{7}$

    C.  $\dfrac{1}{5}$

    D.  $\dfrac{1}{2}$

    E.  2

24. What is the distance between the points $(-2, 8)$ and $(4, -5)$ in the standard $(x, y)$ coordinate plane?

    F.  5
    G.  $\sqrt{37}$
    H.  12
    J.  $\sqrt{181}$
    K.  $\sqrt{205}$

25. What is the $x$-coordinate of the point in the standard $(x, y)$ coordinate plane where the lines $y = 5x + 1$ and $y = 3x - 3$ intersect?

    A.  $-9$
    B.  $-2$
    C.  1
    D.  2
    E.  17

26. What is the slope-intercept form of $4x - 8 - 2y = 0$?

    **F.**  $y = -2x - 4$
    **G.**  $y = -2x + 4$
    **H.**  $y = 2x - 4$
    **J.**  $y = 4x - 2$
    **K.**  $y = 2x + 4$

27. In the standard $(x, y)$ coordinate plane, the distance between the points $(4, 3)$ and $(8, b)$ is 5. Which of the following could be the value of $b$?

    **A.**  3
    **B.**  5
    **C.**  6
    **D.**  7
    **E.**  $\sqrt{63}$

28. In the standard $(x, y)$ coordinate plane, $P(-3, -1)$ will be reflected over the $y$-axis. What will be the coordinates of the image of $P'$?

    **F.**  $(-3, 1)$
    **G.**  $(-1, 3)$
    **H.**  $(1, -3)$
    **J.**  $(1, 3)$
    **K.**  $(3, -1)$

29. A circle in the standard $(x, y)$ coordinate plane intersects the $x$-axis at $(-7, 0)$ and $(1, 0)$. The radius of the circle is 5 coordinate units. Which of the following could be the center of the circle?

    **I.**  $(-3, -3)$
    **II.**  $(-3, 0)$
    **III.**  $(-3, 3)$

    **A.**  I only
    **B.**  II only
    **C.**  III only
    **D.**  I and III only
    **E.**  I, II, and III

30. Which of the following pairs of functions describes the graph below?

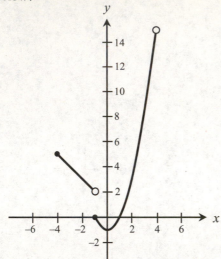

F. $f(x) = x+1, \ -4 \le x < -1$
   $g(x) = x^2 +1, \ -1 < x \le 4$

G. $f(x) = -x+1, \ -4 \le x < -1$
   $g(x) = x^2 -1, \ -1 \le x < 4$

H. $f(x) = 3x+2, \ -4 \le x < -1$
   $g(x) = x^2 -1, \ -1 < x \le 4$

J. $f(x) = -x-1, \ -4 \le x < -1$
   $g(x) = x^2 +1, \ -1 < x \le 4$

K. $f(x) = 2x-1, \ -4 \le x < -1$
   $g(x) = x^2 -1, \ -1 < x \le 4$

31. Let $f(x) = \sqrt{x}$ and $g(x) = 10x + b$. In the standard $(x,y)$ coordinate plane, $y = f(g(x))$ passes through $(4,6)$. What is the value of $b$?

A. $-4$
B. $-14$
C. $-36$
D. $-37$
E. $-38$

32. Parabola $A$ is defined by the equation $y = 3x^2 + 3$. Which of the following could be an equation for parabola $B$?

F.  $y = -\left(\dfrac{3}{2}\right)x^2 + 3$

G.  $y = 3x^2 - 3$

H.  $y = \dfrac{3}{2}x^2 + 3$

J.  $y = 3x^2 - x$

K.  $y = 6x^2 + 3$

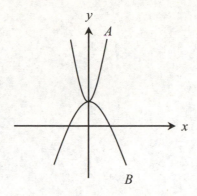

33. The 2 circles $(x + 5)^2 + (y + 5)^2 = 25$ and $(x - 5)^2 + (y - 5)^2 = 25$ are graphed in the standard $(x, y)$ coordinate plane below. Which of the following circles, when graphed, will be tangent to those 2 circles?

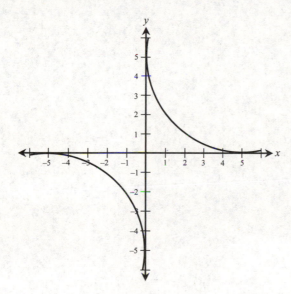

I.   $x^2 + y^2 = 1$

II.  $x^2 + y^2 = 100$

III. $(x - 5)^2 + (y + 5)^2 = 25$

A. I only
B. II only
C. III only
D. I and III only
E. I, II, and III

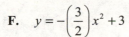

SUMMIT
EDUCATIONAL
GROUP

# Plane Geometry

- ❑ Vocabulary and Foundations

- ❑ Angles

- ❑ Parallel Lines

- ❑ Isosceles and Equilateral Triangles

- ❑ Perimeter and Area of Triangles

- ❑ Right Triangles

- ❑ Similar and Congruent Triangles

- ❑ Quadrilaterals

- ❑ Circles

- ❑ Volume and Surface Area

# Vocabulary and Foundations

❑ To **bisect** means to divide into two equal parts.

❑ A **vertex** is a corner or a point where lines meet.

❑ A **line** is straight, one-dimensional, and extends infinitely in two directions.

❑ A **line segment** is part of a straight line between two points that does not extend beyond these points.

❑ **Perimeter** is the sum of the lengths of the sides of a figure.

❑ **Area** is a measure of the two-dimensional size of a figure.

❑ Objects are **congruent** if they have the same shape and size.

❑ Points are **collinear** if they lie on the same line.

❑ **Supplementary angles** have a sum of 180 degrees.

❑ An **exterior angle** is the angle between a side of a figure and an adjacent side extended outward.

exterior angle

❑ A **polygon** is a closed figure having 3 or more sides.

❑ A **regular polygon** has all sides equal and all angles equal. A regular pentagon, for example, has five equal side and five equal angles.

❑ **Adjacent** sides or angles are next to each other.

❑ The **arc** of a circle is a portion of the circumference.

❑ Common geometric symbols and notations:

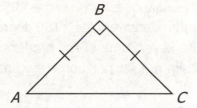

Line segments are denoted by their endpoints. This figure shows line segments $\overline{AB}$ and $\overline{BC}$.

*B* is the vertex of the angle formed by these two line segments.

90° angles are indicated by a small square at the vertex.

Angles are denoted by the vertex, or by three points with the vertex in the middle. In the figure, $\angle B = 90°$, or $\angle ABC = 90°$.

Tick marks are used to indicate line segments that have equal length, or are "congruent." In the figure, $AB = BC$.

Triangles are denoted by the letters at their corners, or "vertices." The triangle in the figure is $\triangle ABC$.

# Angles

About half of the non-trigonometry angle questions on the ACT will ask that you find one angle of a triangle given other interior and exterior angles. "180 degrees in a triangle" and "180 degrees in a straight line angle" are keys. Some of the harder angle questions require that you solve for the interior angles of certain regular polygons (e.g., regular pentagon).

❑ Memorize the following properties of angles.

Right Angle:

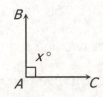

$x =$ _____

Circle:

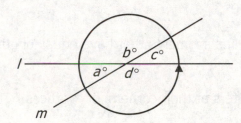

$a + b + c + d =$ _____

Vertical Angles:

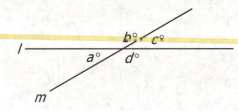

$a =$ _____ ; $b =$ _____

Triangle:

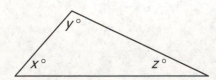

$x + y + z =$ _____

Quadrilateral:

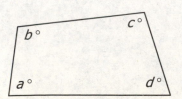

$a + b + c + d =$ _____

❑ The sum of the interior angles of any polygon = $(n-2) \times 180°$, where $n$ is the number of sides.

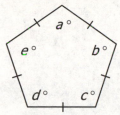

$a + b + c + d + e =$ _____

$a =$ _____

You can also calculate the sum of the interior angles of a polygon by dividing the polygon into triangles and then multiplying the number of triangles by 180°.

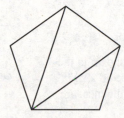

❑ Label all angles in figures as described in the questions. Calculate and label other angles as well. If the figure is not provided, draw one and label it!

## PUT IT TOGETHER

1.  In the figure below, what is the value of *x*?

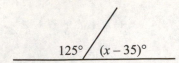

    A.  20
    B.  55
    C.  90
    D.  145
    E.  160

2.  Triangle $\triangle XYZ$ and collinear points *X*, *Y*, and *W* are shown in the figure below. The measure of $\angle X$ is 55°, the measure of $\angle ZYW$ is $(7b)°$, and the measure of $\angle XYZ$ is $(2b)°$. What is the measure of $\angle Z$ ?

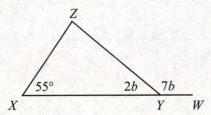

    F.  20°
    G.  40°
    H.  85°
    J.  95°
    K.  140°

3.  In the figure below, regular hexagon *UVWXYZ* is inscribed in the circle. What is the measure of $\angle UZV$ ?

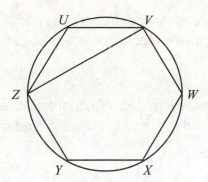

What is the measure of $\angle ZUV$?

A.  15°
B.  30°
C.  45°
D.  60°
E.  75°

# Parallel Lines

(1 per test, (E)(M)(H))

Parallel line questions typically present a diagram – parallelograms, trapezoids, and a variety of parallel lines cut by a transversal – and require a solid understanding of which angles are equal and which are supplementary.

❑ When a line crosses through parallel lines, it creates several sets of equal angles and supplementary angles. The "big" angles are equal and the "small" angles are equal. The sum of a "big" angle and a "small" angle is 180°.

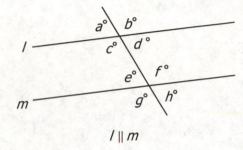

$l \parallel m$

| | |
|---|---|
| $a = d$ | **vertical angles** |
| $d = e$ | **alternate interior angles** |
| $a = e$ | **corresponding angles** |
| $a = h$ | **alternate exterior angles** |
| $a = d = e = h$ | |
| $b = c = f = g$ | |

❑ When a problem contains parallel lines, identify and label all equal angles. Calculate any remaining angles where possible. If a figure is not drawn, draw one!

If $l \parallel m$, and one angle is given as shown, label the unmarked angles in the figure below.

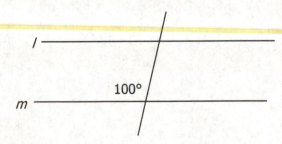

❑ A **parallelogram** is a quadrilateral in which opposite sides are parallel and opposite sides and angles are equal. A **trapezoid** is a quadrilateral in which one pair of opposite sides is parallel. If the non-parallel sides of a trapezoid are equal in length, then the figure is called an **isosceles trapezoid**.

Questions with parallelograms and trapezoids are often parallel line questions. Use your parallel line and angle rules to calculate all the angles.

**PUT IT TOGETHER**

1.  In the figure below, parallel lines *l* and *m* intersect parallel lines *s* and *t*.  If it can be determined, what is the value of *a* + *b*?

    A.  140°
    B.  180°
    C.  220°
    D.  280°
    E.  360°

    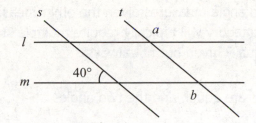

2.  In parallelogram *LMNO*, the measure of ∠*MNO* is 73° and the measure of ∠*LMO* is 80°.  What is the measure of ∠*LMN* ?

    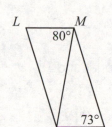

    F.  73°
    G.  83°
    H.  100°
    J.  107°
    K.  153°

3.  In the figure below, the measure of ∠*ABE* is less than the measure of ∠*DEG* .  Given this information, which of the following CANNOT be true?

    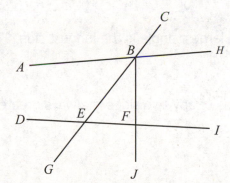

    A.  $\overline{BF} \perp \overline{DF}$
    B.  ∠*ABC* + ∠*DEG* = 180°
    C.  $\overline{AB} \cong \overline{EF}$
    D.  ∠*DEG* = ∠*BEF*
    E.  △*BEF* is a right triangle.

# Isosceles and Equilateral Triangles

(0-1 per test, (E)(M) H )

❑ Isosceles and equilateral triangle questions test your knowledge of the definitions and your ability to calculate side lengths and angle measures given the other measures of the triangle. Harder questions in this category will typically require multiple steps and additional knowledge or skills. Figures are usually given but not always.

❑ In an **isosceles** triangle, two sides are equal, and the two angles opposite those sides are equal.

The straight line that bisects the vertex angle of an isosceles triangle is the perpendicular bisector of the base.

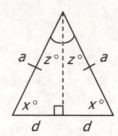

❑ In an **equilateral** triangle, all three sides are equal and each of the angles is 60°.

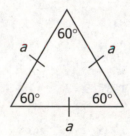

❑ Once you know you have an isosceles or equilateral triangle, label and calculate all sides and angles. If no figure is given, draw one!

❑ In any triangle, the side opposite the largest angle is the longest side. The side opposite the smallest angle is the shortest side.

❑ In any triangle, the sum of the lengths of any two sides is always greater than the length of the third side.

## PUT IT TOGETHER

1. For all triangles $\triangle ABC$ where side $\overline{AB}$ is shorter than side $\overline{BC}$, such as the figure shown below, which of the following statements must be true?

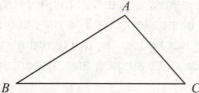

Guesstimate. If one angle in a triangle is very acute, how long is the side opposite?

   A. The measure of $\angle A$ is less than the measure of $\angle C$.
   B. The measure of $\angle A$ is greater than the measure of $\angle C$.
   C. The measure of $\angle A$ is equal to the measure of $\angle C$.
   D. The measure of $\angle A$ is greater than or equal to the measure of $\angle C$.
   E. The measure of $\angle A$ is less than or equal to the measure of $\angle C$.

2. In the figure below, the area of square $BCDE$ is 36. $\triangle ABC$ is equilateral. What is the perimeter of the entire figure?

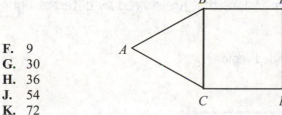

   F. 9
   G. 30
   H. 36
   J. 54
   K. 72

3. In $\triangle XYZ$, the measure of $\angle Y$ is $56°$, and $\angle X$ and $\angle Z$ are congruent. What is the measure of $\angle X$?

Draw the figure, including all the information you've been given.

   A. $56°$
   B. $62°$
   C. $68°$
   D. $78°$
   E. $124°$

# Perimeter and Area of Triangles

(0-2 per test, E Ⓜ Ⓗ)

Area questions are more common than perimeter questions, but neither is typically tested in a direct, simple way on the ACT. Instead of actual side lengths, a question might provide algebraic expressions for the lengths or provide ratios of side lengths. The question might complicate the figure by combining a triangle with another figure. Or, the figure might lie on a coordinate grid. Knowing the formulas, having a toolbox of strategies, and recognizing common question types are all important.

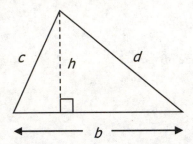

Area = _____

Perimeter = _____

❑ Choose numbers when the figure doesn't give you specific dimensions.

❑ OVERLAPPING FIGURE questions.  Look for dimensions that are shared by different figures when different shapes overlap.

In the figure below, what is the area of the shaded region?

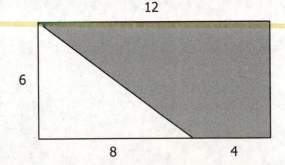

12

6

8　　4

**PUT IT TOGETHER**

1.  Triangle *JFK* is similar to *MLK*. *JF* is 10 inches long, *FK* is 24 inches long, and *KJ* is 26 inches long. The shortest side of *MLK* is 15 inches long. What is the perimeter, in inches, of *MLK*?

    A.  75
    B.  90
    C.  120
    D.  135
    E.  180

2.  The base and sides of a regular pyramid are equilateral triangles. The side length of the base is 4 inches. What is the surface area, in square inches, of the pyramid?

    F.  4
    G.  12
    H.  $12\sqrt{3}$
    J.  16
    K.  $16\sqrt{3}$

3.  In the figure below, *ABCD* is a square with side length 6, and $AE = BF = DG = 2$. What is the ratio of the area of *EFG* to the area of *ABCD*?

    A.  $\dfrac{5}{24}$

    B.  $\dfrac{5}{18}$

    C.  $\dfrac{5}{12}$

    D.  $\dfrac{5}{9}$

    E.  $\dfrac{5}{7}$

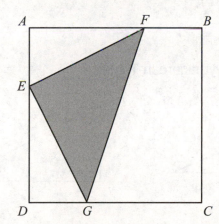

> Break the figure into more familiar shapes. For what shapes can you find areas?

# Right Triangles

(1-2 per test, Ⓔ Ⓜ Ⓗ)

For easier right triangle questions (non-trigonometry), you'll be asked to solve for a side of a given right triangle. The solution requires applying the Pythagorean Theorem or the special right triangle rule. Harder questions, though, involve multiple steps, where solving for a side of a triangle is only a part of the solution. Challenging questions might involve overlapping figures, similar triangles, and shapes where you'll have to draw in the triangle.

❑ The hypotenuse is the longest side of a right triangle. It is opposite the right angle.

The two non-right angles have a sum of 90°.

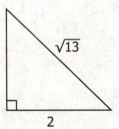

❑ Pythagorean Theorem: $a^2 + b^2 = c^2$

Use the Pythagorean Theorem to find the length of the missing leg of each right triangle.

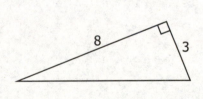

❑ Save time by recognizing common Pythagorean Triples.

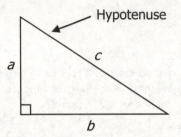

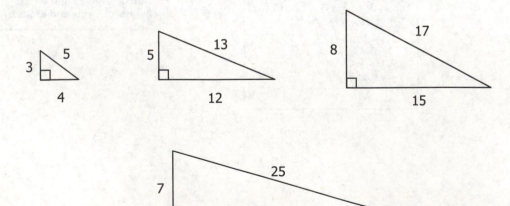

❑ A 45-45-90 triangle is an isosceles right triangle whose sides are in the ratio of $1:1:\sqrt{2}$ .

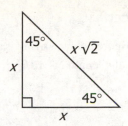

❑ A 30-60-90 triangle is a right triangle whose sides are in the ratio of $1:\sqrt{3}:2$ .

A 30-60-90 right triangle is half of an equilateral triangle.

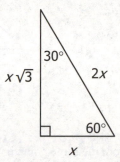

Find the lengths of the missing sides of each of the right triangles below.

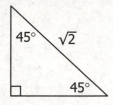

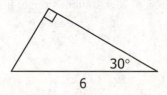

**PUT IT TOGETHER**

1.  In the figure below, $\triangle ABC$ is a right isosceles triangle. If $BC = 2$, what is the length of $\overline{AB}$?

    A.  $\dfrac{\sqrt{2}}{2}$

    B.  $\sqrt{2}$

    C.  2

    D.  $2\sqrt{2}$

    E.  4

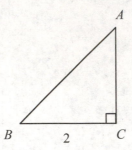

2.  Starting from the same point, a husband and wife drive in different directions to work. The husband first drives 12 miles due south, and then drives 15 miles due west, where he arrives at work. The wife drives 7 miles due east, and then drives 24 miles due north, where she arrives at work. When they are both at work, what is the sum, rounded to the nearest mile, of each of their straight line distances from home?

    F.  39
    G.  44
    H.  45
    J.  46
    K.  58

> Draw a diagram to visualize the word problem.

3.  In the figure below, $\overline{AB} \cong \overline{BC}$, and $\angle ABC \cong \angle BCA$. If the base of the triangle has a length of $s$, what is the height of the triangle in terms of $s$?

    A.  $\dfrac{s\sqrt{3}}{4}$

    B.  $\dfrac{s\sqrt{3}}{2}$

    C.  $s\sqrt{2}$

    D.  $s\sqrt{3}$

    E.  $2\sqrt{3}s$

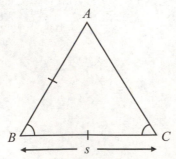

> Try Choosing Numbers for *s*.

# Similar and Congruent Triangles    (1 per test, E Ⓜ H)

Most similar triangle questions give two similar triangles, either in words or in a figure, and you have to set up a proportion to solve them. Slightly more difficult questions require that you first recognize the similar triangles and then solve using proportionality of sides. Congruent triangle questions appear infrequently, are typically difficult, and require you to identify or use the congruence of two triangles.

❑ **Similar triangles** have corresponding angles that are equal and corresponding sides that are proportional. Similar triangles have the same shape but not necessarily the same size.

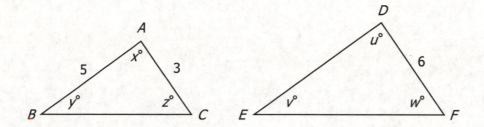

If the two triangles above are similar, what is the length of side $\overline{DE}$ ? _____

❑ A line segment that intersects two sides of a triangle and is parallel to the third side creates two similar triangles.

A line segment connecting midpoints of two sides of a triangle is parallel to the third side of the triangle.

If $E$ is the midpoint of $\overline{BC}$,
$D$ is the midpoint of $\overline{AC}$, and
$\overline{AB} = x$, what is the length of
$\overline{DE}$ in terms of $x$? _____

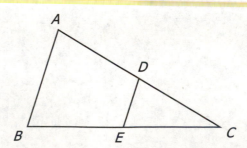

❑ **Congruent trianlges** are equal in size and shape. Corresponding sides and angles are equal.

Fill in the missing angle
measures and side lengths.

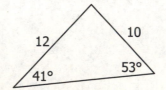

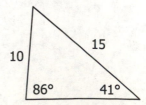

**PUT IT TOGETHER**

1.  In the figure below, △*ABC* is similar to △*XYZ*, with the side
    lengths given in feet. What is the perimeter, in feet, of △*XYZ*?

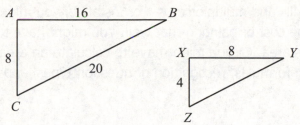

    A.  16
    B.  22
    C.  24
    D.  25
    E.  28

2.  The lengths of corresponding sides of two similar right triangles
    are in the ratio of 3 to 5. The shortest side of the larger triangle is
    120 units long. What is the length, in units, of the shortest side of
    the smaller triangle?

    F.  200
    G.  160
    H.  80
    J.  72
    K.  24

3.  In the figure below, $\overline{AB} \parallel \overline{DE}$. If $AB = 8$, $AE = 3$, and
    $EC = 9$, what is the length of $\overline{DE}$?

    A.  $4\frac{1}{2}$
    B.  5
    C.  6
    D.  $6\frac{1}{4}$
    E.  8

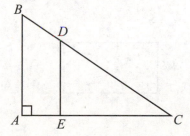

> A triangle with an interior line
> parallel to one side often
> indicates a similar triangles
> question.

# Quadrilaterals

(3-4 per test, Ⓔ Ⓜ Ⓗ)

While there are easy questions that require direct application of the area and perimeter formulas, most in this category involve other skills and multiple steps. For instance, you might have to calculate the area of a wall and then the cost of painting that wall. You might have to plot a rhombus on a coordinate grid and find its area. Or you might have to calculate an area given certain ratios. In all cases, familiarity with formulas, recognition of question types, and facility with strategies are all essential.

❑ A **trapezoid** is a quadrilateral with only one pair of parallel sides. The parallel sides are the bases. In an isosceles trapezoid, the non-parallel sides are equal.

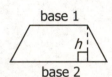

Area = _____

❑ A **parallelogram** is a quadrilateral in which opposite sides are equal and opposite angles are equal. Its diagonals bisect each other.

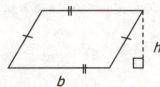

Area = _____

❑ A **rhombus** is a parallelogram with sides of equal length. Its diagonals are perpendicular bisectors of each other.

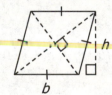

Area = _____

❑ A **rectangle** is a parallelogram with four right angles.

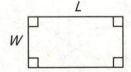

Perimeter = _____

Area = _____

❑ A **square** is a rhombus with four right angles. All sides are congruent.

Perimeter = _____

Area = _____

❑ To find the area or perimeter of an irregular shape, divide the shape using familiar shapes.

Perimeter: _____

Area: _____

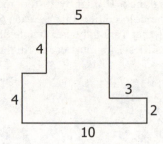

## PUT IT TOGETHER

1.  Tara is making a 10-foot by 20-foot rectangular mural out of rectangular colored tiles that are each 6 inches by 4 inches. Assuming that Tara only uses whole tiles, what is the minimum number of tiles Tara must use to fill the entire mural space?

    **Pay attention to units of measurement.**

    A.  900
    B.  1200
    C.  1600
    D.  1800
    E.  2400

2.  In the figure below, all of the line segments meet at right angles, and all of the measurements are given in meters. In meters, what is the perimeter of the figure?

    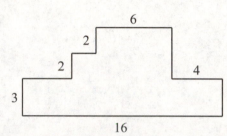

    F.  38
    G.  42
    H.  46
    J.  52
    K.  60

3.  The area of a trapezoid is given by the formula $A = \frac{1}{2}h(b_1 + b_2)$, where $h$ is the height and $b_1$ and $b_2$ are the lengths of the parallel bases. What is the area, in square inches, of the trapezoid given below?

    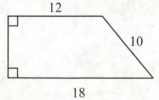

    A.  84
    B.  90
    C.  96
    D.  108
    E.  120

**4.** A parallelogram drawn in the standard $(x,y)$ coordinate plane has its vertices at $(-6,-4)$, $(0,-4)$, $(3,0)$, and $(-3,0)$. What is the area of the parallelogram in square coordinate units?

**F.** 12
**G.** $12\sqrt{2}$
**H.** $16\sqrt{2}$
**J.** 24
**K.** 30

**5.** In the figure below, $F$ lies $\dfrac{1}{4}$ of the way from $A$ to $B$ on rectangle $ABCD$, and $AF = CH$. $E$ bisects $AD$ and $G$ bisects $BC$. The area of parallelogram $EFGH$ is what fraction of the area of rectangle $ABCD$?

**A.** $\dfrac{1}{4}$

**B.** $\dfrac{3}{8}$

**C.** $\dfrac{1}{2}$

**D.** $\dfrac{5}{8}$

**E.** $\dfrac{3}{4}$

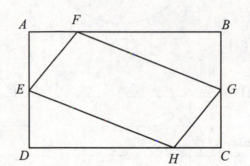

> **Choose Numbers on geometry problems when you aren't given specific values.**

**6.** Trapezoid $ABCD$ can be divided into 12 equilateral triangles of side length 2, as shown below. What is the area of $ABCD$?

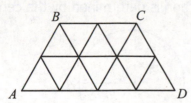

**F.** 12
**G.** $12\sqrt{3}$
**H.** $24\sqrt{3}$
**J.** 48
**K.** $48\sqrt{3}$

# Circles

Circle questions appear in multiple contexts, including direct application of formulas, overlapping and shaded regions, circumference and revolutions, and sector and arc length questions. Knowing the approximation of $\pi$ as 3.14 is important since some questions ask for the best approximation of an answer.

❑  Area = _____

❑  Circumference = _____

❑  Diameter = _____

❑  $\pi$ = _____

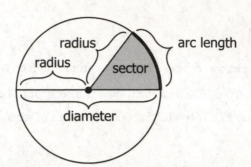

Complete the table below.

| Area | Circumference | Radius | Diameter |
|------|---------------|--------|----------|
| $16\pi$ | | | |
| | $10\pi$ | | |
| | | $\sqrt{2}$ | |
| | | | 5 |

❑  The area of a sector is a fraction of the area of the circle. Similarly, an arc length is a fraction of the circumference. In both cases, the fraction is determined by the central angle.

Area of Sector $AOB = \dfrac{x}{360}\left(\pi r^2\right)$

Length of Arc $AB = \dfrac{x}{360}\left(2\pi r\right)$

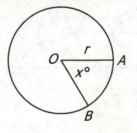

In the figure, the circle with center $O$ has a radius of 6.

What is the length of arc $AB$? _____

What is the area of sector $AOB$? _____

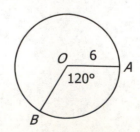

**PUT IT TOGETHER**

1.  A large circle with radius 2 inches is shown in the figure below. 2 smaller circles with radius $r$ inches are removed from the large circle. What is the area, in square inches, of the shaded region remaining after the smaller circles are removed?

    **A.**  $\pi - \pi r^2$
    **B.**  $2\pi - \pi r^2$
    **C.**  $2\pi - 2\pi r^2$
    **D.**  $4\pi - 2\pi r^2$
    **E.**  $4\pi - 4\pi r^2$

    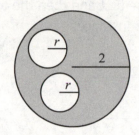

2.  A wheel with a radius of $\dfrac{20}{\pi}$ inches is rolling in a straight line along the ground. Assuming the wheel does not jump or skid, how many inches will the wheel travel in 21 revolutions?

    **F.**  $42\pi$
    **G.**  $420$
    **H.**  $\dfrac{420}{\pi}$
    **J.**  $\dfrac{840}{\pi}$
    **K.**  $840$

    > Distance traveled = Circumference times number of revolutions

3.  In the figure below, the circle centered at $A$ has a radius of 12 centimeters. The area of the sector created by central angle $\angle BAC$ is $24\pi$ cm$^2$. What is the measure of $\angle BAC$?

    > Starting with the radius, what else can you calculate?

    **A.**  $30°$
    **B.**  $45°$
    **C.**  $60°$
    **D.**  $120°$
    **E.**  $135°$

    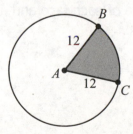

# Volume and Surface Area

(1-2 per test, E Ⓜ Ⓗ)

Questions in this category generally require direct application of the formulas either in the forward or backward direction. Many are presented in real world contexts such as pools and silos. Occasionally, you'll have to find the volume first and then the total weight or cost based on some given cost or weight per cubic foot, for instance.

❑ Cube

Volume = _____

Surface Area = _____

❑ Rectangular Box

Volume = _____

Surface Area = _____

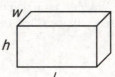

❑ Cylinder

Volume = $\pi r^2 h$

Surface Area = $2\pi rh + 2\pi r^2$

The formulas for volume and surface area of cylinders are provided in cylinder questions.

❑ To find the surface area of any solid, find the area of each face and add the areas all together.

## PUT IT TOGETHER

1.  A formula for the surface area, *SA*, of a right circular cylinder is
    $SA = 2\pi r^2 + 2\pi rh$, where *r* is the radius and *h* is the height. A
    cylindrical grain silo, whose base is shown below, has a height of
    25 meters. Assuming that the silo has a flat top and a flat bottom,
    what is the surface area, in square meters, of the grain silo?

    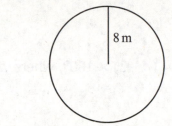

    8 m

    A.  $208\pi$
    B.  $400\pi$
    C.  $416\pi$
    D.  $432\pi$
    E.  $528\pi$

2.  Two neighbors both have rectangular swimming pools in their
    backyards. One neighbor's pool has dimensions that are twice as
    great as the dimensions of the other's pool. What is the ratio of the
    volumes of the two pools?

    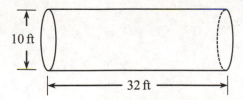

    Try Choosing Numbers for the
    pool dimensions.

    F.  1:1
    G.  2:1
    H.  4:1
    J.  8:1
    K.  16:1

3.  The cylindrical storage tank shown below, which lies horizontally
    underground, has diameter 10 feet and length 32 feet and is filled
    with gasoline.

    10 ft

    32 ft

    If 1 cubic foot of gasoline weighs approximately 47 pounds, then
    how much is the weight, in pounds, of the gasoline in the tank?

    (Note: the volume of a right circular cylinder is given by $\pi r^2 h$,
    where *r* is the radius and *h* is the height.)

    A.  Less than 60,000
    B.  Between 60,000 and 80,000
    C.  Between 80,000 and 100,000
    D.  Between 100,000 and 120,000
    E.  More than 120,000

# Plane Geometry Summary

Angles

❑ Right angle = 90°

❑ Straight line angle = 180°

❑ Sum of interior angles of triangle = 180°

❑ The sum of the interior angles of any polygon = $(n-2) \times 180°$, where $n$ is the number of sides.

Parallel Lines

❑ When a line crosses through parallel lines, it creates several sets of equal angles and supplementary angles.

Isosceles and Equilateral Triangles

❑ In an isosceles triangle, two sides are equal, and the two angles opposite those sides are equal.

❑ In an equilateral triangle, all three sides are equal and each of the angles is 60°.

❑ In any triangle, the side opposite the largest angle is the longest side. The side opposite the smallest angle is the shortest side.

❑ In any triangle, the sum of the lengths of any two sides is always greater than the length of the third side.

Perimeter and Area of Triangles

❑ Area of triangle = $\frac{1}{2}(\text{base} \times \text{height})$

Right Triangles

❑ Pythagorean Theorem: $a^2 + b^2 = c^2$

Similar and Congruent Triangles

❑ Similar triangles have corresponding angles that are equal and corresponding sides that are proportional. Similar triangles have the same shape but not necessarily the same size.

❑ Congruent trianlges are equal in size and shape. Corresponding sides and angles are equal.

## Quadrilaterals

❑ A trapezoid is a quadrilateral with only one pair of parallel sides. The parallel sides are the bases. In an isosceles trapezoid, the non-parallel sides are equal.

❑ A parallelogram is a quadrilateral in which opposite sides are equal and opposite angles are equal. Its diagonals bisect each other.

❑ A rhombus is a parallelogram with sides of equal length. Its diagonals are perpendicular bisectors of each other.

❑ A rectangle is a parallelogram with four right angles.

❑ A square is a rhombus with four right angles. All sides are congruent.

## Circles

❑ Area of circle = $\pi r^2$

❑ Circumference = $2\pi r$

❑ The area of a sector is a fraction of the area of the circle. Similarly, an arc length is a fraction of the circumference. In both cases, the fraction is determined by the central angle.

## Volume and Surface Area

❑ Cube
Volume = $s^3$

Surface Area = $6s^2$

❑ Rectangle
Volume = $l \times w \times h$

Surface Area = $2lw + 2lh + 2wh$

❑ Cylinder
Volume = $\pi r^2 h$

Surface Area = $2\pi rh + 2\pi r^2$

# Plane Geometry Practice

## Angles

Questions 1-3:    E
Question 4:     M

1. In the figure below, ∠*ABC* and ∠*CBD* are supplementary. If the measure of ∠*ABC* is three times the measure of ∠*CBD*, what is the measure of ∠*ABC*?

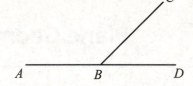

    **A.** 135°
    **B.** 120°
    **C.** 75°
    **D.** 60°
    **E.** 45°

2. Through how many degrees does the minute hand of a clock rotate in one and a half hours?

    **F.** 180
    **G.** 270
    **H.** 360
    **J.** 540
    **K.** 630

3. The figure below shows quadrilateral *CDEF*. What is the measure of ∠*D*?

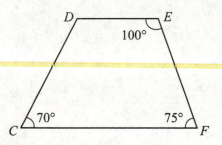

    **A.** 95°
    **B.** 105°
    **C.** 115°
    **D.** 135°
    **E.** 295°

4.  In the figure below, points $A$, $C$, and $D$ are collinear, $B$, $C$, $E$, and $G$ are collinear, and $F$, $E$, and $D$ are collinear. If the measure of $\angle EFG = 30°$ and the measure of $\angle ACB = 40°$, what is the measure of $\angle CDE$ ?

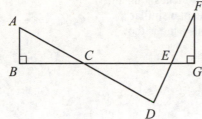

F.  60°
G.  65°
H.  75°
J.  80°
K.  90°

## Parallel Lines

Question 5:      E
Question 6:      M

5.  In the figure below, lines $L_1$ and $L_2$ are parallel and are crossed by transversal $L_3$. What is the value of $x + y$?

A.  110°
B.  140°
C.  180°
D.  210°
E.  250°

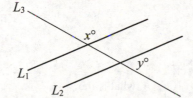

6.  In the figure below, two parallel lines are intersected by two transversals that intersect at point $C$. Two angles are marked. What is the measure of $\angle DCE$ ?

F.  45°
G.  55°
H.  60°
J.  65°
K.  75°

## Isosceles and Equilateral Triangles

Questions 7-8:      M

7.  An isosceles triangle $\triangle ABC$ has one side that is 7 inches long and another that is 14 inches long. If the shortest side of a similar triangle $\triangle DEF$ is 5 inches long, which of the following is the length of another side of $\triangle DEF$ in inches?

    A.  5
    B.  7
    C.  8
    D.  9
    E.  10

8.  If the lengths of two sides of a triangle are 4 and 11, which of the following could be a length of the third side?

    F.  3
    G.  4
    H.  7
    J.  11
    K.  16

## Perimeter and Area of Triangles

Questions 9-10:      M

9.  A triangle has sides with lengths $4x, 5x,$ and $7x$. If $x = 4$, what is the perimeter of the triangle?

    A.  14
    B.  54
    C.  64
    D.  128
    E.  172

10. In right triangle $\triangle DEF$, the legs have lengths of $x$ and $x+3$. In terms of $x$, what is the area of the triangle?

    F.  $2x+3$
    G.  $3x+9$
    H.  $\dfrac{x^2+3x}{2}$
    J.  $x^2+3x$
    K.  $x^2+3x+3$

## Right Triangles

Questions 10-12:    E
Questions 14-16:    M
Question 17:        H

11. A ball is rolled up a ramp with a base that is 24 feet long and an incline that is 25 feet long, as shown below. If the ball is rolled up the ramp and pushed over the edge, how far, in feet, would the ball fall?

    A.  3
    B.  5
    C.  7
    D.  9
    E.  11

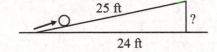

25 ft

?

24 ft

12. A right triangle has legs of lengths 4 and 5. What is the length of the hypotenuse?

    F.  6
    G.  $6\sqrt{2}$
    H.  $\sqrt{41}$
    J.  9
    K.  20

13. A tour plane left the airport at the equator and flew 80 miles due east out over the sea, then turned to the north and flew 40 miles due north. At that point, the plane flew straight back to the airport. Which of the following is the distance, in miles, of the straight flight back to the airport?

    A.  $\sqrt{120}$
    B.  $\sqrt{3200}$
    C.  85
    D.  $\sqrt{8000}$
    E.  100

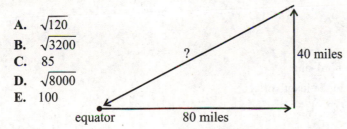

?

40 miles

equator          80 miles

14. Three sides of a triangle are in the ratio of $8 : 8\sqrt{3} : 16$. What is the largest angle of the triangle?

    F.  60
    G.  90
    H.  120
    J.  140
    K.  150

**15.** In the figure below, the corners of square *EFGH* are at the midpoints of the sides of square *ABCD*. If the length of $\overline{AB}$ is $8\sqrt{2}$ units, what is the length of $\overline{EF}$ in units?

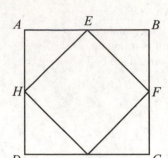

A. 8
B. 12
C. $12\sqrt{2}$
D. 15
E. 16

**16.** In the figure below, right triangles △*BCD* and △*ABC* share a side along $\overline{BC}$. What is the length of $\overline{AC}$?

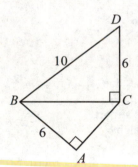

F. $2\sqrt{6}$
G. $2\sqrt{7}$
H. 6
J. 8
K. 10

**17.** In the circle below, $\overline{AO}$ is a radius, $\overline{BD}$ is a chord, and $\overline{AC} \perp \overline{BD}$. If the length of $\overline{AO}$ is 5 inches, and the length of $\overline{AC}$ is 8 inches, what is the length, in inches, of $\overline{CD}$?

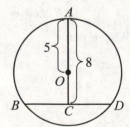

A. 4
B. $4\sqrt{2}$
C. $4\sqrt{3}$
D. 6
E. 12

## Similar and Congruent Triangles

Questions 18-19:    M

18. In the figure below, $\triangle DEF \sim \triangle RST$. If the measure of $\angle EDF$ is 40° and the measure of $\angle RST$ is 100°, what is the measure of $\angle DFE$?

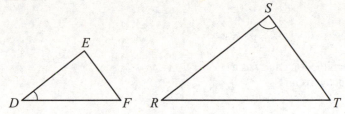

    **F.**  30°
    **G.**  40°
    **H.**  45°
    **J.**  50°
    **K.**  55°

19. In the figure below, $\overline{AB}$ is parallel to $\overline{DE}$, the length of $\overline{AD}$ is 6, and the length of $\overline{EC}$ is $2\sqrt{3}$. What is the length of $\overline{AB}$?

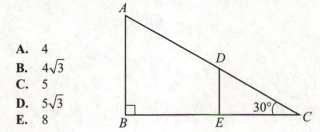

    **A.**  4
    **B.**  $4\sqrt{3}$
    **C.**  5
    **D.**  $5\sqrt{3}$
    **E.**  8

## Quadrilaterals

Question 20:      E
Questions 21-23:    M

20. In the figure below, the length of $\overline{AB}$ is 3 inches, and the area of the parallelogram is 19.5 square inches. What is the height, in inches, of the parallelogram?

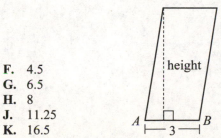

    **F.**  4.5
    **G.**  6.5
    **H.**  8
    **J.**  11.25
    **K.**  16.5

21. A rectangle has one side length of 16 centimeters and another side length that is 15 centimeters less than three times the length of the first side. What is the perimeter of the rectangle?

    A. 34 cm
    B. 62 cm
    C. 66 cm
    D. 72 cm
    E. 98 cm

22. A rectangular classroom is 12 feet wider than it is long and has a perimeter of 136 feet. How many feet long is the room?

    F. 18
    G. 24
    H. 28
    J. 36
    K. 40

23. What is the area of the shaded portion of the figure drawn below?

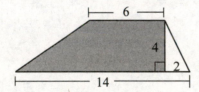

    A. 20
    B. 24
    C. 28
    D. 32
    E. 36

## Circles

Questions 24-25:   M
Questions 26-28:   H

24. Two circles have circumferences of $12\pi$ and $8\pi$. Which of the following gives the ratio of the area of the larger circle to the area of the smaller circle?

    F. $4:9\pi$
    G. $4:3$
    H. $9:4$
    J. $9:4\pi$
    K. $144\pi:64$

**25.** Two concentric circles with center *A* are shown in the figure below. The inner circle has a radius of 4, and the distance from *B* to *C* is 12. What is the difference between the area of the larger circle and the area of the smaller circle?

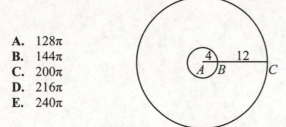

    **A.** 128π
    **B.** 144π
    **C.** 200π
    **D.** 216π
    **E.** 240π

**26.** In the figure below, two smooth wheels are turning clockwise and rotating a belt that is wrapped around them. The larger wheel has a radius of 4 inches and the smaller one has a radius of 2 inches. For every 360° the larger wheel rotates, how many degrees does the smaller wheel rotate?

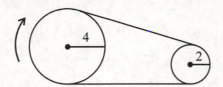

    **F.** 180°
    **G.** 540°
    **H.** 720°
    **J.** 1080°
    **K.** 1440°

**27.** A 12-inch by 16-inch rectangle is inscribed into a circle as shown below. What is the area, in square inches, of the shaded region?

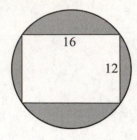

   **A.**  $10\pi - 192$
   **B.**  $100\pi - 216$
   **C.**  $100\pi - 192$
   **D.**  $400\pi - 192$
   **E.**  $400\pi$

**28.** A certain game is played by dropping marbles onto a special board with point values labeled, as shown below. The radius of the smallest circle is 2 inches. The radius of each circle is twice as large as the one inside it. If a marble is dropped randomly, what is the chance that it will land in the 10-point area or the 40-point area?

   **F.**  $\dfrac{17}{128}$

   **G.**  $\dfrac{13}{64}$

   **H.**  $\dfrac{8}{13}$

   **J.**  $\dfrac{7}{10}$

   **K.**  $\dfrac{1}{2}$

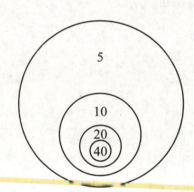

## Volume and Surface Area

Question 29:     M
Question 30:     H

**29.** A construction crew has to fill the wooden form below with concrete. The dimensions, in feet, are as marked, and all edges meet at right angles. How much concrete, in cubic feet, is needed to fill the form exactly to the top?

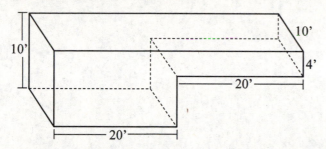

    **A.**  1920
    **B.**  2440
    **C.**  2560
    **D.**  2800
    **E.**  3280

**30.** A rectangular solid has side lengths of $a$, $2a$, and $3b$. In terms of $a$ and $b$, what is the surface area of the rectangle?

    **F.**  $6a^2b$
    **G.**  $2a^2 + 9ab$
    **H.**  $2a^2 + 18ab$
    **J.**  $4a^2 + 9ab$
    **K.**  $4a^2 + 18ab$

## Miscellaneous

Questions 31-35:    E
Questions 36-37:    M
Questions 38-40:    H

**31.** In △ABC below, $\overline{AB} \cong \overline{BC}$. What is the measure of ∠ABC?

    **A.**  50°
    **B.**  55°
    **C.**  60°
    **D.**  65°
    **E.**  75°

**32.** In the figure below, square *ABCD* is inscribed in a circle. If the diameter of the circle is 8, what is the length of a side of the square?

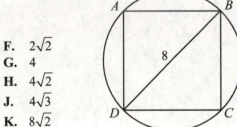

    **F.**  $2\sqrt{2}$
    **G.**  4
    **H.**  $4\sqrt{2}$
    **J.**  $4\sqrt{3}$
    **K.**  $8\sqrt{2}$

**33.** A rug measuring 5 feet by 12 feet is cut diagonally. What is the length, in feet, of the diagonal cut?

    **A.**  13
    **B.**  15
    **C.**  15.5
    **D.**  17
    **E.**  18

**34.** In the figure below, square *ABCD* is divided into four equally sized smaller squares. If a smaller square has a side length of 6, what is the length of the diagonal of *ABCD* (not shown)?

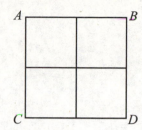

**F.**  12
**G.**  $6\sqrt{2}$
**H.**  $12\sqrt{2}$
**J.**  16
**K.**  $20\sqrt{2}$

**35.** In the figure below, line *L* is tangent to a circle. If the radius $\overline{AB}$ is 12, and the length of $\overline{BC}$ is 5, what is the length of $\overline{AC}$?

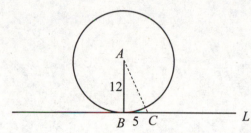

**A.**  $5\sqrt{3}$
**B.**  10
**C.**  12
**D.**  13
**E.**  15

**36.** Billy has a set of identical rectangular blocks with dimensions as shown below. When he is not playing with them, his mother stacks them in a cupboard with dimensions of 18×15×20 inches. If all of the blocks completely fill the cupboard, leaving no extra space, how many blocks does Billy have?

**F.**  27
**G.**  81
**H.**  135
**J.**  270
**K.**  1350

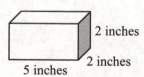

37. A farmer's rectangular field is 600 ft by 80 ft and is all grazing
    land for a cow. The farmer decides to build a circular pig sty with a
    radius of 8 ft in the field. How much land, in square feet, is left for
    grazing?

    A.  2800 + 8π
    B.  48000 − 64π
    C.  60000 − 100π
    D.  40000 − 64π
    E.  48000

38. A circle has a radius of 5. What is the measure of an arc on that
    circle that is intercepted by a central angle of 144°?

    F.  4π
    G.  10
    H.  10π
    J.  25
    K.  25π

39. In the figure below, △DEF is inscribed in △ABC and $\overline{BD} \cong \overline{BF}$ .
    Three angles are as marked. What is the measure of ∠AED?

    A.  40°
    B.  45°
    C.  50°
    D.  55°
    E.  60°

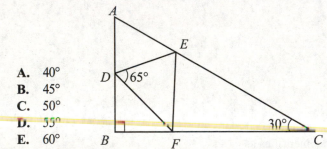

40. In the figure below, points A, C, and D are collinear, and B, C, and
    E are collinear. Which of the following conclusions CAN be
    justified by the given information?

    F.  ∠ABC ≅ ∠CBD
    G.  $\overline{CE} \cong \overline{CD}$
    H.  $\overline{AB} \perp \overline{BD}$
    J.  ∠BDE > 90
    K.  $\overline{AB}$ is parallel to $\overline{ED}$ .

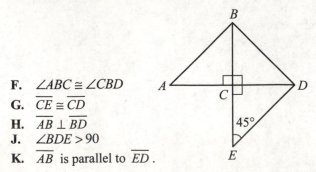

# Trigonometry

- SOH CAH TOA

- Trig Identities

- The Unit Circle

- Graphs of Sine and Cosine

- Laws of Sines and Cosines

# SOH CAH TOA

(2-3 per test, E Ⓜ Ⓗ)

Trigonometry is tested lightly on the ACT. In fact, there are a total of four trig questions on the entire test. Typically, two of those questions will ask that you "solve" a right triangle by using the sine, cosine, and tangent functions or their inverses. All of these questions can be solved by applying SOHCAHTOA, the acronym that describes the relationships between basic trig functions and the ratios of sides of a right triangle.

❑ **SOH CAH TOA** is an acronym that represents the right triangle relationships for sine, cosine, and tangent.

SOH: $Sin\,\theta = \dfrac{length\ of\ \mathbf{O}pposite\ side}{length\ of\ \mathbf{H}ypotenuse}$

CAH: $Cos\,\theta = \dfrac{length\ of\ \mathbf{A}djacent\ side}{length\ of\ \mathbf{H}ypotenuse}$

TOA: $Tan\,\theta = \dfrac{length\ of\ \mathbf{O}pposite\ side}{length\ of\ \mathbf{A}djacent\ side}$

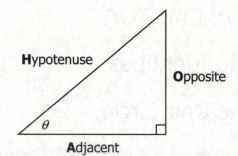

❑ The inverses of those functions do the reverse. They allow you to find an angle measure from the ratio of the side lengths. The inverses of these functions are written $sin^{-1}$, $cos^{-1}$, and $tan^{-1}$, or as arcsin, arcos, and arctan.

$Sin^{-1}\,\dfrac{opposite}{hypotenuse} = \theta$

$Cos^{-1}\,\dfrac{adjacent}{hypotenuse} = \theta$

$Tan^{-1}\,\dfrac{opposite}{adjacent} = \theta$

❑ You can use SOH CAH TOA on inverse trig questions as well.

$sin^{-1}\dfrac{3}{5} = $ _____

$cos^{-1}\dfrac{3}{5} = $ _____

$tan^{-1}\dfrac{4}{3} = $ _____

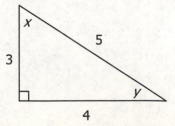

**PUT IT TOGETHER**

1.  In the right triangle shown below, which of the following statements is true?

    A.   $\cos A = \dfrac{8}{15}$

    B.   $\sin A = \dfrac{8}{15}$

    C.   $\tan A = \dfrac{15}{8}$

    D.   $\cos C = \dfrac{8}{17}$

    E.   $\tan C = \dfrac{15}{17}$

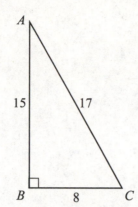

2.  If $0 \le \theta \le \dfrac{\pi}{2}$ and $\cos\theta = \dfrac{12}{13}$, then $\sin\theta = ?$

    Draw a right triangle and fill in side lengths with the information given.

    F.   $\dfrac{1}{5}$

    G.   $\dfrac{5}{13}$

    H.   $\dfrac{5}{12}$

    J.   $\dfrac{12}{13}$

    K.   $\dfrac{13}{12}$

**3.** An airplane is on an upward straight-line trajectory, with an angle of incline measuring 42°, as shown in the figure below. The airplane must climb 890 feet from its current altitude in order to reach its cruising altitude. Which of the following expressions gives the distance, in feet, from the airplane's current position to its position when it reaches its cruising altitude?

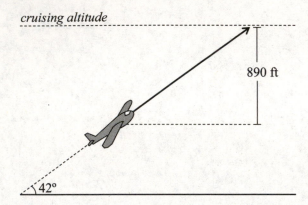

A. $\dfrac{890}{\sin 42°}$

B. $\dfrac{890}{\cos 42°}$

C. $\dfrac{\sin 42°}{890}$

D. $\dfrac{\cos 42°}{890}$

E. $\dfrac{890}{\tan 42°}$

**4.** A ship leaving from an island motors on a constant bearing, or angle, so that after traveling 23 nautical miles, it will reach a harbor 8 miles to the East and an unknown distance to the North, as shown in the figure below. Which of the following expressions gives the bearing of the ship?

(Note: 1 nautical mile = 0.869 miles)

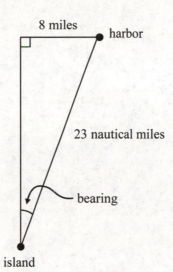

**F.** $\mathrm{Sin}^{-1}\dfrac{8}{23}$

**G.** $\mathrm{Tan}^{-1}\dfrac{8}{23\times0.869}$

**H.** $\mathrm{Sin}^{-1}\dfrac{8}{23\times0.869}$

**J.** $\mathrm{Cos}^{-1}\dfrac{8}{23\times0.869}$

**K.** $\mathrm{Tan}^{-1}\dfrac{8\times0.869}{23}$

# Trig Identities

Occasionally, a trig question will ask you to simplify an expression through the use of some of the fundamental trig identities.

❑ Tangent:  $\tan\theta = \dfrac{\sin\theta}{\cos\theta}$

❑ Cotangent:  $\cot\theta = \dfrac{\cos\theta}{\sin\theta} = \dfrac{1}{\tan\theta}$

❑ Secant:  $\sec\theta = \dfrac{1}{\cos\theta}$

❑ Cosecant:  $\csc\theta = \dfrac{1}{\sin\theta}$

❑ $\sin^2\theta + \cos^2\theta = 1$

   When you see both a $\sin^2$ and $\cos^2$ in a trig expression, try to manipulate the expression to get $\sin^2 + \cos^2$, so you can replace it with 1.

❑ Rarely, a different trig identity will be introduced, but it'll be provided for you, so you don't need to memorize a whole list of identities.

   If $\cos x = \dfrac{1}{2}$, what is the value of $\cos 2x$? _____

   (note:  $(\cos x)^2 = \dfrac{1 + \cos 2x}{2}$ )

## PUT IT TOGETHER

1. For $0 < x < \dfrac{\pi}{2}$, which of the following is equivalent to $\dfrac{\cos x}{\tan x}$?

   A. $\sin x$

   B. $\dfrac{1}{\sin x}$

   C. $\dfrac{1}{\cos x}$

   D. $\dfrac{\cos^2 x}{\sin x}$

   E. $\dfrac{\cos x}{\sin x}$

2. For $0 \le \theta \le \pi$, if $2\sin^2\theta = y - 2\cos^2\theta$, what is the value of $y$?

   F. $\dfrac{\pi}{2}$

   G. $2$

   H. $\pi$

   J. $\dfrac{3\pi}{2}$

   K. $6$

> Rearrange equations to create expressions that are more familiar and useful.

# The Unit Circle

(0-1 per test, E Ⓜ Ⓗ)

The Unit Circle can be a challenging topic, but for the most part, you can do well on ACT trig questions with just the basics. Questions in this category take different forms: Some revolve around understanding the relationship between degrees and radians; others require that you solve for an angle whose terminal side lies in quadrants 2, 3, or 4; others require an understanding that angles of different size can share a terminal side.

❑  The Unit Circle

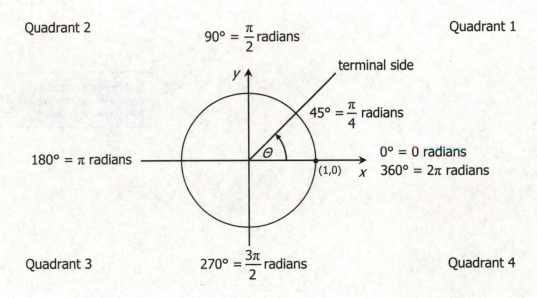

❑  Angles can be measured in both degrees and radians.  180 degrees is equal to $\pi$ radians.

❑  To convert from radians to degrees, multiply by $\dfrac{180}{\pi}$. To convert from degrees to radians multiply by $\dfrac{\pi}{180}$.

What is the value of 240° in radians?  _____

What is the value of $\dfrac{\pi}{2}$ radians in degrees?  _____

❑ The value of the *x* and *y* coordinates where the **terminal** side of the angle intersects the unit circle equals the cosine and sine of the angle, respectively. Use SOH CAH TOA to see this.

The signs of the cosine functions in each quadrant mirror the signs of the *x* coordinates. Similarly, the signs of the sine functions mirror the signs of the *y* coordinates.

Terminal side $\overline{OA}$ has length of 1 unit.

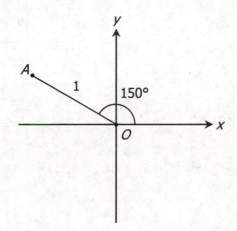

1.  Draw a right triangle with $\overline{OA}$ as the hypotenuse.

2.  Using right triangle rules, find the other side lengths of the right triangle.

3.  What are the coordinates of point *A*? _____

4.  Find the sine and cosine of 150°.

    cos 150° = _____

    sin 150° = _____

❑ Angles can be bigger than 360 degrees, and they can be negative.

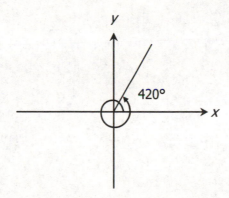

List two angles that are coterminal with 405°: _____  _____

List two angles that are coterminal with −210°: _____  _____

Is $\cos \dfrac{9\pi}{4}$ positive or negative? _____

❑ Memorize the following 1$^{st}$ quadrant common sine and cosine values.

| Angle Measure | Sine | Cosine |
|---|---|---|
| 0° = 0 radians | 0 | 1 |
| 30° = $\frac{\pi}{6}$ radians | $\frac{1}{2}$ | $\frac{\sqrt{3}}{2}$ |
| 45° = $\frac{\pi}{4}$ radians | $\frac{\sqrt{2}}{2}$ | $\frac{\sqrt{2}}{2}$ |
| 60° = $\frac{\pi}{3}$ radians | $\frac{\sqrt{3}}{2}$ | $\frac{1}{2}$ |
| 90° = $\frac{\pi}{2}$ radians | 1 | 0 |

## PUT IT TOGETHER

1. If $\dfrac{\pi}{2} < \theta < \pi$ and $\sin\theta = \dfrac{5}{13}$, then $\cos\theta = ?$

    A.  $\dfrac{12}{13}$

    B.  $\dfrac{5}{12}$

    C.  $\dfrac{5}{13}$

    D.  $-\dfrac{5}{12}$

    E.  $-\dfrac{12}{13}$

> Draw a right triangle and fill in side lengths with the information given.
>
> What quadrant is the terminal side of the angle in?
>
> What is the sign of cosine in this quadrant?

2. Angle $F$ has a measure of $\dfrac{37\pi}{6}$ radians. Angle $G$ and Angle $F$ are coterminal. Angle $G$ could have which of the following measures?

    F.  30°
    G.  45°
    H.  60°
    J.  120°
    K.  210°

# Graphs of Sine and Cosine

(0-1 per test, E  M (H))

The rare graph question will give you a trig function or the graph of a trig function and ask that you determine the period and/or the amplitude.

❑  $y = \sin x$

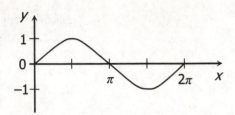

Period (one cycle) = $2\pi$

Amplitude (height) = 1

$\sin(0) = 0$

$\sin\left(\dfrac{\pi}{2}\right) = 1$

❑  $y = \cos x$

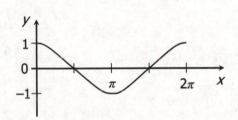

Period (one cycle) = $2\pi$

Amplitude (height) = 1

$\cos(0) = 1$

$\cos\left(\dfrac{\pi}{2}\right) = 0$

❑  The amplitude shows how "tall" the graph is. The amplitude is governed by the coefficient in front of the function. In the function $y = A\sin Bx$, $A$ is the amplitude.

Notice that $y = 2\sin x$ has an amplitude of 2, or 2 times the amplitude of $y = \sin x$.

The maximum value of the function $y = 2\sin x$ is 2.

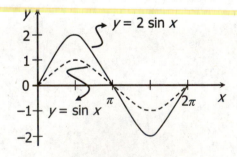

❑  The period is how long it takes for the graph to go through one complete cycle.

In the function $y = A\sin Bx$, $\dfrac{2\pi}{B}$ is the period.

$y = \sin 2x$ has a period of $\pi$, which is $\dfrac{1}{2}$ the period of $y = \sin x$.

Notice that the relationship between the period and the coefficient is inverse.

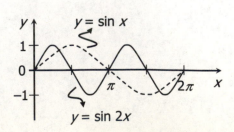

## PUT IT TOGETHER

1.  The function $y = \sin x$ is shown on the graph below. Let $p$ equal the interval over which the curve completes one entire cycle before repeating itself over the next interval (for $y = \sin x$, $p = 2\pi$). For the function $y = \sin \dfrac{x}{2}$ (not shown), what is the value of $p$?

    A.  $\dfrac{\pi}{2}$

    B.  $\dfrac{2\pi}{3}$

    C.  $\pi$
    D.  $2\pi$
    E.  $4\pi$

    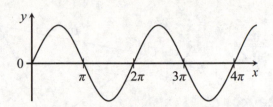

2.  Which of the following trigonometric functions has an amplitude of 4?

    (Note: A trigonometric function's amplitude is half the positive difference between its maximum and minimum values.)

    F.  $f(x) = 4\sin x$

    G.  $f(x) = \sin 4x$

    H.  $f(x) = \dfrac{\sin x}{4}$

    J.  $f(x) = \cos \dfrac{x}{4}$

    K.  $f(x) = \cos 4x$

# Laws of Sines and Cosines

(0-1 per test, E  M  (H))

Occasionally, one of the four trig questions will require that you use the Law of Sines or the Law of Cosines to solve for an angle or side of a non-right triangle. These questions are easy to spot because the question will provide you with the formula. You just need to plug in appropriately and solve.

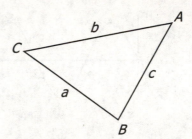

☐ Law of Sines:    $\dfrac{a}{\sin A} = \dfrac{b}{\sin B} = \dfrac{c}{\sin C}$

☐ Law of Cosines:  $c^2 = a^2 + b^2 - 2ab\cos c$

## PUT IT TOGETHER

1. $\overline{AB}$ is a line segment along one bank of a stream and point $C$ is on the opposite bank. If the measure of $\angle A$ equals 30°, the measure of $\angle C$ equals 45°, and the length of $\overline{BC}$ is 400 feet, what is the length, in feet, of $\overline{AB}$?

   (Note: Law of Sines: $\dfrac{a}{\sin A} = \dfrac{b}{\sin B} = \dfrac{c}{\sin C}$)

   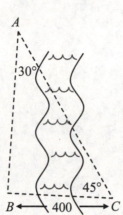

   A. 200
   B. $200\sqrt{2}$
   C. 275
   D. $300\sqrt{3}$
   E. $400\sqrt{2}$

2. As shown in the figure below, $\triangle ABC$ has two sides of length 4 inches and one side of length $x$ inches. The degree measure of the angle between $\overline{AB}$ and $\overline{AC}$ is $\theta$. In terms of $x$, what is the value of $\cos\theta$?

   (Note: The Law of Cosines states that for any triangle, if $a$, $b$, and $c$ are the lengths of the sides opposite $\angle A$, $\angle B$, and $\angle C$, respectively, then $a^2 = b^2 + c^2 - 2bc \cos\angle A$.)

   F. $\dfrac{x^2 + 32}{32}$

   G. $\dfrac{x^2 - 32}{32}$

   H. $\dfrac{x^2 - 16}{32}$

   J. $\dfrac{32 - x^2}{32}$

   K. $\dfrac{16 - x^2}{32}$

   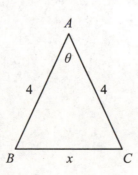

# Trigonometry Summary

SOH CAH TOA

☐  $\sin \theta = \dfrac{\text{opposite}}{\text{hypotenuse}}$

☐  $\cos \theta = \dfrac{\text{adjacent}}{\text{hypotenuse}}$

☐  $\tan \theta = \dfrac{\text{opposite}}{\text{adjacent}}$

☐  $\sin^{-1} \dfrac{\text{opposite}}{\text{hypotenuse}} = \theta$

☐  $\cos^{-1} \dfrac{\text{adjacent}}{\text{hypotenuse}} = \theta$

☐  $\tan^{-1} \dfrac{\text{opposite}}{\text{adjacent}} = \theta$

Trig Identities

☐  Tangent:   $\tan \theta = \dfrac{\sin \theta}{\cos \theta}$

☐  Cotangent:   $\cot \theta = \dfrac{\cos \theta}{\sin \theta} = \dfrac{1}{\tan \theta}$

☐  Secant:   $\sec \theta = \dfrac{1}{\cos \theta}$

☐  Cosecant:   $\csc \theta = \dfrac{1}{\sin \theta}$

☐  $\sin^2 \theta + \cos^2 \theta = 1$

## Unit Circle

❑ Angles can be measured in both degrees and radians. 180 degrees is equal to $\pi$ radians

❑ The value of the $x$ and $y$ coordinates where the terminal side of the angle intersects the unit circle equals the cosine and sine of the angle, respectively.

❑ Angles can be bigger than 360 degrees, and they can be negative.

## Graphs of Sine and Cosine

❑ The amplitude shows how "tall" the graph is. The amplitude is governed by the coefficient in front of the function. In the function $y = A\sin Bx$, $A$ is the amplitude.

❑ The period is how long it takes for the graph to go through one complete cycle.

In the function $y = A\sin Bx$, $\dfrac{2\pi}{B}$ is the period.

## Laws of Sines and Cosines

❑ Law of Sines: $\dfrac{a}{\sin A} = \dfrac{b}{\sin B} = \dfrac{c}{\sin C}$

❑ Law of Cosines: $c^2 = a^2 + b^2 - 2ab\cos c$

# Trigonometry Practice

## SOH CAH TOA

Questions 1-5:     M
Question 6:        H

1.  In the right triangle shown below, $a$, $b$, and $c$ are the lengths of the sides. What is the value of $\sin\theta$?

    A.  $\dfrac{c}{b}$

    B.  $\dfrac{c}{a}$

    C.  $\dfrac{b}{a}$

    D.  $\dfrac{a}{b}$

    E.  $\dfrac{a}{c}$

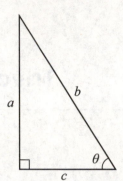

2.  In the triangle below, the length of $\overline{BC}$ is 6 inches and $\cos B = \dfrac{4}{5}$.

    What is the length, in inches, of the hypotenuse of the right triangle $\triangle ABC$?

    F.  3.8
    G.  7.0
    H.  7.5
    J.  8.0
    K.  15.0

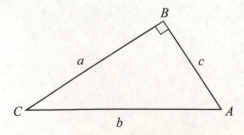

3.  In the right triangle below, which of the following expressions is equal to $\cos\angle C$ ?

    A.  $\dfrac{c}{a}$

    B.  $\dfrac{c}{b}$

    C.  $\dfrac{a}{b}$

    D.  $\dfrac{a}{c}$

    E.  $\dfrac{b}{a}$

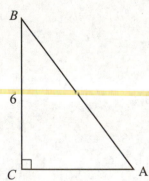

4.  For the right triangle below, what is the value of $\sin B + \cos B$?

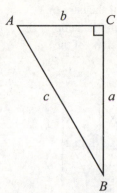

F.  $\dfrac{b}{a}$

G.  $\dfrac{a}{c}$

H.  $\dfrac{a+b}{c}$

J.  $\dfrac{b-c}{a}$

K.  $\dfrac{a}{b+c}$

5.  The sun shines over the top of a building, casting a shadow over an area located on the opposite side of the building. The distance between the top of the building and the edge of the shadow is 60 feet, as shown in the figure below. What is the height, in feet, of the building?

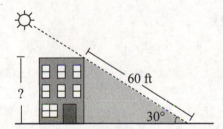

A.  10
B.  15
C.  30
D.  35
E.  52

6.  In the figure below, $\tan \theta = 1$. What is the length of $\overline{OA}$?

F.  $\sqrt{2}$
G.  $\sqrt{3}$
H.  3
J.  $2\sqrt{3}$
K.  $3\sqrt{2}$

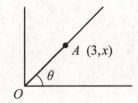

## Trig Identities

Questions 7-9:     H

7.  A runway lamp is located 18 meters from the center of the base of
    an airplane control tower. If the angle of elevation from the lamp
    to the top of the tower is 53°, what is the height, in meters, of the
    tower?

    A.  18 sec 53°
    B.  18 tan 53°
    C.  18 sin 53°
    D.  18 cot 53°
    E.  18 cos 53°

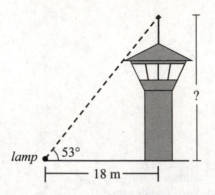

8.  Given that $\sin(\alpha + \beta) = (\sin\alpha)(\cos\beta) + (\cos\alpha)(\sin\beta)$, which of the
    following expressions is equivalent to $\sin\left(\dfrac{5\pi}{12}\right)$?

    (Note: $\dfrac{5\pi}{12} = \dfrac{3\pi}{12} + \dfrac{2\pi}{12}$ )

    F.  $\dfrac{1}{2}$

    G.  $\dfrac{\sqrt{8}}{4}$

    H.  $\dfrac{\sqrt{3}}{2}$

    J.  $\dfrac{\sqrt{6} + \sqrt{2}}{4}$

    K.  $\dfrac{\sqrt{3} + 1}{2}$

9. If $a$ and $c$ are positive, $0 < \theta < \pi$, and $\cos\theta = -\dfrac{a}{c}$, then what is $\cot\theta$?

   A.  $\dfrac{c}{a}$

   B.  $\dfrac{a}{\sqrt{c^2 - a^2}}$

   C.  $\dfrac{a}{\sqrt{c^2 - a^2}}$

   D.  $-\dfrac{\sqrt{c^2 - a^2}}{a}$

   E.  $-\dfrac{a}{\sqrt{c^2 - a^2}}$

## The Unit Circle

Question 10:      M
Questions 11-13:  H

10. The formula $\left[\dfrac{90(x+y)}{z}\right]$ is used to represent the measure of the

    angle, in degrees, at the intersection of two roads. What is the measure of this angle in radians?

    F.  $\dfrac{\pi(x+y)}{2z}$

    G.  $\dfrac{(x+y)}{2z}$

    H.  $\dfrac{\pi(x+y)}{180z}$

    J.  $\dfrac{\pi}{2z}$

    K.  $\dfrac{\pi}{180z}$

**11.** If $0 < \theta < \pi$ and $\tan\theta = -\dfrac{4}{3}$, then $\sin\theta = ?$

    **A.** $\dfrac{5}{3}$

    **B.** $\dfrac{4}{5}$

    **C.** $\dfrac{3}{4}$

    **D.** $\dfrac{3}{5}$

    **E.** $-\dfrac{4}{5}$

**12.** If $90° \le x° \le 180°$ and $4\sin^2 x = 3$, what is the value of $\cos x$?

    **F.** $\dfrac{\sqrt{3}}{2}$

    **G.** $\dfrac{\sqrt{2}}{2}$

    **H.** $\dfrac{1}{2}$

    **J.** $-\dfrac{\sqrt{3}}{2}$

    **K.** $-\dfrac{1}{2}$

**13.** What is the value of $x$ if $16\cos^2 x + 1 = 5$ and $0° \le x° \le 90°$?

    **A.** $0°$

    **B.** $30°$

    **C.** $45°$

    **D.** $60°$

    **E.** $90°$

## Graphs of Sine and Cosine

Question 14:      H

14. The graph of $y = \tan x$ is shown below. What is the period of function $\tan x$?

F. $\dfrac{2}{\pi}$

G. $\dfrac{\pi}{2}$

H. $\pi$

J. $\dfrac{3\pi}{2}$

K. $2\pi$

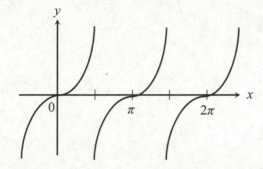

## Laws of Sines and Cosines

Question 15:      H

15. Two asteroids are traveling through space, each on a straight-line path toward Planet Brutus, as shown below. The angle between the trajectories from each asteroid to Planet Brutus is 48°. At the moment when Asteroid $A$ is 40 miles from Planet Brutus and Asteroid $B$ is 30 miles from Planet Brutus, how far apart are the two asteroids?

(Note: The law of cosines states that for any triangle with vertices $A$, $B$, and $C$ and the sides opposite those vertices with lengths $a$, $b$, and $c$, respectively, $c^2 = a^2 + b^2 - 2ab\cos C$.)

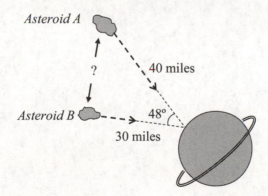

A. $\sqrt{40^2 + 30^2 + 2(40)(30)\cos 42°}$

B. $\sqrt{40^2 + 30^2 + 2(40)(30)\cos 48°}$

C. $\sqrt{40^2 + 30^2 - 2(40)(30)\cos 42°}$

D. $\sqrt{40^2 + 30^2 - 2(40)(30)\cos 48°}$

E. $\sqrt{40^2 + 30^2 - 2\cos 42°}$

## Miscellaneous

Questions 16-18:   M
Questions 19-25:   H

16. If $\dfrac{3\pi}{2} < \theta < 2\pi$ and $\tan\theta = -\dfrac{5}{12}$, then $\cos\theta = ?$

   F.   $-\dfrac{12}{13}$

   G.   $-\dfrac{5}{13}$

   H.   $\dfrac{5}{13}$

   J.   $\dfrac{5}{12}$

   K.   $\dfrac{12}{13}$

17. For the triangle shown below, $\dfrac{\cos Q}{\tan P}$ is equivalent to:

   A.   $\dfrac{p}{r}$

   B.   $\dfrac{q}{r}$

   C.   $\dfrac{p^2}{rq}$

   D.   $\dfrac{q^2}{pr}$

   E.   $\dfrac{r}{q}$

18. For what values of $\theta$, if $0° \le \theta < 360°$, does $\tan\theta = -1$?

   F.   $0°$ and $360°$ only
   G.   $90°$ and $180°$ only
   H.   $45°$ and $225°$ only
   J.   $135°$ and $315°$ only
   K.   $45°$, $135°$, $225°$, and $315°$

**19.** If $\tan\theta = \dfrac{x}{2}$ and $0 < \theta < \dfrac{\pi}{2}$, then what is $\sin\theta$?

A. $\dfrac{2}{x+2}$

B. $\dfrac{x}{\sqrt{x^2+4}}$

C. $\dfrac{2}{\sqrt{x^2+4}}$

D. $\dfrac{\sqrt{x^2+4}}{2}$

E. $\dfrac{\sqrt{x^2+4}}{x}$

**20.** A spotlight is mounted onto the ground pointing upward to the top of a flagpole that is 60 feet high. The angle of elevation of the beam of light originating from the spotlight is 49°. What is the distance, in feet, between the spotlight and the base of the flagpole?

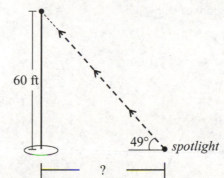

F.  60 tan 49°

G.  60 cot 49°

H.  60 sin 49°

J.  60 sec 49°

K.  60 cos 49°

**21.** A search light shines directly down from a helicopter onto level ground as shown in the diagram below. If the helicopter is 50 feet above the ground surface, which of the following expressions could be used to calculate the width of the illuminated portion of the ground surface?

A.  50 tan 40°

B.  $\dfrac{50}{\tan 20°}$

C.  $\dfrac{100}{\tan 20°}$

D.  50 tan 20°

E.  100 tan 20°

**22.** In the figure shown below, $\overline{CD}$ intersects $\overline{AB}$ to form two right triangles, $\triangle ABC$ and $\triangle BCD$, which share a common side $\overline{BC}$. What is $\sin \theta$?

(Note: $\sin (x - y) = \sin x \cdot \cos y - \sin y \cdot \cos x$ for all $x$ and $y$)

F. $\dfrac{11}{52}$

G. $\dfrac{33}{80}$

H. $\dfrac{33}{65}$

J. $\dfrac{48}{65}$

K. $\dfrac{63}{65}$

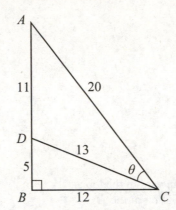

**23.** The equations of the two functions graphed below are

$$f(x) = a_1 \sin x \quad \text{and} \quad g(x) = a_2 \cos \frac{3}{2} x.$$

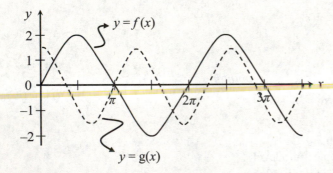

Which of the following is true of $a_1$ and $a_2$?

A. $a_1 < 0 < a_2$

B. $a_1 < a_2 < 0$

C. $a_2 < a_1 < 0$

D. $0 < a_1 < a_2$

E. $0 < a_2 < a_1$

**24.** Angle $X$ has a measure of $\dfrac{9\pi}{4}$ radians. Angle $X$ and Angle $Y$ are coterminal. Angle $Y$ could have which of the following measures?

F.   225°
G.   180°
H.   135°
J.   90°
K.   45°

**25.** A bird flies upward from the ground at a constant angle of ascent. At an altitude of 120 feet, it has flown 150 feet horizontally, as illustrated below. Which of the following expressions gives the angle of the bird's ascent?

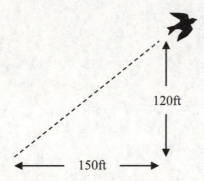

120ft

150ft

A.   $\arcsin\left(\dfrac{120}{150}\right)$

B.   $\arcsin\left(\dfrac{150}{120}\right)$

C.   $\arccos\left(\dfrac{150}{120}\right)$

D.   $\arctan\left(\dfrac{120}{150}\right)$

E.   $\arctan\left(\dfrac{150}{120}\right)$

SUMMIT
EDUCATIONAL
GROUP

# Science Overview

- ❏ The Science Test
- ❏ Format and Scoring
- ❏ Attractors
- ❏ Setting Your Goal
- ❏ Working Through the Science Test
- ❏ General Tips

# The Science Test

| Format | 40 questions |
|--------|--------------|
|        | Multiple-choice |
|        | 4 answer choices |
| Content | Biology |
|         | Chemistry |
|         | Physics |
|         | Geology |
|         | Astronomy |
|         | Meteorology |
| Scoring | Science Test Score: 1-36 |
| Time | 35 minutes |

❑ The Science Test does not focus on your knowledge of scientific facts. Instead, it tests how well you can use the skills of scientific reasoning.

❑ Almost all of the questions in the Science Test can be answered by referring only to the material presented in the relevant passages.

However, between 1 and 5 questions per test may rely upon scientific knowledge not contained in their passages.

A few questions may require mathematic calculations. In addition to identifying trends or finding averages, you may occasionally have to use algebra or geometry skills.

# Format and Scoring

❏ You receive 1 raw point for a correct answer. You lose nothing for incorrect answers. Your **raw score** is calculated by adding up raw points. Your raw score is then converted to a **scaled score** from 1-36.

❏ You are asked to work through several passages. Each test contains:

12-16 Data Representation questions. Each passage typically has 5 questions.

18-22 Research Summary questions. Each passage typically has 6 questions.

6-8 Conflicting Viewpoints questions. Each passage typically has 7 questions.

❏ **Data Representation** passages describe scientific phenomena. They typically present graphs and tables which quantify the relationships between 2-4 different variables. Data Representation questions will ask you to describe the relationships between the variables.

❏ **Research Summary** passages describe scientific experiments and their results. They typically detail the experiment's hypothesis, design, and quantifiable results. Research Summary questions will ask you about the experiment's design, execution, and conclusions.

❏ **Conflicting Viewpoints** passages present two or more theories about various scientific phenomena. Not all theories can be correct. These questions will not necessarily ask you to determine which theory is correct, but they will ask you to describe each viewpoint and its relationships to the others.

❏ The instructions are the same on every ACT. Familiarize yourself with the instructions before you take the test. At test time, you can skip the instructions and focus on the problems.

**DIRECTIONS:** There are seven passages in this test. Each passage is followed by several questions. After reading a passage, choose the best answer to each question and fill in the corresponding oval on your answer document. You may refer to the passages as often as necessary.
You are NOT permitted to use a calculator on this test.

# Attractors

❑   Spot and avoid attractor answer choices.

The test writers anticipate typical student mistakes and include those mistakes as answer choices. In other words, they set traps for the unsuspecting student. We call these answer choices "attractors." Attractors show up most often on medium and difficult problems.

Try to spot the attractor answer choices in the following problems.
Consider how a student might mistakenly choose each attractor answer.

A high school physics class videotaped a member of the diving team jumping off of a stationary platform. Cameras were located both above and below the surface of the water to track his position over the course of the jump, including the time that he spent underwater.

The class recorded information until the diver surfaced from the pool. "Point A" was a sticker placed on his body that the class used to determine his position. The class used the data from the video to create Figure 1 below.

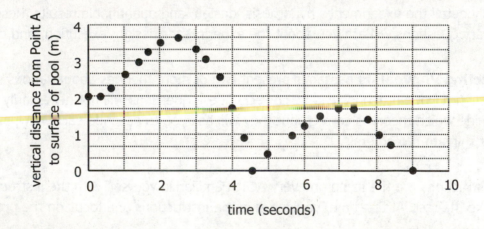

Figure 1

1. According to Figure 1, the diver was briefly at rest at all of the following times EXCEPT:

   A.  0 seconds
   B.  2.5 seconds
   C.  4.5 seconds
   D.  7 seconds

2. Which of the following BEST describes what is occurring to the diver between 4.5 and 6.5 seconds?

   F.  He was surfacing for air.
   G.  He was jumping off the board for a second time.
   H.  He was traveling through the air towards the water.
   J.  He was underwater and traveling downwards.

# Setting Your Goal

❑ You don't have to get every question right to score well.

To score a 21 on the Science Test – which is above the national average – you need to answer only 23 of the 40 questions correctly. That's only 58%, or just over half of the questions! On your regular school tests, 58% is a failing grade, but on the ACT, it's above average!

❑ Use the table below to set a target for the number of questions you need to answer correctly to hit your goal score for the Science Test.

| Science Scaled Score | Science Raw Score | Percent Correct |
|---|---|---|
| 36 | 40 | 100% |
| 35 | 39 | 98% |
| 33 | 38 | 95% |
| 32 | 37 | 93% |
| 31 | 36 | 90% |
| 29 | 35 | 88% |
| 28 | 33-34 | 84% |
| 27 | 32 | 80% |
| 26 | 31 | 78% |
| 25 | 29-30 | 74% |
| 24 | 28 | 70% |
| 23 | 26-27 | 66% |
| 22 | 24-25 | 61% |
| 21 | 23 | 58% |
| 20 | 21-22 | 54% |
| 19 | 19-20 | 49% |
| 18 | 17-18 | 43% |
| 17 | 14-16 | 35% |
| 16 | 13 | 33% |
| 15 | 11-12 | 28% |
| 14 | 9-10 | 23% |
| 13 | 8 | 20% |
| 12 | 6-7 | 15% |
| 11 | 5 | 13% |

❑ For most students, attempting every problem on the ACT will prevent them from scoring to their potential. Solving every question means you'll have to rush, which means you're more likely to make careless mistakes.

Having a realistic goal makes the test more manageable. With less pressure to answer every question, you can spend more time on easy and medium problems and less time on the difficult ones.

Remember, you get one raw point for each question, whether it's the simplest basic problem or the most challenging problem. Whether it takes you ten seconds or three minutes to answer, it's still one point.

❑ Create a Plan of Attack for the Science Test.

Using your goal score and the score table, complete the Plan of Attack below. This will help you determine your best pace while working through the test.

Most of your time and energy should be spent on the questions needed to achieve your goal score. Assume that you will likely miss some of the questions you attempt, and use educated guessing on the rest.

---

**Science Test Plan of Attack**

My overall ACT Goal: _____

My Science Test Goal: _____

How many questions do I need to answer correctly (raw score)? _____

How many questions should I attempt? _____

---

# Working Through the Science Test

❑ Focus on one passage at a time.

If you get to a challenging problem, move on to the next question, but do not progress to the next passage until you have completed all of the questions for your current passage.

❑ Adjust your pacing to the passage types. You have an average of 5 minutes per passage, but some passages may take longer, so you should move more quickly through others.

Data Representation passages are typically the most straightforward. Move through these quickly. Try to complete each Data Representation passage within 4 minutes.

Research Summary passages can be complex and are typically more challenging and time-consuming. Try to complete each Research Summary passage within 5 minutes.

Conflicting Viewpoints passages are typically similar to Reading passages, though they have fewer questions. Try to complete each Conflicting Viewpoints passage within 7 minutes.

❑ It's important to learn which types of passages and questions you tend to find easy, and which ones you find harder to solve. This will help you determine your best pace for finishing the Science Test on time.

# General Tips

☐ Move quickly through the Science passages by adjusting your strategies to each passage type. Plenty of practice will help you to work with more speed and efficiency.

☐ Don't worry if you're unfamiliar with the subject of a passage.

Usually, all the information you need about a subject will be contained within the passage. The Science Test rarely has questions that require outside knowledge of science facts.

☐ You don't need a calculator on the Science Test.

You are not allowed to use a calculator on the Science Test, but don't let this cause you stress — it's actually good news. It means that there are very few calculations on the test. The rare questions that require math will only require rough estimates that you can do in your head or in the margins of the test booklet.

**Science**

- ❑ The Scientific Method
- ❑ Data Representation
  - o Interpretation
  - o Relationship
  - o Additional Data
  - o Connection
- ❑ Research Summary
  - o Data
  - o Experimental Design
  - o Evaluation
- ❑ Conflicting Viewpoints
  - o Detail
  - o Perspective
  - o Assessment

# The Scientific Method

The Scientific Method is the process that scientists use to ask and answer questions. This is done by creating and proving (or disproving) theories. For example, to find out why the volume of a substance is changing, you would make and test theories about what is causing the change (e.g., temperature, time, location). The goal of most science is to explain the chain of causation that brings about certain events.

❑ Understand what each step of the Scientific Method is supposed to achieve.

**Step 1:** Ask a Question

The Scientific Method begins with a hypothesis, which is an educated guess a scientist makes to explain observations.

For the purposes of the ACT, think about this step in terms of what is being measured or discussed in the passage.

**Step 2:** Conduct Experiments

An experiment tests a hypothesis by measuring how one variable affects another.

On the ACT, this is an important step in Research Summary passages.

**Step 3:** Interpret Data

The results of experiments are analyzed to find trends or patterns in the data.

An important skill for many ACT Science questions is being able to summarize the results of an experiment by putting data into words.

**Step 4:** Draw Conclusions

A conclusion is a logical judgment made from the collected data that either proves or disproves the hypothesis.

In simple terms, this step is used to determine what can be learned from the results of the experiment.

❑ Summarize Science passages in terms of the Scientific Method. This will put information in context, so it is more relatable and understandable.

Read the following description of an experiment and answer the questions that follow:

After the 4th of July, a student becomes interested in how and why fireworks have different colors. The student thinks that different chemicals determine the different colors of the explosions. The student decides to devise a laboratory experiment. Using all safety precautions, the student obtains several different chemicals: sodium chloride, sodium bromide, copper chloride, and copper sulfate. Each chemical is dissolved in water to create a solution with a concentration of 1M. The student then lights a Bunsen burner. Each of the chemical solutions is sprayed into the flame of the Bunsen burner. As each chemical is sprayed, the student observes changes in the color of the flame:

Sodium chloride burns orange.

Sodium bromide burns orange.

Copper chloride burns green.

Copper sulfate burns green.

The student uses this data to determine that only the metal (sodium or copper) determines what color a chemical will burn inside of a firework.

What is the question being asked?

How does the student design an experiment to answer that question?

What data did the student collect?

What is the conclusion?

❑ Learn to apply the Scientific Method to different types of passages. Each type of Science passage focuses on different steps of the Scientific Method:

Data Representation passages focus on step 3. They present data in tables and graphs and ask questions about trends, patterns, and specific data points.

Research Summary passages focus on steps 2, 3, and 4. They ask you to consider experimental designs and the data collected.

Conflicting Viewpoint passages focus on steps 1 and 4. They present scientific questions and ask you to compare different conclusions.

# Data Representation Overview

❑ The ACT Science Test usually has 3 Data Representation passages.

Each Data Representation passage usually has 5 questions.

❑ Data Representation passages may look intimidating, because they often include large, complicated charts and graphs. However, they are typically the simplest passages in the Science Test.

Most Data Representation questions can be quickly solved by locating specific data in the passage.

❑ Follow these guidelines while working through Data Representation passages:

- Briefly scan the passage. Skim any explanatory text that may introduce the passage. Pay close attention to any key terms in italics.

- Pay close attention to the axes, scales, and units on charts and graphs. Do not spend time analyzing the data yet; all passages will have much more information than is needed to solve the questions. At most, note if there is a clear relationship between variables.

- Try to spend no more than half a minute scanning the passage for the information that will help guide you through the questions.

- Let each question guide you. Pay attention to the terms and variables in each question, which will direct you to the labels and axes in the charts and graphs of the passage. You may have to look at the answer choices for more clues about where to find information.

❑ These passages are your opportunity to move quickly. A brisk pace is important because you will need more time to work through the more complicated Research Summary and Conflicting Viewpoints passages.

❑ Data Representation passages include the following question types:

- Interpretation

- Relationship

- Additional Data

- Connection

# Interpretation

❑ Interpretation questions ask you to identify or summarize information presented in the passage.

❑ Interpretation questions typically appear in the following forms:

> According to Figure 1, population increased the most during which time period?
>
> Based on Table 2, the resonant frequency of Material A was closest to...
>
> On the basis of the data provided, one could generalize that...

❑ These questions can often be solved very quickly, as long as you have an understanding of the data and have identified the labels on the charts and tables.

| Table 1 | | |
|---|---|---|
| Time (s) | Speed (m/s) | Height (m) |
| 0.0 | 0.0 | 1000 |
| 2.0 | 19.6 | 980.4 |
| 4.0 | 39.2 | 921.6 |
| 6.0 | 58.8 | 823.6 |
| 8.0 | 78.4 | 686.4 |
| 10.0 | 98.0 | 510.0 |
| 12.0 | 117.6 | 294.4 |
| 14.0 | 137.2 | 39.6 |
| 14.3 | 140.00 | 0.0 |
| 16.0 | 0.0 | 0.0 |

Table 1 describes an object dropped from a height of 1km above the ground.

4 seconds after the object begins to fall, what is its speed?

_____

How far does the object fall between 8 and 14 seconds after it is dropped?

_____

❑ Some interpretation questions require an understanding of the topic. You may have to use logic or your own scientific knowledge in order to explain the data shown in the passage.

> Based on the data in Table 1, why does the speed decrease between 14.3 and 16 seconds after the object is dropped?

_____

For these questions, it may help to imagine the story behind the data. By visualizing an experiment, you can use your general scientific knowledge to understand what the data represents.

❑ Interpretation questions are very common in Data Representation passages. Because these questions are usually relatively simple, these passages can be finished quickly, which will give you more time to work through Research Summary and Conflicting Viewpoints passages.

## PUT IT TOGETHER

*Sediment* is made of particles, such as sand and soil, that have been deposited by a natural process.

*Metamorphic rock* is formed as a result of dramatic temperature and/or pressure changes.

*Sedimentary rock* is formed when sediment hardens.

*Igneous rock* is formed as molten magma solidifies.

*Extrusive (volcanic)* rock is formed on the outer surface of the earth while *intrusive (plutonic)* rock is formed beneath the Earth's surface.

Figure 1 illustrates the cycle followed by each type of rock. Figure 2 shows characteristics of types of igneous rocks.

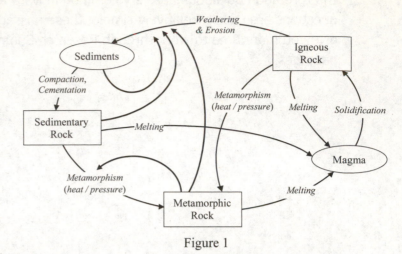

Figure 1

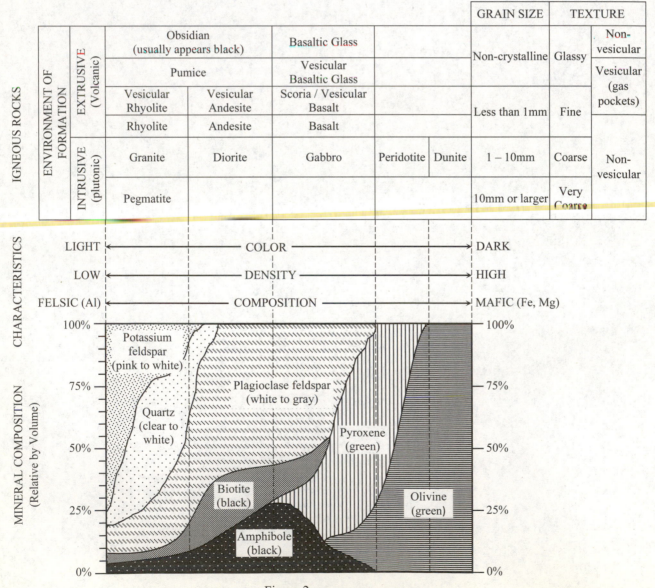

| ENVIRONMENT OF FORMATION | | | | | | GRAIN SIZE | TEXTURE | |
|---|---|---|---|---|---|---|---|---|
| EXTRUSIVE (Volcanic) | Obsidian (usually appears black) | | Basaltic Glass | | | Non-crystalline | Glassy | Non-vesicular |
| | Pumice | | Vesicular Basaltic Glass | | | | | Vesicular (gas pockets) |
| | Vesicular Rhyolite | Vesicular Andesite | Scoria / Vesicular Basalt | | | Less than 1mm | Fine | |
| | Rhyolite | Andesite | Basalt | | | | | |
| INTRUSIVE (plutonic) | Granite | Diorite | Gabbro | Peridotite | Dunite | 1 – 10mm | Coarse | Non-vesicular |
| | Pegmatite | | | | | 10mm or larger | Very Coarse | |

(IGNEOUS ROCKS)

CHARACTERISTICS

LIGHT ← COLOR → DARK

LOW ← DENSITY → HIGH

FELSIC (Al) ← COMPOSITION → MAFIC (Fe, Mg)

Figure 2

1.  According to Figure 2, an igneous rock with light color and a high mineral composition would be:

    A.  Biotite.
    B.  Olivine.
    C.  Potassium Feldspar.
    D.  Pyroxene.

*In Data Representation passages, the questions will guide you through the data.*

2.  The data in Figure 2 supports which of the following statements about the relative grain size and texture of igneous rock and the location that the rock was formed?

    F.  Rocks formed on the Earth's surface are composed of small grains with smooth textures.
    G.  Rocks formed under the Earth's surface are composed of small grains with smooth textures.
    H.  Rocks formed on the Earth's surface are composed of large grains with coarse textures.
    J.  Rocks formed under the Earth's surface are composed of large grains with smooth textures.

3.  According to Figure 1, weathering and erosion most directly lead to the formation of:

    A.  magma.
    B.  sedimentary rocks.
    C.  sediments.
    D.  metamorphic rock.

4.  Which of the following correctly ranks the following igneous rock species from low to high mineral composition according to Figure 2?

    *Use Process of Elimination.*

    F.  Potassium Feldspar, Biotite, Quartz, Amphibole
    G.  Amphibole, Biotite, Quartz, Potassium Feldspar
    H.  Biotite, Quartz, Amphibole, Potassium Feldspar
    J.  Quartz, Biotite, Potassium Feldspar, Amphibole

5.  Which of the following cycles would be a correct conclusion supported by Figure 1?

    A.  Melted sedimentary rock that undergoes weathering and erosion becomes magma.
    B.  Solidified magma that undergoes weathering and erosion becomes sedimentary rock.
    C.  Melted metamorphic rock forms sediment.
    D.  Solidified magma that undergoes heat and/or pressure changes forms metamorphic rock.

# Relationship

❏ Relationship questions ask you to determine the effects of changing a variable.

❏ Relationship questions typically appear in the following forms:

> According to Chart 1, as distance increased, the temperature... (increased / decreased)
>
> Based on Table 2, as mass increased, density... (increased / remained the same)
>
> In Study 1, as time increased, pressure... (increased only / decreased, then increased)

❏ A **direct** relationship is one in which variables either both increase or both decrease.

This is also known as "direct variation" or "positive correlation."

A graph of a direct relationship is not necessarily a straight line. If you can draw an increasing or decreasing line or curve (line of best fit) that basically follows a direct trend, then you can call it a direct relationship.

❏ An **inverse** relationship is one in which one variable increases as the other decreases.

This is also known as "inverse variation" or "negative correlation."

❏ Variables may be unrelated if there are no trends in the data.

Unrelated variables may cause a wide scattering of data points or a flat line.

| Table 1 | |
|---|---|
| $CO_2$ pressure (mm Hg) | $CO_2$ volume (liters) |
| 470 | 356 |
| 615 | 272 |
| 700 | 239 |
| 810 | 206 |
| 895 | 187 |

Draw a chart to plot the data points in Table 1:

Based on Table 1, what happens to volume when pressure decreases? _____

What is the type of relationship between pressure and volume? _____

❑ Some variables have more complex relationships. Look for patterns and trends in data.

The figure below demonstrates a 32-year survey of the populations of the snowshoe hare and its only natural predator, the Canadian lynx, within a certain region of wilderness.

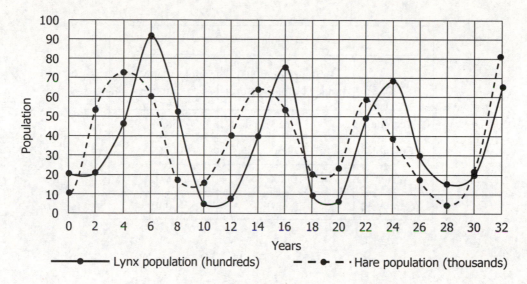

Figure 1

During which 2-year span did the hare population rise most rapidly?

During which 2-year span did the lynx population fall most rapidly?

When the lynx population is at a peak, what happens to the hare population?

Approximately how many years pass between the population peaks of the hare population? When, after the 32-year mark, will the next population peak likely occur?

If the hare population were to reach 0, what would likely happen to the lynx population?

If the lynx population were to reach 0, what would likely happen to the hare population?

## PUT IT TOGETHER

A team of researchers studied the relationship between the boiling points and vapor pressures of several liquids. Table 1 lists the boiling point and molecular mass of each of the liquids. The vapor pressures of these liquids are graphed in Figure 1.

| Table 1 | | |
|---|---|---|
| Substance | Boiling Point (°C) (under 1 atm pressure) | Molecular Mass (amu) |
| Acetone | 56.53 | 58.08 |
| Ethanol | 78.50 | 46.07 |
| Water | 100.00 | 18.02 |
| Acetic Acid | 118.10 | 60.05 |

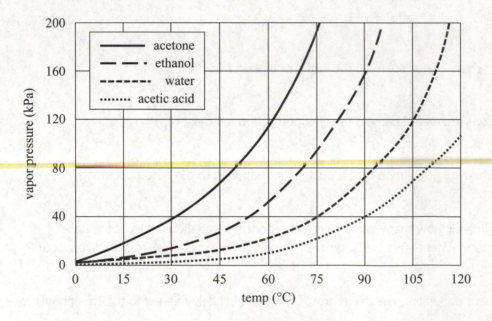

Figure 1

1.  Which of the following statements best describes the relationship between vapor pressure and temperature?

    A.  Vapor pressure increases as temperature increases.
    B.  Vapor pressure decreases as temperature increases.
    C.  Vapor pressure increases, and then decreases as temperature increases.
    D.  Vapor pressure decreases, and then increases as temperature increases.

2.  Does the data in Table 1 support the conclusion that boiling point increases with molecular mass?

    F.  Yes, because the substance with the highest boiling point has the greatest molecular mass.
    G.  Yes, because the substance with the lowest boiling point has the smallest molecular mass.
    H.  No, because the substance with the highest boiling point has the smallest molecular mass.
    J.  No, because there is no pattern between the values for boiling point and molecular mass.

3.  A plot of boiling points versus molecular mass is best represented by which of the following graphs?

    A.
    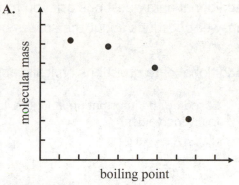

    B.
    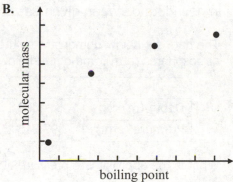

    C.
    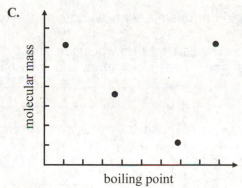

    D.
    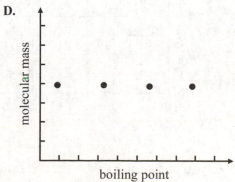

# Additional Data

❑ Additional data questions ask you to identify the patterns formed by sets of data and to answer questions about the spaces between the data points and outside the data set.

❑ Additional data questions typically appear in the following forms:

Based on the information in Figure 1, _____ will be closest to which of the following values?

Based on Table 1, _____ is closest to which of the following?

❑ Fill in new data between given data points by finding midpoints.

The data set below demonstrates the relationship between water pressure, measured in atmospheres (atm), and depth below sea level in meters:

| Table 1 | | | | | |
|---|---|---|---|---|---|
| Depth (m) | -4000 | -3000 | -2000 | -1000 | 0 |
| Pressure (atm) | 397.815 | 298.611 | 199.407 | 100.204 | 1 |

What is the approximate pressure at 1500m below sea level? _____

❑ Add data points that fall outside the given data by extending patterns or trends.

The data set below demonstrates the relationship between altitude above sea level, measured in kilometers, and atmospheric pressure.

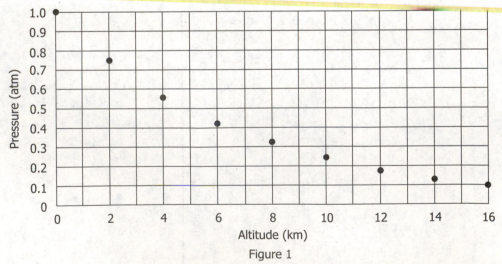

Figure 1

Based on Figure 1, estimate the atmospheric pressure at 20km above sea level: _____

Suppose a region is 1km below sea level (but not underwater). Based on the data in

Figure 1, estimate the atmospheric pressure in this region: _____

❑ Some additional data questions ask you to analyze new information in the context of the passage's information and data.

These questions may seem intimidating, but they usually only require you to recognize patterns and trends. Once you identify how the new information relates to the passage's data, you can easily solve by interpolating or extrapolating.

In the table below, experimenters charted the characteristics of a special class of elementary particles called *leptons*.

| Table 1 | | | | |
|---|---|---|---|---|
| Name | Symbol | Charge | Antiparticle | Mass (MeV/c$^2$) |
| Electron | e$^-$ | -1 | e$^+$ | 0.511 |
| Electron neutrino | $v_e$ | 0 | $\overline{v}_e$ | nearly massless, but non-zero |
| Muon | μ$^-$ | -1 | μ$^+$ | 105.7 |
| Muon neutrino | $v_μ$ | 0 | $\overline{v}_μ$ | .0980 < x < 0.170 |
| Tau | T- | -1 | T$^+$ | 1,777 |
| Tau neutrino | $v_T$ | 0 | $\overline{v}_T$ | 13.5 < x < 15.5 |

Scientists discovered a new lepton that they named the "alpha neutrino." Based upon Table 1, what was the most likely charge for this particle? _____

Experimenters split one of the leptons from the table into two unequal fragments. If one of the resulting fragments had a mass of 780 MeV/c$^2$, from which lepton did it originate?

A.  electron
B.  muon neutrino
C.  tau neutrino
D.  tau

## PUT IT TOGETHER

The periodic table is organized to illustrate trends in the behavior of elements as atomic number increases. Table 1 shows the period and family of elements, which correspond to the periodic table's rows and columns, respectively.

By definition, the first ionization energy of an element is the energy required to remove the highest energy electron from a neutral atom in the gaseous state.

| Table 1 | | | | | |
|---|---|---|---|---|---|
| Element | Period | Family | Atomic Radii (pm) | Electronegativity | 1st Ionization Energy (kJ/mol) |
| Lithium | 2 | 1 | 155 | 0.98 | 520 |
| Carbon | 2 | 4 | 77 | 2.55 | 1087 |
| Fluorine | 2 | 7 | 57 | 3.98 | 1681 |
| Sodium | 3 | 1 | 190 | 0.93 | 496 |
| Silicon | 3 | 4 | 118 | 1.9 | 787 |
| Chlorine | 3 | 7 | 97 | 3.16 | 1251 |
| Potassium | 4 | 1 | 235 | 0.82 | 419 |
| Germanium | 4 | 4 | 122 | 2.01 | 762 |
| Bromine | 4 | 7 | 114 | 2.96 | 1140 |

1.  Which of the following is the best estimate of the electronegativity of an element found in period 2 and family 2?

    A.  0.52
    B.  0.85
    C.  1.50
    D.  2.85

2.  The best estimate of the 1st ionization energy of an element in period 1 and family 1 is:

    F.  600 kJ/mol.
    G.  500 kJ/mol.
    H.  400 kJ/mol.
    J.  300 kJ/mol.

> Look at the 1st Ionization Energy of each element in family 1. What is the trend as the period decreases?

3.  If an element has an electronegativity of 0.70 and an atomic radius of 250 pm, then it is most likely found in:

    A.  Family 1.
    B.  Family 2.
    C.  Family 4.
    D.  Family 6.


4.  Which of the following is most likely the measure of the atomic radius of an element found in period 5 and family 4?

    F.  50 pm
    G.  75 pm
    H.  100 pm
    J.  125 pm

# Connection

❑ Connection questions ask you to compare data across sets.

❑ Connection questions typically appear in the following forms:

Based on Figure 2 and Table 1, the tensile strength for Material A is most likely closest to which of the following?

Based on Table 1 and Figure 1, what is the correct order of the four documented species, from the most dimorphic to the least dimorphic?

❑ In order to draw connections across data sets, you must identify which variables the sets have in common. By matching a shared value, you can compare corresponding data.

Some questions will also require you to draw connections between data sets and the background information.

Table 1 demonstrates the relationship between a driver's speed and *stopping sight distance*, the distance a driver must be able to see in order to identify a 6-inch-wide obstacle in the road and safely stop before hitting it. Table 2 shows the actual distance traveled between braking and a complete stop, on wet and dry pavement.

| Table 1 | | | Table 2 | | |
|---|---|---|---|---|---|
| Speed (mph) | Stopping Sight Distance (ft) | | Speed (mph) | Braking Distance (ft) | |
| | Desirable | Minimum | | Wet | Dry |
| 20 | 107 | 107 | 20 | 63 | 52 |
| 25 | 147 | 139 | 25 | 92 | 71 |
| 30 | 196 | 177 | 30 | 130 | 91 |
| 35 | 248 | 218 | 35 | 172 | 120 |
| 40 | 313 | 267 | 40 | 225 | 148 |
| 45 | 383 | 319 | 45 | 284 | 179 |
| 50 | 461 | 376 | 50 | 357 | 212 |
| 55 | 538 | 432 | 55 | 417 | 249 |
| 60 | 634 | 502 | 60 | 493 | 288 |
| 65 | 724 | 549 | 65 | 581 | 330 |
| 70 | 840 | 613 | 70 | 686 | 375 |

When driving with a minimum sight distance of 500 ft, how long is the braking distance on dry pavement? _____

At what speed is the minimum stopping sight distance less than the braking distance under wet conditions? Under dry conditions? If driving under those conditions, what will happen in an emergency braking situation?

## PUT IT TOGETHER

Scientists charted the effects of rearing density and temperature on the survival rates of zebrafish in captivity. In the wild, the average temperature of their environment is 28°C. Temperature and rearing density were tested in separate experiments, and were not varied at the same time.

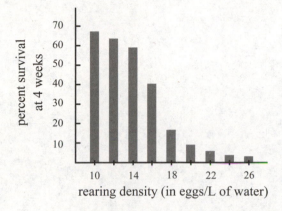

Figure 1

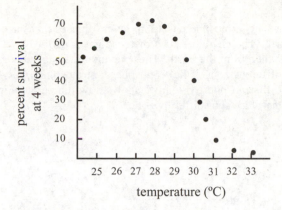

temperature (°C)

Figure 2

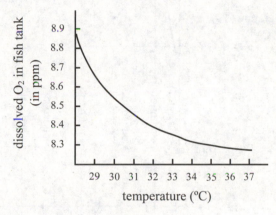

temperature (°C)

Figure 3

Tell the story behind the data.

**Why does survival decrease as rearing density increases?**

**Why does survival increase then decrease as temperature increases?**

1. When the survival rate of the hatchlings is at 40%, which of the following is closest to the level of dissolved $O_2$ in the tank?

   A. 8.3 ppm
   B. 8.5 ppm
   C. 8.7 ppm
   D. 8.8 ppm

2. The percent survival of zebrafish with a rearing density of 20 eggs/L is closest to their percent survival at which temperature?

   F. 26.5 °C
   G. 28.0 °C
   H. 31.2 °C
   J. 33.1 °C

3. According to Figure 1 and Figure 2, which of the following environments is likely to be most harmful to zebrafish survival?

   A. Rearing density: 10 eggs/L
      Temperature: 28°C
   B. Rearing density: 26 eggs/L
      Temperature: 27°C
   C. Rearing density: 10 eggs/L
      Temperature: 33°C
   D. Rearing density: 26 eggs/L
      Temperature: 33°C

# Checkpoint Review

The atmosphere is a thin layer of gases that surrounds the Earth. The characteristics of these gases differ based on their distance from the Earth. These layers are also categorized into 4 different zones: the troposphere, stratosphere, mesosphere, and thermosphere. Figure 1 shows how temperature, pressure, and water vapor differ by zone.

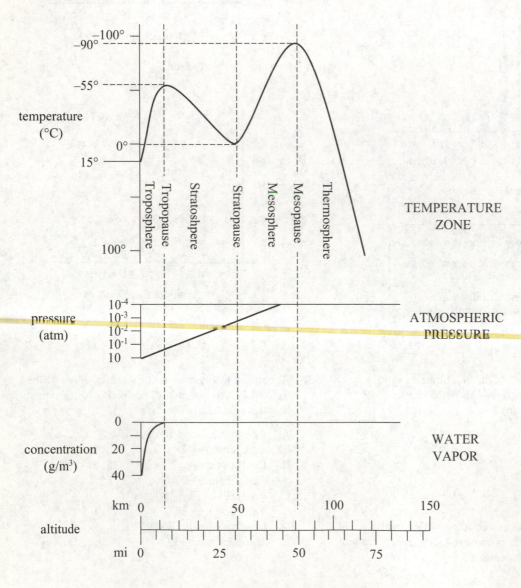

Figure 1

# Checkpoint Review

1. Which of the following data is represented on the horizontal axis of Figure 1?

   A. Temperature, pressure, and concentration
   B. atm, $g/m^3$, and °C
   C. Concentration and sea level
   D. Altitude

2. Is the statement "The atmospheric pressure increases with altitude" supported by the data in Figure 1?

   F. Yes, because atmospheric pressure increases exponentially as altitude increases.
   G. Yes, because the maximum value of atmospheric pressure exists at the highest altitude.
   H. No, because the same value for altitude is indicated for all values of atmospheric pressure.
   J. No, because atmospheric pressure decreases exponentially as altitude increases.

3. According to Figure 1, approximately how many miles above sea level is the Mesosphere located?

   A. 26 mi
   B. 42 mi
   C. 50 mi
   D. 80 mi

4. According to Figure 1, which of the following statements best describes the relationship, if any, between the temperature of a temperature zone and the altitude?

   F. As the altitude of the zone increases, the temperature increases in the Troposphere and Stratosphere and decreases in the Mesosphere and Thermosphere.
   G. As the altitude of the zone increases, the temperature increases in the Troposphere and Mesosphere and decreases in the Stratosphere and Thermosphere.
   H. As the altitude of the zone increases, the temperature increases in the Mesosphere and Thermosphere and decreases in the Troposphere and Stratosphere.
   J. As the altitude of the zone increases, the temperature increases in the Stratosphere and Thermosphere and decreases in the Troposphere and Mesosphere.

5. Special identification is given to the narrow zones that separate the temperature zones. These smaller zones use the suffix "pause." What is the zone that separates the Stratosphere from the Mesosphere?

   A. Tropopause
   B. Stratopause
   C. Mesopause
   D. Thermopause

# Research Summary Overview

❑ The ACT Science Test usually has 3 Research Summary passages.

Each Research Summary passage usually has 6 questions.

❑ Research Summary passages are often the most challenging passages in the Science Test.

These passages usually take more time than typical Data Representation passages. Research Summary questions can also require more careful consideration, and there is a greater likelihood that questions will depend on your own understanding of scientific concepts.

❑ All question types that appear in Data Representation passages may also appear in Research Summary passages. Research Summary passages also have questions based on the design and evaluation of experiments.

❑ Follow these guidelines while working through Research Summary passages:

• Quickly read through the passage in order to understand the experiment. Make sure that you can identify the independent and dependent variables (what the experimenters are adjusting and what they are measuring).

• Pay attention to the axes, scales, and units on charts and graphs. Do not spend time analyzing the data yet; all passages will have much more information than is needed to solve the questions. At most, note if there is a clear relationship between variables.

• Overall, try to spend no more than a minute reading through the passage for the information that will allow you to understand the experiment and will guide you through the questions.

• Let each question guide you. Pay attention to the terms and variables in each question, which will direct you to the labels and axes in the charts and graphs of the passage. Often, questions will ask you to consider multiple aspects of experimental design, data, and conclusions.

❑ Research Summary passages include the following question types:

- Data

- Experimental Design

- Evaluation

❑ Identifying a question's type will help you determine the level at which you should analyze the passage.

Data questions, which are the same types of questions that appear with Data Representation passages, can be solved with the information in the charts and tables that appear in the passage.

Experimental design questions require you to understand the experiment or study described in the passage. These questions usually require an understanding of the scientific method.

Evaluation questions require a broad view of the experiment or study described in the passage.

# Data

❑ Data questions require you to look at the information presented in the passage to find data points, identify relationships and patterns, and make connections.

All question types that commonly appear with Data Representation passages can be considered data questions when they appear in Research Summary passages.

❑ Data questions typically appear in the following forms:

Based on the results of Study 1, which material had the highest absorbency?

In Experiment 1, had a sample with a pH of 4 been tested, the reaction rate would have been closest to...

According to Study 2, the temperatures of object A and object B were closest to the same value at which of the following times?

❑ Most data questions can be solved quickly, as long as you have an understanding of the data and have identified the labels on the charts and tables.

## PUT IT TOGETHER

A researcher conducted experiments to test chemical and physical characteristics of soil composition and measure how each of these characteristics affects tree growth. *Soil texture* refers to the amount of sand, silt, and clay particles in a sample of soil. Scientists group soil textures into *soil texture classes.*

*Study 1*

Samples were taken at various soil depths of multiple texture classes of soil. These samples were analyzed for soil type.

| Table 1 | | | | | |
|---|---|---|---|---|---|
| Soil Depth (inches) | Texture Class | | | | |
| | A | B | C | D | E |
| 0-12 | Sandy loam | Loam | Loam | Silty clay loam | Silty clay loam |
| 12-24 | Sandy loam | Loam | Loam | Clay loam | Silty clay loam |
| 24-36 | Sandy loam | Loam | Loam | Sandy loam | Clay loam |
| 36-48 | Loam | Sandy loam | Sandy loam | Sandy loam | Loam |

*Study 2*

Samples at various texture classes and soil depths were analyzed to determine the eventual tree heights.

| Table 2 | | | | | |
|---|---|---|---|---|---|
| Texture Class | Bulk Density (g/cm3) at Soil Depth (inches) | | | | Tree Height (feet) |
| | 0-12 inches | 12-24 inches | 24-36 inches | 36-48 inches | |
| A | 1.59 | 1.74 | 1.78 | 1.79 | 19-37 |
| B | 1.51 | 1.57 | 1.66 | 1.69 | 10.5-32.5 |
| C | 1.52 | 1.65 | 1.67 | 1.69 | 12-34.5 |
| D | 1.48 | 1.56 | 1.61 | 1.71 | 2.5-17 |
| E | 1.35 | 1.54 | 1.63 | 1.66 | 5.5-28 |

1. According to Study 2, what texture class of soil produced the trees of greatest height?

   A. Texture Class A
   B. Texture Class B
   C. Texture Class C
   D. Texture Class E

2. Sandy loam is found:

   F. at depths of 0-12 inches.
   G. in Texture Class A soil.
   H. at depths of 24-48 inches.
   J. at various depths and soil texture classes.

3. According to Study 2, which of the following best describes bulk density as soil depth increases?

   A. Bulk density increases only.
   B. Bulk density decreases only.
   C. Bulk density increases, then decreases.
   D. Bulk density remains the same.

4. If a sample of Texture Class A soil was obtained with a bulk density of 1.58 g/cm3, at what depth was the sample most likely taken?

   F. 0-12 inches
   G. 12-24 inches
   H. 24-36 inches
   J. 36-48 inches

5. According to the results of Study 1 and Study 2, which of the following conclusions can be made about tree height?

   A. The tallest trees grew in soil with silty clay loam at depths of 0-12 inches.
   B. The tallest trees grew in soil with silty clay loam at depths of 12-24 inches.
   C. The shortest trees grew in soil with sandy loam at depths of 0-12 inches.
   D. The shortest trees grew in soil with clay loam at depths of 12-24 inches.

SUMMIT
EDUCATIONAL
GROUP

# Experimental Design

❑ Experimental design questions ask you to consider how an experiment works. These range from straightforward questions about the basic construction of the experiment to more complex questions about why the experiment was designed in a particular way.

❑ Experimental design questions typically appear in the following forms:

In which of the following ways was the design of Experiment 1 different from that of Experiment 3?

In Study 1, what is the most likely reason the students used a temperature-controlled water bath?

Which of the following is a weakness of the design of Experiment 2?

❑ Note what the experimenter is changing and measuring. Experiments are designed to examine how changing the independent variable affects the dependent variable.

An **independent variable** is directly manipulated by the experimenter. This is typically the *x*-axis in a graph.

A **dependent variable** is not directly manipulated by the experimenter. The dependent variable is what the experimenter is measuring. This is typically the *y*-axis in a graph.

A student conducts an experiment measuring the relationship between heat and volume.

In the study, three beakers containing the same amount of room temperature water were placed over heat sources of varying intensity. The student measured the temperature of the water in each beaker at regular intervals.

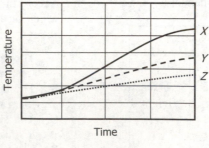

Figure 1

In the study, which variable is directly manipulated? _____

In the study, which variable is dependent? _____

❑  A **controlled variable** is kept constant. In an experiment, all variables that are not the independent or dependent variables should remain constant. This ensures that no other factors can unintentionally affect the dependent variable.

In an experiment with multiple trials or groups, one of these may be a **control** – a set of data whose independent variable the experimenter does not alter, in order to create a baseline to which other trials or groups can be compared.

In the study, what variables should be controlled in order to ensure accurate data?

_____

Suppose that the student conducting the study used an additional trial beaker of room temperature water. This beaker was not placed over a heat source. If the temperature of the water in this beaker changed during the experiment, how could this affect the experimenters' interpretation of the data?

_____

Experimenters often need controls to ensure that what is happening is really due to the independent variable and not some other factor.

## PUT IT TOGETHER

A pharmaceutical company conducted a study to measure the effectiveness of *Drug X,* a new medication intended to treat exercise-induced asthma. This condition causes sufferers' throats to constrict, limiting the amount of oxygen they inhale.

For this study, researchers recruited 1,000 volunteers between the ages of 18 and 30. Out of these participants, 200 were given a placebo pill which did not contain any of the drug. The remaining 800 volunteers were given concentrations of *Drug X* in proportions that corresponded to their body weights.

### Study 1

Before starting the medication or placebo, participants were asked to run at a 7 mph pace for 20 minutes. Before running, the researchers used an *oximeter* to measure the concentration of oxygen in participants' blood. Oxygen levels were then re-measured after exercise. The results of this experiment are shown in Table 1.

Change in blood $O_2$ concentration is calculated:
final $O_2$ concentration – initial $O_2$ concentration

| Table 1 | | |
|---|---|---|
| weight of participant (lbs) | number of participants | avg. change in blood $O_2$ concentration (mmHg) |
| 80-100 | 70 | -30 |
| 101-120 | 130 | -25 |
| 121-140 | 350 | -20 |
| 141-160 | 200 | -26 |
| 161-180 | 170 | -28 |
| 181-200 | 80 | -38 |

### Study 2

Five weeks after beginning the medication or placebo on a daily basis, the same participants were again asked to run at a 7 mph pace for 20 minutes. Blood-oxygen concentration was measured before and after the run. The results of this trial are shown in Table 2.

| Table 2 | | |
|---|---|---|
| placebo data | | |
| weight of participant (lbs) | number of participants | avg. change in blood $O_2$ concentration (mmHg) |
| 80-100 | 20 | -29 |
| 101-120 | 60 | -26 |
| 121-140 | 80 | -18 |
| 141-160 | 40 | -27 |
| 161-180 | 0 | N/A |
| 181-200 | 0 | N/A |
| *Drug X* data | | |
| 80-100 | 50 | -19 |
| 101-120 | 70 | -16 |
| 121-140 | 270 | -15 |
| 141-160 | 160 | -18 |
| 161-180 | 170 | -26 |
| 181-200 | 80 | -37 |

### Study 3

Five weeks after Study 2, participants returned for the last experiment. This was identical to Study 2, except that participants received two times the concentration of *Drug X* that they had received before. The placebo group was not re-tested in this study. The results are shown in Table 3 below.

| Table 3 | | |
|---|---|---|
| *Drug X* data | | |
| weight of participant (lbs) | number of participants | avg. change in blood $O_2$ concentration (mmHg) |
| 80-100 | 50 | -5 |
| 101-120 | 70 | -8 |
| 121-140 | 270 | -8 |
| 141-160 | 160 | -10 |
| 161-180 | 170 | -21 |
| 181-200 | 80 | -35 |

1. Which of the following is a control group in this experiment?

   A. participants weighing more than 160 lbs
   B. participants who took the placebo
   C. participants who took *Drug X*
   D. there is no control group

2. What is the most likely reason why the researchers ran the exercise test before and after volunteers took the medication?

   F. To show change over time
   G. To measure the difference that *Drug X* made in blood $O_2$ concentration
   H. To induce a severe asthma attack
   J. To establish resting heartrates

3. Which of the following are independent variables in Study 2 and Study 3?

   I. blood $O_2$ concentration
   II. gender of participants
   III. amount of *Drug X* received

   A. I only
   B. II only
   C. III only
   D. I and III

4. Which of the following is a weakness of the control group?

   F. Not all participant weights are represented.
   G. They were given no medication.
   H. There were too many people in the group.
   J. There were no participants over the age of 30.

5. What is the most likely reason that the researchers required the participants to run at a steady pace for a specific time period?

   A. They wanted to ensure that all heartrates were the same.
   B. They wanted to standardize participants' breathing rates.
   C. They wanted to make sure all participants had the same $O_2$ concentration.
   D. They wanted to create similar conditions affecting all participants.

> What did the researchers directly manipulate? What were they seeking to measure?

# Evaluation

❑ Evaluation questions ask you to consider an experiment's overall results. Usually, these questions rely on your understanding of the relationships between variables.

❑ Evaluation questions typically appear in the following forms:

A biologist claimed that _____. Are the results from Study 1 consistent with her claim?

It was hypothesized that _____. Is this consistent with the results of Experiment 1?

Which of the following statements about _____ is supported by the results of Study 2?

❑ These questions may ask if the experimenter's original hypothesis was verified or not. The answers typically include two "Yes" options and two "No" options, each with different justifications.

Students in a chemistry class wanted to compare the heat energy that could be produced from peanuts, cashews, and almonds. In separate trials, a gram of each substance was burned in an insulated environment, where the energy heated a 100mL beaker of water. The students measured the maximum change in the water temperature while the samples were burnt. All trials were conducted in a room with a stable temperature of 20°C, and the water began at 20°C for each trial. In order to calculate the energy (in joules) produced by burning each sample, students used the following formula:

*joules = mass of the water × temperature increase × 4.2 J/(g°C)*

|  | temperature increase of water (°C) | energy (joules) |
|---|---|---|
| almond | + 14.9 | 6276 |
| cashew | + 19.9 | 8368 |
| peanut | + 9.96 | 4184 |

Which of the following statements are supported by the results of this study?

A. Almonds and cashews have less oil than peanuts.
B. Almonds produced two times the energy that peanuts produced.
C. One gram of almonds produced less energy than two grams of peanuts.
D. Cashews increased the water temperature by the least amount.

A student hypothesized that burning the cashew would heat the water more quickly than would burning the peanut or almond. Is this hypothesis consistent with the results of the experiment?

F. Yes, because the water reached the highest temperature.
G. Yes, because the cashew released the most energy when burned.
H. No, because the cashew heated the water more slowly than the almond.
J. No, because time was not a variable measured in this experiment.

❑ These questions may introduce new information about the experimental design and ask how the new information affects the results.

### PUT IT TOGETHER

Over a period of 20 years, researchers studied the water quality and animal populations of a large lake ecosystem in Connecticut. Prior to the beginning of the study, the lake had a stable pH of 6.5.

*Study 1*

Researchers conducted a study to determine the *tolerance* of animal species in the lake environment for various pH ranges in captivity. The researchers began by establishing average birthrates and life expectancies for each species in aqueous environments with a pH of 6.5, as a control value. Later, researchers conducted similar experiments, varying the pH of the environment. The birthrates and life spans of each animal type were averaged. A species with data within 80% of both the control birthrate and life expectancy was deemed "tolerant" to a given pH environment. The results of this study are shown in Table 1.

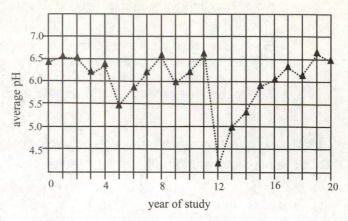

Figure 1

*Study 3*

Researchers monitored the populations of two fish, trout and bass, over the course of the study. Every 3 months, researchers would spend 8 hours catching, tagging, and releasing fish within the lake. The data is shown in Figure 2 below.

| Table 1 | | | | | | |
|---|---|---|---|---|---|---|
| | pH tolerance | | | | | |
| | 6.5 | 6.0 | 5.5 | 5.0 | 4.5 | 4.0 |
| trout | ✓ | ✓ | ✓ | ✓ | | |
| bass | ✓ | ✓ | | | | |
| perch | ✓ | ✓ | ✓ | ✓ | ✓ | |
| frogs | ✓ | ✓ | ✓ | ✓ | ✓ | ✓ |
| salamanders | ✓ | | | | | |

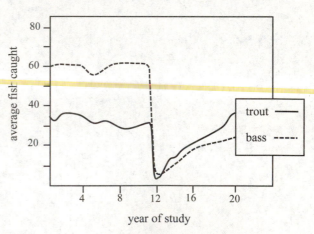

Figure 2

*Study 2*

Researchers tested the pH levels in the lake on the first day of each month for the entire 20-year study. Decreases of more than 1 pH per year were attributed to manmade pollution, while fluctuations less than this likely occurred naturally. The data from this study was used to create Figure 1.

> How does the data in Figure 1 relate to the date in Figure 2? What would explain the similarities?

1. A biologist stated that bass would be the only animals in the lake negatively affected if the pH dropped to 5.0. Is this consistent with the data in Table 1?

   A. Yes, because bass are constantly immersed in water.
   B. Yes, because all other animals are tolerant of this pH.
   C. No, because salamanders are not tolerant of this pH.
   D. No, because both salamanders and trout are not tolerant of this pH.

2. An ecology student hypothesized that, over the course of the study, there would always be a higher population of bass than trout in the lake. Does Figure 2 support this claim?

   F. Yes, because there were always more bass caught.
   G. Yes, because bass were more tolerant at the various pH levels.
   H. No, because there are always more trout caught.
   J. No, because trout surpassed bass soon after year 12.

3. An environmental group stated that, during the course of the study, two factories opened in the vicinity of the lake. Both operated for one calendar year before they were forced to shut down due to their negative effects upon the pH of the lake. According to Study 2, which of the following could be the years that these factories opened?

   A. Year 3 and Year 8
   B. Year 4 and Year 8
   C. Year 8 and Year 11
   D. Year 4 and Year 11

4. An ecologist claimed that, when a body of water drops more than 1.5 pH units over the course of a year, it takes longer for it to neutralize its pH than it does for the water to become acidic. Are the results of Study 2 consistent with this claim?

   F. Yes, because it took less time for the pH to return to 6.5.
   G. Yes, because it took more time for the pH to return to 6.5.
   H. No, because it took the same amount of time.
   J. No, because it cannot be determined from the data.

5. Which of the following statements about fish populations is supported by both Table 1 and Figure 2?

   A. Bass prey upon frogs.
   B. Perch populations recovered more quickly than bass from the most drastic pH change.
   C. Decreased acidity harms bass and trout populations.
   D. Increased acidity harms bass and trout populations.

# Checkpoint Review

*Biosorption* is a natural process by which some living organisms bind contaminants into their cellular structure, removing them from the surrounding environment. This technique may present an inexpensive way to extract heavy metals from drinking water. Scientists performed the following experiments to determine the most effective way to use a fungus, *Rhizopus nigricans,* to remove lead ions ($Pb^{2+}$) from aqueous solutions.

## Experiment 1

Figure 1 depicts the experimental setup scientists assembled to test the $Pb^{2+}$ biosorption rate of *Rhizopus nigricans* fungus pellets in a set amount of solution. A self-stirred vessel agitated a solution of $H_2O$ and $Pb(NO_3)_2$ at a constant speed. Every 10 minutes, the experimenters tested the concentration of lead present in the solution using a $Pb^{2+}$ meter. All trials began with the same concentration of $Pb^{2+}$, while the biomass (amount, in grams) of the fungus was varied. The results are shown in Table 1.

## Experiment 2

Figure 2 shows the apparatus used to test the effectiveness of $Pb^{2+}$ removal using *Rhizopus nigricans* pellets in a continuous system of filtration. Using a peristaltic pump, scientists pushed an aqueous solution of $Pb(NO_3)_2$ through a filter of glass marbles and fungal pellets within a glass column. The purpose of the marbles was to keep the pellets stationary in the column, creating a filter through which the aqueous solution was propelled. The flow rate of the apparatus was controlled by adjusting the diameter of a plug at the bottom of the column. In each trial, the initial concentration of $Pb^{2+}$ and fungal pellets was constant, while the flow rate was varied. Each trial recycled the aqueous $Pb(NO_3)_2$ through the system for 80 minutes, and a $Pb^{2+}$ meter was used to chart the lead concentration in the solution over time. The result of this experiment are shown in Table 2.

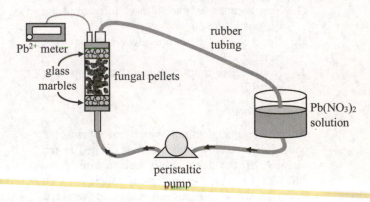

Figure 3

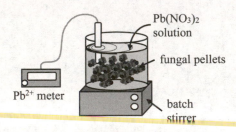

Figure 1

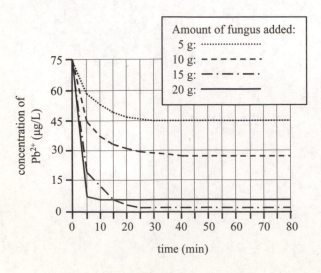

Figure 2

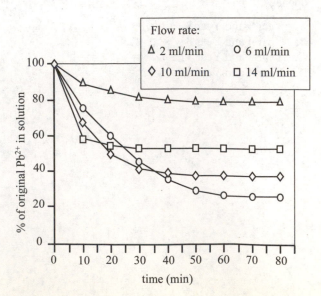

Figure 4

# Checkpoint Review

1.  According to the description, what would *most likely* occur if the experimenters had not included the glass marbles in the setup for Experiment 2?

    A.  The solution would flow in the wrong direction.
    B.  The fungal pellets could migrate out of the glass column.
    C.  The experiment would be completed more quickly.
    D.  Nothing would occur differently.

2.  Which of the following is a dependent variable in Experiment 2?

    F.  Time
    G.  Original concentration of $Pb^{2+}$
    H.  Amount of fungus in the system
    J.  Percent of original $Pb^{2+}$ present in solution

3.  According to Figures 2 and 4, which of the following saw the quickest decline in $Pb^{2+}$ concentration?

    A.  Flow rate: 14 ml/minute at 0-10 min
    B.  Flow rate: 14 ml/minute at 70-80 min
    C.  5g fungus at 0-5 min
    D.  20g fungus at 0-5 min

4.  Which of the following would an experimenter need to know about Experiment 2 in order to replicate it exactly?

    F.  How long to run the filtration system
    G.  The original concentration of the $Pb(NO_3)_2$ solution
    H.  The amount of fungus and $Pb(NO_3)_2$ used
    J.  Both G and H

5.  Which of the following situations is MOST analogous to the experimental setup in Experiment 1?

    A.  A filtration system for a fishtank which continually pumps the water through a charcoal filter to eliminate toxins
    B.  A device is put in a washing machine while it is running to capture unwanted particles from the water
    C.  A food dye is added to a water pitcher to change its color
    D.  A new species of mold begins to cause respiratory illnesses

6.  What is the control group for Experiment 1?

    F.  0g fungal pellets
    G.  10g fungal pellets
    H.  75 µg/L $Pb^{2+}$
    J.  There is no control group

# Conflicting Viewpoints Overview

❑ The ACT Science Test usually has 1 Conflicting Viewpoints passage.

Each Conflicting Viewpoints passage usually has 7 questions.

❑ Conflicting Viewpoints passages typically resemble the paired passages from the Reading Test. In most cases, you can work through the passage in much the same way as you would a Reading paired passage.

Occasionally, these passages will be presented as experiments, much like Research Summary passages. In these cases, multiple experimenters will offer differing views on the outcome of the experiment.

❑ Follow these guidelines while working through Conflicting Viewpoints passages:

- Quickly read through the passage. The questions will generally not require as much depth of understanding as those in the Reading Test. However, you should still complete the reading before you move on to the questions.

- Before the viewpoints, there will be a brief description that provides context for the passage. This information is regarded as fact and will not be disputed by the scientists.

- Pay close attention to diagrams and to any technical terms you have not encountered before. When you come across these terms in each of the theories, mark them so you can find them again easily.

- If the passage includes an experiment with diagrams, note where they appear in the passage. Sometimes the diagrams describe scientific fact or experimental design, but sometimes they only represent one side's opinion.

❑ For some students, it is easier to work on one viewpoint at a time, rather than reading through all of the viewpoints and then moving on to the questions. You may find that you can stay more focused by reading one viewpoint, answering only the questions that relate to it, and then moving on to the next viewpoint.

However, most students find that they have a better understanding of each viewpoint if they read all of them, compare and contrast, and then answer the questions.

❑ You should plan to spend more time on the Conflicting Viewpoints passage than you will on any other single passage in the Science Test, because you cannot answer many of the questions until you understand the viewpoints.

❑ Conflicting Viewpoints passages include the following question types:

- Detail

- Perspective

- Assessment

# Detail

❑ Detail questions require you to identify single data points, facts, or aspects of theories and models.

❑ Detail questions typically appear in the following forms:

> The Miasma Theory does NOT include the hypothesis that...
>
> Which of the following is the most consistent with the Germ Theory?
>
> According to the passage, a similarity between the Ecocyte Hypothesis and the Three-Domain System is that both theories...

❑ Read the passage before trying to answer the questions. Detail questions are generally the simplest type of question asked with Conflicting Viewpoint passages, yet they are still not easy to answer without an understanding of the passage's facts and ideas.

## PUT IT TOGETHER

Two scientific theories developed to answer the question, "Could the planet Mars support life?"

### Theory 1

There is no conclusive evidence to support the belief that the planet Mars is capable of supporting living organisms. Mars lacks an atmosphere like Earth's. Its environment is hostile in temperature (down to negative 143 degrees Celsius) and there is no protection from fierce solar radiation.

Water, necessary for life as we know it, is found on Mars only in the form of ice, which has not proven to sustain life. Many compounds known to exist along with living organisms, such as carbonates, are undetected on Mars; the types that are detected there can also be produced by inorganic activity. Methane present in the atmosphere, on Earth an indication of living organisms, could just as easily have been produced by inorganic processes as by bacteria.

It is claimed that chondrules, found within a Martian meteorite, are wormlike bacteria of extremely small size, yet it is unlikely that life could exist on such a microscale. DNA and RNA, the building blocks of life, establish a minimum size requirement observed in all life on Earth. Since chondrules are below this limit, they most likely are an inorganic byproduct.

### Theory 2

The explorations of NASA's Viking Mission on Mars amassed an extensive collection of soil and atmospheric samples. The evidence from these samples strongly suggests that the planet supports life.

To test for the presence of living organisms, Martian soil was blended with a radioactive material, carbon-14. If the soil were inhabited by living organisms, they would digest radioactive material. Chemical reactions between organisms and carbon-14 would produce certain gases. These gases were indeed detected by Viking researchers.

Atmospheric tests showed the presence of methane in the Mars atmosphere. Methane, abundant in Earth's atmosphere, is produced by organisms, though it can also be produced by inorganic means, like the tectonic shift of Earth's continental plates. However, the quantity of methane detected in the atmosphere surrounding Mars leads to the conclusion that some of it had to be produced by living organisms.

The litmus test for the existence of life is the presence of liquid water. Two theories suggest the existence of water on Mars. One states that the climate on Mars was warmer in the past. Higher temperatures would have meant the planet's current ice caps were at one point vast rivers and seas. Photographs that seem to depict ancient riverbeds support that theory. The second opinion is Mars has always been a cold planet covered in ice. But the ice, uniquely lower in density in solid than in liquid form, floated as a protective layer above liquid water, which flowed beneath.

The most conclusive piece of evidence for the existence of life on Mars was the discovery of chondrules within an ancient meteorite rock in Antarctica. Chondrules are living organisms formed within rocks when water is allowed to seep into the structure. The meteor not only contained chondrules, but also fossilized worms, organic matter, and magnetite, a product of bacteria exposed to magnetism.

1.  The lack of magnetic fields on Mars disclaims what substance as evidence of life on Mars?

    A.  Water
    B.  Methane
    C.  Magnetite
    D.  Carbonates

2.  Viking tested Martian soil with radioactive materials to see if:

    F.  gases would be released.
    G.  water would be found.
    H.  methane would be found.
    J.  chondrules would be found.

# Perspective

❑ Perspective questions require you to understand a theory, model, or hypothesis from the viewpoint of the scientist or student.

These questions will not ask you to judge whether a theory is correct or incorrect.

❑ The most basic perspective questions will test your understanding of a single viewpoint by asking you compare it to another idea.

Scientists discuss two different views on the cause of global climate change.

### Scientist 1

Although carbon dioxide is the most plentiful gas attributed to warming in our atmosphere, it is not the most problematic. In the recent past, other gases have been responsible for the warming of the atmosphere. Some of these "other" gases include methane, nitrous oxide, and chlorofluorocarbons. Soot caused by carbon dioxide pollution has the ability to reflect some of the cosmic energy back into space; this pollution creates a type of shield against the energy that causes warming. Secondly, technology has been developed and implemented specifically to reduce the hazards of carbon dioxide. As society has not yet begun to address the harmful effects of these other gases, they have now become the primary cause of current global warming.

### Scientist 2

Byproducts from the burning of fossil fuels react with oxygen in the air and produce carbon dioxide. Production of carbon dioxide due to industrial emissions has steadily increased. In addition, forests, which take carbon dioxide out of the air, are shrinking, and therefore more carbon dioxide remains in the atmosphere.

Carbon dioxide absorbs energy, but only in a specific range of wavelengths. Much of the energy that would otherwise leave the earth falls within this range and is trapped in the atmosphere by the carbon dioxide buildup. Some energy from the sun, however, has wavelengths shorter than this range and is not absorbed by the carbon dioxide.

Scientist 1 states that:

A. although carbon dioxide is one component of global warming, it is not the most harmful component.
B. although carbon dioxide is not the only gas that contributes to global warming, it does have the most harmful effects.
C. planting more trees would solve the problem of global warming.
D. the production of carbon dioxide has increased over time.

❑ More complex Perspective questions will require you to compare multiple viewpoints. The viewpoints may share common ground, even if they disagree on particular details.

Both scientists would agree that:

A.  gases other than carbon dioxide cause the most harm to Earth's atmosphere.
B.  carbon dioxide poses the biggest threat to Earth in the form of global warming.
C.  carbon dioxide is one cause of global warming.
D.  carbon dioxide absorbs energy from the sun.

Scientist 1 and Scientist 2 disagree on which statement?

F.  Carbon dioxide is a factor in global warming.
G.  Carbon dioxide soot plays a helpful role in blocking harmful energy from the sun.
H.  Other gases are more responsible for global warming than carbon dioxide is.
J.  Fixing the hole in the ozone layer would solve the problem of global warming.

❑ Some of the more challenging Perspective questions will present you with additional scientific data, and ask how a particular scientist would utilize that data or how the data would affect a viewpoint.

Which scientist would support a global action to plant and conserve more forests as a primary way to fight global warming?

A.  Scientist 1 only
B.  Scientist 2 only
C.  Both scientists 1 and 2
D.  Neither scientist 1 nor 2

## PUT IT TOGETHER

Most solid structures have a highly organized molecular arrangement known as a crystalline structure. When the temperature of a solid rises, this rigid structure of molecules begins to vibrate increasingly until the structure is broken down and the molecules can begin to flow. The molecules are then classified as being in the liquid state of matter. This liquid state has drastic differences in physical properties from the solid state, and therefore this change is classified as a *first-order phase transition*.

Glass is a substance whose state of matter is difficult to classify. Scientists discuss two possible explanations for the classification of glass as a state of matter.

### Scientist 1

Substances in the liquid state have measurable viscosity, or resistance to flow. Typically, as temperature of liquids drop, viscosity will increase. If this increase in viscosity happens quickly, then the liquid becomes a syrup as it cools. The disordered arrangement of the thick syrup will not allow a strict crystal structure to form, which prevents a first-order phase transition from happening. The resulting substance, although not a crystalline solid, does retain sufficient rigidity to have solid structure and is therefore categorized as an amorphous solid. The fact that old buildings always have panes of glass that are thicker on the bottom than at the top is often given as evidence against this classification. However, this is not due to the flow of glass at all—in fact, it was the convention of builders historically to place glass panes with the thicker edge at the bottom. All evidence shows glass to be an amorphous solid.

### Scientist 2

The true state of matter of glass is actually that of a super-cooled liquid. Super-cooled liquids are substances that exist at a temperature below their freezing point, while still holding the characteristics of a liquid. Although seemingly rigid like solids, these substances have not actually crystallized back into the organized structure of solids. They continue to flow at a very slow rate. This can be seen in the windows of old buildings: the glass is always thicker at the bottom than at the top. Over long periods of time, the window glass flows and settles.

Also, under certain conditions, glass can be forced into a crystalline state, at which point it becomes opaque. This is a very different condition from transparent glass, and therefore this shows the two to be different substances. Under normal conditions, glass has not reached this crystalline state, and therefore remains in the liquid state of matter. Glass is not a solid, amorphous or otherwise, but instead it is correctly categorized as a super-cooled liquid.

> Before you answer the questions, make sure you know what information is agreed on (introductory paragraphs) and summarize both scientists' viewpoints.

1. Scientist 2 defines the solid state of matter by:

   A. cold temperatures.
   B. a disorganized molecular structure.
   C. high densities.
   D. an organized crystalline structure of molecules.

2. According to the passage a first-order phase transition:

   F. occurs as a substance cools or heats.
   G. is marked by differences in the properties of the substances before and after the change.
   H. occurs only as a substance changes from a solid to liquid, or a liquid to gas.
   J. is the first phase change that occurs.

3. Suppose that historians uncovered proof that builders incorporated a method of building where glass panes were always placed with the thick edge at the top of windows. Which scientist would be best supported by this claim?

   A. Scientist 1 only
   B. Scientist 2 only
   C. Both Scientist 1 and Scientist 2
   D. Neither Scientist 1 nor Scientist 2

4. Both scientists would most likely agree that glass:

    F. has a more highly organized molecular structure than most solids do.
    G. does not retain the ordered structure of crystalline solids.
    H. holds some of the properties of liquids such as flow.
    J. will not undergo a first order phase transition.

5. Scientist 1 would most likely state that the highly ordered structure of a solid is not reached by glass because:

    A. the temperature drops too quickly for the structure to form.
    B. the viscosity of glass increases too quickly and does not allow the organized structure to form.
    C. the substance never reaches its freezing point.
    D. the substance is not rigid enough.

6. Scientist 2's views differ from Scientist 1's views in that Scientist 2:

    F. believes glass to undergo a first order phase transition.
    G. thinks glass acts as an extremely slow moving liquid and not a rigid solid.
    H. argues that glass has no rigidity at all.
    J. claims that the viscosity of glass does not increase as temperature drops.

7. Which of the following was discussed by Scientist 2 and ignored by Scientist 1?

    A. The flow of liquid in the panes of old glass
    B. The rigid nature of glass
    C. The process of forcing glass molecules into a crystalline structure
    D. The melting point of glass

# Assessment

❑ Assessment questions will ask you to judge how well a viewpoint is supported by certain facts or discoveries.

❑ Most of these questions will ask you to determine whether certain observations strengthen or weaken a particular viewpoint.

To answer one of these questions, you must both interpret the observation and also determine whether it aligns with the viewpoint.

Below are two scientific theories on how the universe began.

Scientist 1

Approximately 13.7 billion years ago, the universe existed as a hot, dense, and infinitely small zone. All matter in the universe was condensed into a single point. At this incredible density, our known laws of physics do not apply. Some event, currently unknown, sparked a rapid expansion of this matter. The universe quickly expanded into a jumble of electrons, quarks, and other subatomic particles. As they cooled, these particles converged into more massive protons and neutrons. Upon further cooling, protons and electrons formed hydrogen and helium atoms. Proto-stars and galaxies appeared, born from these amassed atoms. The first stars eventually burned themselves out, tossing out heavy elements formed in their cores into the universe. These discharges would in turn become the start of new stars and planets. The universe continues to grow outward. Analysis of radiation wavelengths shows that most observable galaxies are moving away from each other. As time goes on, the universe will continually expand, growing colder and less dense.

Scientist 2

The Steady State theory claims that the universe is expanding but keeps a constant average density over time. This phenomenon could only occur if, as matter expanded and dispersed, more matter is being created to keep the ratio of mass to volume consistent. This theory therefore claims that the amount of matter in the universe is not constant, as the Big Bang theory insinuates; instead, matter is constantly created. The energy source of this matter is as yet unknown. The amount of matter created is so small that it is immeasurable, therefore the lack of data does not disprove the theory.

Which statement below, if true, would support the Big Bang theory and not the Steady State theory?

A. The density of the universe has remained constant since it began.
B. The universe is not expanding.
C. The mass of the universe has remained constant since it began.
D. The universe is moving in closer together.

❑ Some assessment questions will ask you which viewpoint, if any, would be strengthened or weakened by additional information. These questions may require you to cross-reference more than one hypothesis, which is easier to do if you have effectively mapped the passage already.

Finding new information that could prove there was a definite time when our universe did not exist would support which theory?

A.  Big Bang theory only
B.  Steady State theory only
C.  Both the Big Bang theory and the Steady State theory
D.  Neither the Big Bang theory nor the Steady State theory

## PUT IT TOGETHER

The fields of robotics and computer animation have made great strides toward approximating human likeness in machines. However, as the appearance and functionality of humanoid creations get closer to those of natural humans, scientists have discovered a distinct revulsion response in human observers. Two scientists discuss theories as to why this reaction occurs.

In graphs that plot the emotional response of humans against the anthropomorphic levels of robots, we have observed a steep decline of comfort among humans while they view near-human robots. The technical term for this dip is called the *uncanny valley*. Most humans will feel measurable repulsion toward creations in this aesthetic sphere, and will not be able to form an empathetic response towards a robot that exhibits these characteristics.

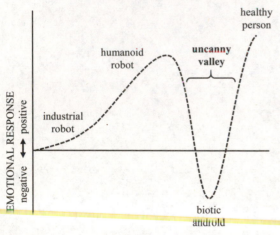

Figure 1

### Scientist 1

As the similarities between robots and humans increase, an evolutionary response is triggered in order to avoid contamination by viruses, bacteria, or other parasites. Humans are more likely to catch diseases from organisms with similar genetic backgrounds; for instance, it is highly unlikely that a person would catch a sickness from a grasshopper. However, pathogens are shared easily between humans, leading us to feel discomfort when those around us are visibly sick or exhibiting physical defects. Robots that come close to approximating human likeness and behavior are placed into the same group as pathogen-bearers— in fact, the more human a robot appears, the more sensitive we are to its defects, which we instinctively treat as signifying poor health.

### Scientist 2

Humanoid robots have the potential to cause a feeling of discomfort due to the conflicting sensory clues perceived by the observer. The human brain organizes information into categories, called *schemas*—when these categories are violated, we feel a distinct sense of eeriness. Researchers have demonstrated that the neural response to a *category-inconsistent* robot (meaning, one that combines robotic behavior with human-like appearance, or vice versa) suggests increased levels of prediction error. Humans and other living creatures rely upon a certain amount of stereotype and prediction to navigate their environments. Since category-inconsistent robots blur the boundary between two distinct cognitive schemas, humans exhibit a repulsion response as a defense mechanism, and are less likely to build an empathetic bond with the robot. From the point of view of an animal in an environment, being able to stereotype, or accurately predict, the behavior of another creature facilitates survival. The prediction error caused by category-inconsistent robots makes humans uncomfortable and on-edge, with increased adrenaline making them more prepared to engage in fight-or-flight behavior. The solution to this discomfort is a sense of familiarity that is best developed through routine exposure, thus creating new schemas.

1. Engineers who work regularly in the design of humanoid robots have a measurably lower revulsion response to these machines than do the general public. Whose hypothesis does this support?

   A. Scientist 1's.
   B. Scientist 2's.
   C. Both Scientist 1's and Scientist 2's.
   D. Neither Scientist 1's nor Scientist 2's.

2. Scientist 1's viewpoint would be *strengthened* by which of the following experimental findings?

   F. Humans feel the same level of revulsion towards humanoid robots as they do towards sick farm animals.
   G. Humans can contract most insect-borne pathogens and viruses.
   H. A new robot that gets even closer to human likeness does not cause observers discomfort.
   J. Humans have a greater response to sickness in chimps than they have to sicknesses in lizards.

3. Some fast-food restaurants have considered installing humanoid robots as cashiers. If Scientist 2's model is correct, how will the average fast food customer respond to a humanoid robot taking his or her order 20 years after these robots first appear in local restaurants?

   A. With revulsion, because the humanoid robot is still category-inconsistent.
   B. With revulsion, because is no longer category-inconsistent.
   C. Without revulsion, because the humanoid robot is still category-inconsistent.
   D. Without revulsion, because the humanoid robot is no longer category-inconsistent.

4. Scientist 2's model would be most weakened if which of the following observations were made?

   F. People can develop affection for non-humanoid machines, such as cars.
   G. Animals relocated to unfamiliar habitats are less likely to survive.
   H. Humanoid machines have appeared in literature since 1886 and are familiar images in popular culture.
   J. Children often respond to strangers by hiding behind their parents.

# Checkpoint Review

Three scientists discuss their viewpoints about the extinction of *Mammuthus primigenius*, otherwise known as the "woolly mammoth." Woolly mammoths first appear in the fossil record around 150,000 years ago, during the Pleistocene Epoch. This time period encompassed the last great Ice Age, and was known for its especially large animals, or *megafauna*.

## Scientist A

Woolly mammoths were roughly the size of today's African elephants, but had smaller ears to decrease overall heat loss and a coat of thick fur to protect them from the harsh environment. During the time that these animals were active, there was little precipitation and most of the planet's water was frozen. Because of this, the mammoths evolved with a very particular vegetarian diet, as the choices were limited to a few hearty plants that could survive winters that were 5-10°C (41 to 50°F) below our current global averages.

Through the study of glaciers and sediment samples deep within the earth, paleoclimatologists have theorized that the planet's average temperatures began to increase naturally around 14,000 years ago. This drastic climate difference would have greatly affected the woolly mammoth's main food supply— given that each mammoth needed to consume around 130 lbs of specific, mineral-rich vegetation per day, it was a death sentence.

## Scientist B

Undoubtedly, climate change during the woolly mammoth's period of activity in the Pleistocene Era presented great difficulties for the species. Popular depictions of the demise of the mammoth describe the extinction as being due to the growing warmth of the atmosphere and the effects of this heat upon the animal's food sources around 14,000 years ago. While the warmer climate was not favorable for the success of the woolly mammoth, it was only one of many factors that contributed to its disappearance.

There is significant fossil evidence demonstrating the tenacity of this creature throughout periods of extreme climate fluctuation. Around 120,000 years ago, average temperatures across the Earth were at least as warm as they are today, if not warmer. While the woolly mammoth population decreased significantly throughout this time period, they survived by migrating north, to cooler areas. In the end, it was just unlucky chance that probably finished off the species—humans began to hunt the mammoth around 14,000 years ago, when the *megafauna* population was already suffering from the warm climate and competition for food. If humans had not come into existence, it is likely that woolly mammoths would still be walking the earth today.

## Scientist C

Contemporary environmental activists point to the extinction of the woolly mammoth as a rallying point for the fight against global warming. The death of the animal did coincide curiously with a period of unusually warm weather, and a shift in dominant vegetation that killed off its main food sources.

While the evidence of these factors is indisputable, the warmer era that killed off the mammoths is not solely due to normal global warming. New data shows that a comet or meteorite struck North America around 10,000 years ago, resulting in melted ice sheets, widespread fires, and scorching, hurricane-force winds. While the woolly mammoth's species had survived several periods of warmer weather during its existence, such extreme changes would have been impossible to overcome. Weakened by the lack of available vegetation, mammoths that were lucky enough to survive this event would have been easily targeted by humans or other large predators. When humans happened to kill off the last few woolly mammoths, they brought a swifter end to an extinction that would have happened regardless of their interference.

# Checkpoint Review

1.  Which passage, if any, describes physical attributes of the woolly mammoth?

    A.  Scientist A's passage
    B.  Scientist B's passage
    C.  Both passage A and B
    D.  Neither passage A or B

2.  According to Scientist A, the woolly mammoth's diet was:

    F.  omnivorous and varied.
    G.  vegetarian and particular.
    H.  vegetarian and unrestricted.
    J.  carnivorous and precise.

3.  Scientist B's views differ from Scientist A's in that only Scientist B believes that a significant factor in the extinction of the woolly mammoth was:

    A.  warmer climates.
    B.  lack of food.
    C.  water shortages.
    D.  hunting by humans.

4.  From the viewpoints presented in the passages, how would Scientist B most likely react to reading Scientist A's explanation of the extinction of the mammoth?

    F.  Agree with all points
    G.  Agree, but suggest that there was too much focus upon climate change
    H.  Disagree with all points
    J.  Disagree with most points, except for temperature data

5.  Scientist C would describe the viewpoint of contemporary environmental activists as:

    A.  unfounded in scientific reality.
    B.  connecting two very different circumstances.
    C.  completely incorrect.
    D.  the solution to a problem.

6.  Scientist B and Scientist C both agree that:

    F.  woolly mammoths would still exist today, if not for hunting by humans.
    G.  a meteorite or comet contributed to the woolly mammoth's extinction.
    H.  gradual global warming was the most direct reason for the woolly mammoth's extinction.
    J.  prior to their extinction, mammoths had survived climates warmer than their ideal.

7.  Suppose that a recent study discovered that the last mammoths on Earth were not undernourished, and probably had enough to eat. This information damages the viewpoint of:

    A.  Scientist A.
    B.  Scientist B.
    C.  Scientist C.
    D.  All of the above.

# Science Summary

## The Scientific Method

☐ Understand what each step of the scientific method is supposed to achieve.

   Step 1: Ask a Question
   Step 2: Conduct Experiments
   Step 3: Interpret Data
   Step 4: Draw Conclusions

☐ Learn to apply the scientific method to different types of passages. Each type of Science passage focuses on different steps of the scientific method:

   Data Representation passages focus on step 3. They look at data presented in tables and graphs and ask questions about trends, patterns, and specific data points.

   Research Summary passages focus on steps 2, 3, and 4. They ask you to consider the experimental design and the resulting data collected.

   Conflicting Viewpoint passages focus on steps 1 and 4. They look at a scientific question and ask you to compare different conclusions.

## Data Representation

☐ Data Representation passages may look intimidating, because they often include large, complicated charts and graphs. However, they are typically the simplest passages.

☐ These passages are your opportunity to move quickly. This is important because you will need more time to work through the more complicated Research Summary and Conflicting Viewpoints passages.

## Research Summary

☐ Research Summary passages are often the most challenging passages in the Science Test.

☐ These passages usually take more time than typical Data Representation passages. They also require more careful consideration to solve questions, and there is a greater likelihood of questions that depend on your own understanding of scientific concepts.

## Conflicting Viewpoints

☐ Conflicting Viewpoints passages typically resemble the paired passages from the Reading Test. In these cases, you can work through the passage in much the same way as you would a Reading paired passage.

**Science Practice**

## Data Representation

## Passage I

The *orbital eccentricity* of an astronomical object describes the shape of its orbit around another astronomical body. A perfectly circular orbit would have an eccentricity value of 0, and all other eccentricities are positive values. The farther an orbit's shape deviates from a circle, the larger its eccentricity value becomes.

Figure 1 and Table 1 show the values and shapes of different types of orbits.

| Table 1 | |
|---|---|
| type of orbit | eccentricity value |
| circular | $e = 0$ |
| elliptical | $0 < e < 1$ |
| parabolic | $e = 1$ |
| hyperbolic | $e > 1$ |

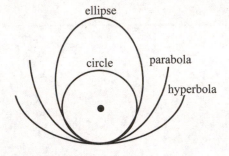

Figure 1

Various properties of celestial bodies within our solar system are shown in Table 2 below.

| Table 2 | | | | |
|---|---|---|---|---|
| celestial object | mean distance from sun (million km) | orbital eccentricity | mass (earth = 1) | density (g/cm³) |
| Sun | --- | --- | 33,000.00 | 1.4 |
| Earth | 149.6 | 0.017 | 1.00 | 5.5 |
| Saturn | 1426.7 | 0.054 | 95.16 | 0.7 |
| Uranus | 2871.0 | 0.047 | 14.54 | 1.3 |
| Neptune | 4498.3 | 0.009 | 17.15 | 1.8 |
| Earth's moon | 149.6 | 0.055 | 0.01 | 3.3 |

The orbital ranges of various astronomical bodies orbiting the Sun are shown in Figure 2 below.

| label | name |
|---|---|
| A | Saturn |
| B | Uranus |
| C | Neptune |
| D | Halley's Comet |
| E | Ceres |
| F | Pluto |

distance from sun (in AU)

distance from sun (in millions of km)

Figure 2

1.  According to Table 1, an acceptable eccentricity value for an elliptical orbit would be:

    A.  −0.14
    B.  0.00
    C.  0.59
    D.  1.08

2.  According to Table 2, which of the following had the least eccentric orbit?

    F.  Saturn
    G.  Earth
    H.  Uranus
    J.  Neptune

3.  A comet travelled in an elliptical orbit around the sun with an eccentricity value of $E_1$. During the course of its normal orbit, the comet encountered a gravitational pull that forced it into a parabolic orbit with a new eccentricity of $E_2$. Which of the following could NOT be true?

    A.  $E_1 = 0.029$
    B.  $E_1 - E_2$ is negative
    C.  $E_2 > E_1$
    D.  $E_2 + E_1 = 2$

4.  According to Figure 2, approximately how far is 1 Astronomical Unit (AU)?

    F.  1500 million m
    G.  1500 million km
    H.  150 million m
    J.  150 million km

5.  If the small black circle represents the Sun, which of the following diagrams most closely reflects the data shown in Figure 2 for the orbits of Saturn, Uranus, and Pluto?

    A.

    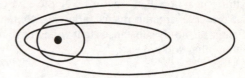

    B.

    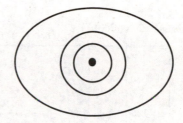

    C.

    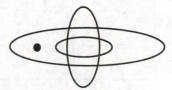

    D.

    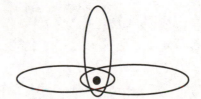

## Data Representation

## Passage II

Scientists extracted soil samples at various depths within a peat bog. Peat bogs offer acidic environments that preserve organic matter, allowing contemporary scientists to study substances that would have decayed within other soil types.

Radiocarbon dating was used to assign ages to the samples, and they were analyzed for levels of various substances. Study 1 charted the relative percentages of pollen types within the sample. Study 2 observed the levels of two elements, Rubidium (Rb) and Zirconium (Zr), within the same soil samples.

Study 1

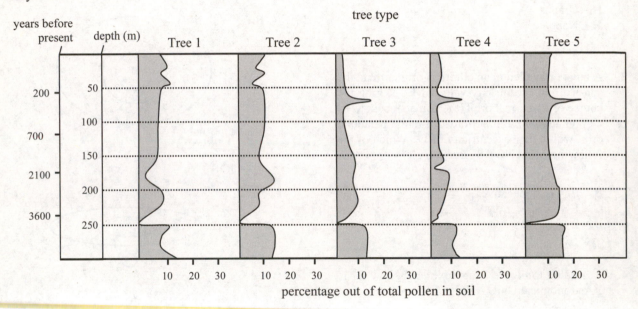

Figure 1

Study 2

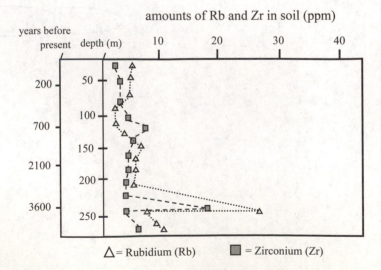

Figure 2

1. According to Figure 2, which substance was more often found at higher levels within the soil samples?

   A. Tree 5 pollen
   B. Zirconium
   C. Rubidium
   D. Not able to be determined

2. According to Figure 1, which of the following trees reached the highest pollen percentage out of the samples studied?

   F. Tree 2
   G. Tree 3
   H. Tree 4
   J. Tree 5

3. A scientist asserted that soil levels of Rb and Zr in excess of 10 ppm may indicate that a major volcanic eruption occurred in the area. Do Figure 1 and Figure 2 support the possibility of such a volcanic event approximately 3700 years ago?

   A. Yes, because Rb and Zr levels increased drastically while pollen decreased, indicating less tree growth.
   B. Yes, because Rb and Zr levels decreased drastically while pollen decreased, indicating less tree growth.
   C. No, because Rb and Zr levels increased drastically while pollen increased, indicating more tree growth.
   D. No, because the study did not consider geological phenomena.

4. In Figure 1, three of the trees show a similar pattern in their pollen graphs at 70 meters below the surface. Which of the following is LEAST likely to be the reason why this occurred?

   F. A temporary increase in pollinators for these trees caused their numbers to spike.
   G. These trees favor arid conditions, and the climate had a temporary dry spell during the time the sample was deposited.
   H. The three tree types began to decrease in number due to an insect infestation.
   J. A forest fire in the area decimated other tree species, allowing the three trees to take over the cleared area.

5. According to Figure 1, what best describes the relationship between the pollen data for Tree 1 and Tree 2 from 0 meters – 50 meters under the surface?

   A. Direct relationship
   B. Inverse relationship
   C. Symbiotic relationship
   D. No relationship

## Data Representation

## Passage III

For an object to move, a force must be applied to oppose both the weight of the object and the friction of the surfaces.

Table 1 gives coefficients of friction for three combinations of surfaces.

Figure 1 shows the force required to move several objects 10 meters.

| Table 1 | | |
|---|---|---|
| Surface 1 | Surface 2 | Coefficient Kinetic Friction |
| steel | steel | 0.57 |
| aluminum | steel | 0.47 |
| lubricated metal | lubricated metal | 0.06 |

Force Required to Oppose Friction

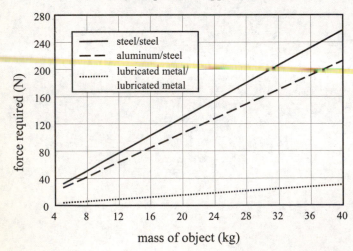

Figure 1

1.  According to Figure 1, what is the force, in Newtons, that is required to move a 28 kg aluminum object 10 meters along a steel surface?

    A. 20 N
    B. 120 N
    C. 150 N
    D. 170 N

2.  If a 40 kg object of an unknown substance with a coefficient of kinetic friction of 0.52 is moved 10 meters along an identical surface, the force required would be:

    F. 30 N.
    G. 120 N.
    H. 230 N.
    J. 250 N.

3.  The information provided in Table 1 indicates that the surface combination with the least frictional force is:

    A. steel on steel.
    B. aluminum on steel.
    C. aluminum on aluminum.
    D. lubricated metal on lubricated metal.

4.  Based on the information in Figure 1, one would conclude that as the mass of an object increases:

    F. the force required to oppose friction decreases.
    G. the force required to oppose friction increases.
    H. the force required to oppose friction increases then decreases.
    J. the force required to oppose friction decreases then increases.

5.  Rank the three surface combinations in order of least friction to highest friction.

    A. lubricated metal/lubricated metal, steel/steel, aluminum/steel
    B. steel/steel, aluminum/steel, lubricated metal/lubricated metal
    C. aluminum/steel , steel/steel, lubricated metal/lubricated metal
    D. lubricated metal/lubricated metal, aluminum/steel, steel/steel

## Data Representation

## Passage IV

The geosphere is the solid or mineral part of the Earth, consisting of layers, from the outer crust down to the inner core, which have separated through density and temperature.

There are two ways to classify the composition of the geosphere – chemically, into crust, mantle, and core, or functionally, in the case of the outer layers (crust and mantle) into lithosphere and asthenosphere.

Figure 1 shows how the pressure and temperature vary by depth.

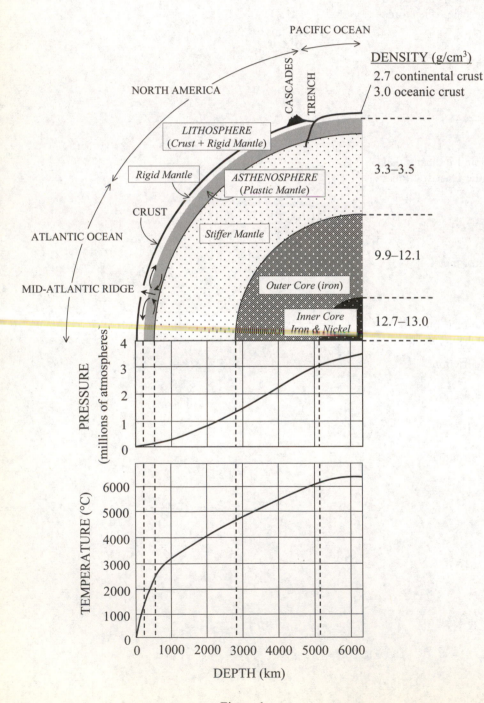

Figure 1

1. The Asthenosphere is known as a plastic mantle due to its non-solidified, molten composition. According to Figure 1, which of the following predictions regarding the pressure and temperature of the Asthenosphere is correct?

   A. The "plastic" nature of the Asthenosphere is due to its relatively low pressure and temperature of approximately 0° C.
   B. The "plastic" nature of the Asthenosphere is due to its relatively low pressure and temperature of approximately 2000° C.
   C. The "plastic" nature of the Asthenosphere is due to its relatively high pressure and temperature of approximately 2000° C.
   D. The "plastic" nature of the Asthenosphere is due to its relatively high pressure and temperature of approximately 6700° C.

2. Based on the data presented in Figure 1, which of the following correctly lists layers of the Earth's interior from lowest to highest density?

   F. Inner Core, Outer Core, Oceanic Crust, Continental Crust, Stiffer Mantle
   G. Inner Core, Outer Core, Stiffer Mantle, Rigid Mantle, Continental Crust
   H. Asthenosphere, Oceanic Crust, Lithosphere, Outer Core, Inner Core
   J. Continental Crust, Oceanic Crust, Asthenosphere, Outer Core, Inner Core

3. According to Figure 1, the temperature of the Outer Core is approximately between:

   A. 1000° C and 2500° C
   B. 2500° C and 5000° C
   C. 4800° C and 6300° C
   D. 6200° C and 6500° C

4. According to Figure 1, which layer of the Earth's interior is found to have a pressure of 1 million atmospheres?

   F. Stiffer Mantle at a depth of 1500 km
   G. Stiffer Mantle at a depth of 2500 km
   H. Inner Core at a depth of 4000 km
   J. Inner Core at a depth of 2500 km

5. According to Figure 1, which of the following statements best describes the relationship, if any, between the pressure, temperature, and density of the Earth's interior?

   A. As the temperature of the Earth's interior increases, both the density and pressure increase.
   B. As the temperature of the Earth's interior decreases, both the density and pressure increase.
   C. As the temperature of the Earth's interior increases, the density increases and pressure decreases.
   D. As the temperature of the Earth's interior increases, the density decreases and pressure increases.

## Data Representation

## Passage V

The stability of an isotope depends upon the number of neutrons present. Stable isotopes will remain unchanged while unstable isotopes will decay at a specified rate. Figure 1 depicts the number of protons versus neutrons for stable isotopes for the first 22 elements. Figure 2 depicts the half-lives (decay rate) for many unstable isotopes.

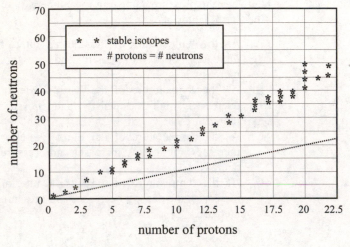

Figure 1

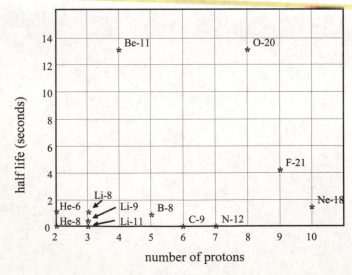

Figure 2

1.  According to the information presented in Figure 1, how does the number of protons relate to the number of neutrons required for a stable atom?

    A.  Stable isotopes have equal numbers protons and neutrons.
    B.  Stable isotopes have fewer neutrons than protons.
    C.  Stable isotopes require more neutrons to be stable as protons increase.
    D.  Stable isotopes require fewer neutrons to be stable as protons increase.

2.  According to the information presented in Figure 2, as the number of protons increase:

    F.  the half lives of unstable isotopes increase.
    G.  the half lives of unstable isotopes decrease.
    H.  the half lives of unstable isotopes remains unchanged.
    J.  the half lives of unstable isotopes show no relationship to number of protons.

3.  A stable isotope with 20 protons could likely have:

    A.  0 neutrons.
    B.  20 neutrons.
    C.  40 neutrons.
    D.  60 neutrons.

4.  Based on the data above, one conclusion that could be drawn for isotopes that have a similar number of protons is that:

    F.  stable isotopes always have fewer neutrons.
    G.  stable isotopes always have two more neutrons.
    H.  stable isotopes may have more or fewer neutrons.
    J.  stable isotopes have roughly twice as many neutrons as protons.

5.  Lithium-8 (Li-8) is an unstable isotope with a half life closest to:

    A.  1.0 second.
    B.  2.5 seconds.
    C.  3.0 seconds.
    D.  4.5 seconds.

## Data Representation

## Passage VI

Long term studies have been done on the use of pesticides throughout the past 60 years. These studies revolve around how resistant certain pests are becoming to pesticide use. Figure 1 shows the number of pests that have become resistant to pesticides over the past 60 years.

Table 1 compares the average doses necessary to kill two common pests in both 1970 and 1980.

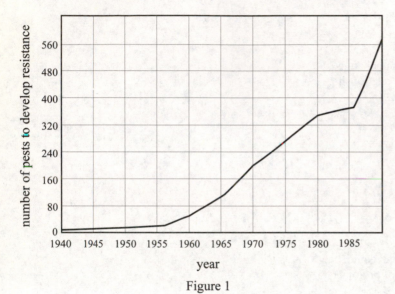

Figure 1

| Table 1 | | | | |
|---|---|---|---|---|
| Pesticide | Average Dose Necessary to Kill (mg per gram larva) | | | |
| | Pest X | | Pest Y | |
| | 1970 | 1980 | 1970 | 1980 |
| DDT | 0.028 | 1.011 | 0.127 | 16.508 |
| Endrin | 0.008 | 0.138 | 0.057 | 12.938 |
| Carbaryl | 0.128 | 0.541 | 0.301 | 54.552 |
| Stobane | 0.053 | 1.037 | 0.732 | 11.134 |
| Toxaphene | 0.041 | 0.444 | 0.464 | 3.517 |

1. What is the trend in the resistances of pests over time?

   A. Pest resistance increased steadily over time.
   B. Pest resistance increased at an increasing rate over time.
   C. Pest resistance decreased steadily over time.
   D. Pest resistance decreased at an increasing rate over time.

2. What is the most reasonable explanation for the higher lethal dose of pesticide needed to kill Pest Y compared to Pest X?

   F. Pest Y is larger and requires more pesticide to kill.
   G. Pest Y's larva is less sensitive to pesticides.
   H. Pest Y is camouflaged and can avoid those spraying the pesticides.
   J. Only some of the pesticides require higher lethal doses for Pest Y.

3. According to Figure 1, the slowest increase in resistance took place during what years?

   A. 1940-1950
   B. 1950-1960
   C. 1960-1970
   D. 1970-1980

4. If studies were done on a pest that revealed it to require a dose of 0.054 mg/g larva to kill it in 1970 and 1.040 mg/g larva in 1980, it was likely to be:

   F. Pest X only.
   G. Pest Y only.
   H. Either pest X or Y.
   J. Neither pest X nor Y.

5. What is one logical piece of information that could have occurred within the data from Figure 1?

   A. During 1950-1980 a disease spread among pests lowering their populations.
   B. During 1980-1987 the government allowed stronger, more effective pesticides to be used.
   C. During 1940-1956 there was a large influx of pests from Canada.
   D. During 1970-1980 the government allowed stronger, more effective pesticides to be used.

## Data Representation

## Passage VII

Students studied the relationship between voltage, current, and resistance in two types of direct current circuits. The setups for the circuits are shown below. Each circuit contains two resistors ($R_1$ and $R_2$), a battery to provide electrical energy, and an ammeter to measure the current. Figure 1 shows a series circuit, and Figure 2 shows a parallel circuit.

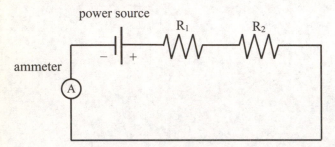

Figure 1

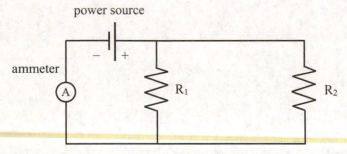

Figure 2

In Fig. 3 below, an Ohm's Law Formula Wheel displays the relationships between voltage, current, power, and resistance. Each quadrant gives the various formulas to find these values.

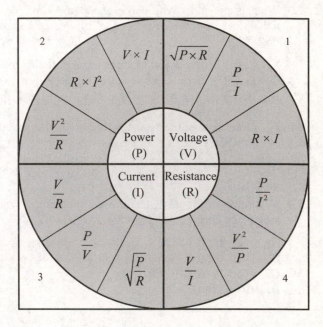

Figure 3

From the trials conducted, researchers generated a table of values for the voltage (V), resistance (R), and current (I). $R_1$ and $R_2$ refer to the specific resistance of each resistor, while $R_{total}$ is a value that represents the total resistance within the circuit.

|        | trial | voltage (V) | $R_1$ ($\Omega$) | $R_2$ ($\Omega$) | $R_{total}$ of circuit ($\Omega$) | I (Amps) |
|--------|-------|-------------|------------------|------------------|-----------------------------------|----------|
|        |       |             |                  |                  | **Table 1** |          |
| Fig. 1 | 1     | 10          | 2                | 4                | 6                                 | 1.67     |
|        | 2     | 12          | 2                | 4                | 6                                 | 2.00     |
|        | 3     | 18          | 2                | 4                | 6                                 | 3.00     |
| Fig. 2 | 1     | 10          | 2                | 4                | .75                               | 13.33    |
|        | 2     | 12          | 2                | 4                | .75                               | 16.00    |
|        | 3     | 18          | 2                | 4                | .75                               | 24.00    |

1.  Which of the following represents a parallel circuit?

    A.  Figure 1
    B.  Figure 2
    C.  Table 1
    D.  Figure 3

2.  According to Table 1, what was the value of the current of Fig. 2 during Trial 3?

    F.  $3.00 \, \Omega$
    G.  $24.00 \, \Omega$
    H.  3.00 Amps
    J.  24.00 Amps

3.  According to Figure 3, which of the following equations is equal to $R \times I^2$ ?

    A.  $\dfrac{V}{I}$

    B.  $\sqrt{P \times R}$

    C.  $\dfrac{V^2}{R}$

    D.  $\dfrac{P}{I^2}$

4.  If a student only had experimental values for $R$ and $I$, how many of the equations from the quadrant 3 of Fig. 3 could be solved?

    F.  1
    G.  2
    H.  3
    J.  None could be solved

5.  According to Table 1, which of the following is most likely the calculation used to find the $R_{total}$ for Figure 2?

    A.  $\dfrac{R_2}{R_1}$

    B.  $\dfrac{1}{R_1} + \dfrac{1}{R_2}$

    C.  $R_1 + R_2$

    D.  None of the above

## Data Representation

## Passage VIII

Biologists have studied the effects of natural human enzymes on biological processes such as digestion. Enzymes are chemicals that speed up specific chemical reactions, although they are not changed themselves during the chemical reaction. Enzymes are not constantly at work in the body; instead, they lie dormant until some trigger releases their power. Figures 1 and 2 present the results of a study on Enzyme X. They show the effects of pH levels on the enzyme's activity and the rate of protein digestion over time (an enzyme-activated reaction).

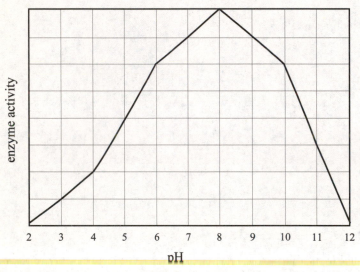

Figure 1

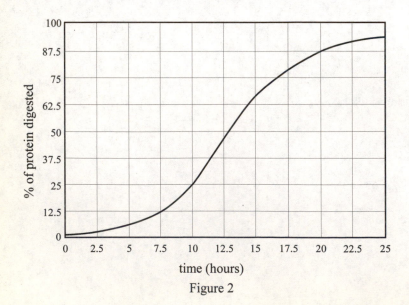

Figure 2

1.  From Figure 2, it can be concluded that the highest
    amount of protein digestion occurred between:

    A.  0-7.5 hours.
    B.  7.5-15 hours.
    C.  15-20 hours.
    D.  20-25 hours.

2.  The data in Figure 1 and Figure 2 supports which of the
    following hypotheses?

    F.  At time 0, a pH of 8 may have existed at the site of
        activity.
    G.  At time 12.5, a pH of 2 may have existed at the site
        of activity.
    H.  At time 12.5, a pH of 8 may have existed at the site
        of activity.
    J.  At time 12.5, a pH of 12 may have existed at the site
        of activity.

3.  What is one question that this study did NOT address?

    A.  The effect of temperature on enzyme activity
    B.  The effect of pH on enzyme activity
    C.  The effect of time on digestion
    D.  The effect of enzymes on digestion

4.  In this study, which of the following variables was the
    dependent variable?

    F.  temperature
    G.  pH
    H.  time
    J.  enzyme activity

5.  It can be concluded from Figure 1 that the optimum pH
    for enzyme activity is:

    A.  between 3 and 5.
    B.  between 5 and 7.
    C.  between 7 and 9.
    D.  between 9 and 11.

## Data Representation

## Passage IX

A marine biology class analyzed the solutes present in a sample of water from the Mediterranean Sea as compared to those within a sample of river water from the Mississippi River in the United States.

The salinity of a body of water refers to the concentration of salt in solution. When it is displayed as a percent, a salinity of 0.5% represents 5 pounds of salt per 1000 pounds of water. Since the process of evaporation directly correlates with the temperature of an ocean, the attributes of temperature, salinity, and rate of evaporation are interconnected. Figure 1 displays the percent composition of different solutes in a sea water sample, while Figure 2 does the same for a sample of river water. Table 1 displays relative temperature and salinity information for three large bodies of water.

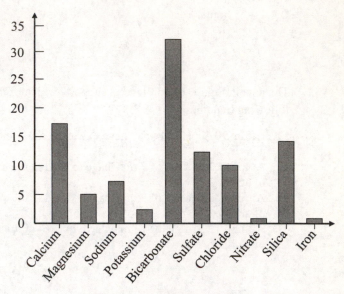

Percent Composition of River Water

Figure 2

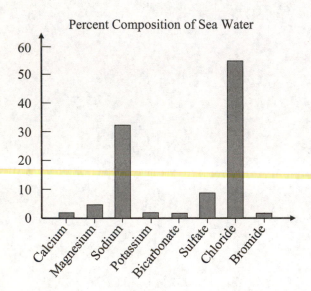

Percent Composition of Sea Water

Figure 1

| Table 1 | | |
|---|---|---|
| Ocean | Relative Temp | Salinity (%) |
| Red Sea/ Persian Gulf | High | 4.0 |
| North Atlantic | High/Moderate | 3.79 |
| Baltic Sea | Low | 1.0 |

1.  The chemical that makes up the highest percent composition of seawater is:

    A. bicarbonate.
    B. magnesium.
    C. sodium.
    D. chloride.

2.  One piece of data that would counter the hypothesis that ocean temperature affects salinity would be:

    F. finding multiple low salinity samples of river water in multiple high temperature river ranges.
    G. finding multiple high salinity samples of river water in multiple high temperature river ranges.
    H. finding multiple high salinity samples of ocean water in multiple cold temperature ocean ranges.
    J. finding multiple high salinity samples of ocean water in multiple high temperature ocean ranges.

3.  The relationship depicted in Table 1 is that:

    A. as ocean temperature rises, salinity rises.
    B. as ocean temperature drops, salinity rises.
    C. as ocean temperature rises, salinity remains steady.
    D. as ocean temperature drops, salinity remains steady.

4.  When added to a solution, bicarbonate raises the pH value. If the sample of river water from Figure 2 was poured into the sample of sea water from Figure 1, which of the following would occur?

    F. The mixture would be more acidic than the sea water alone.
    G. The mixture would be more basic than the river water alone.
    H. The mixture would be less acidic than the sea water alone.
    J. The mixture would be as acidic as the river water alone.

5.  How many pounds of salt are present per 1000 pounds of water in the Baltic Sea?

    A. 0.5
    B. 1
    C. 5
    D. 10

## Data Representation

## Passage X

Figure 1 and Table 1 are tools commonly used by pilots to safely operate airplanes under different conditions. Figure 1 is a *wind component chart*, which is used to calculate the headwind and crosswind components when taking off or landing.

Table 1 is a *takeoff distance table*, which is used to determine the minimum distance needed for takeoff on a runway under ideal conditions.

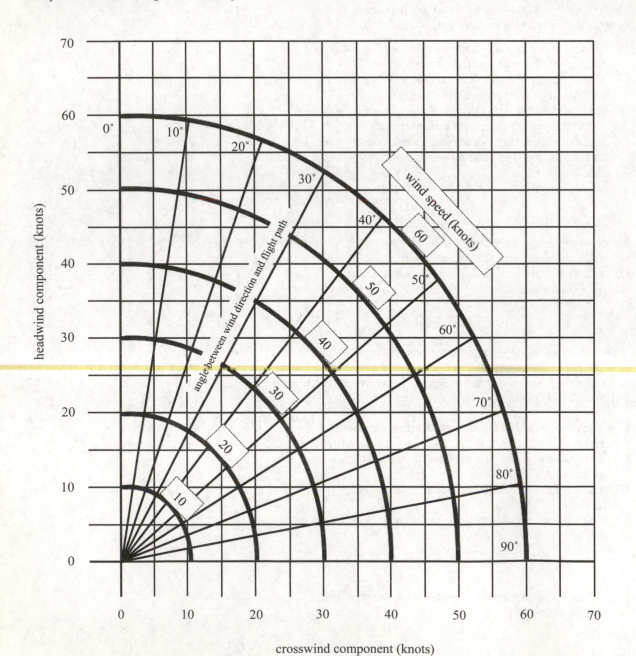

Figure 1

| Table 1 | | | | | | | | | | |
|---|---|---|---|---|---|---|---|---|---|---|
| aircraft weight (lbs) | takeoff speed (knots) | | altitude (ft) | runway temp 0°C | | runway temp 10°C | | runway temp 20°C | | |
| | lift-off | at 50 feet | | ground roll (ft) | to clear 50 ft. obstacle (ft) | ground roll (ft) | to clear 50 ft. obstacle (ft) | ground roll (ft) | to clear 50 ft. obstacle (ft) | |
| 3000 | 66 | 75 | sea level | 627 | 1102 | 692 | 1167 | 767 | 1317 | |
| | | | 1000 | 667 | 1187 | 727 | 1252 | 827 | 1377 | |
| | | | 2000 | 727 | 1287 | 802 | 1327 | 887 | 1497 | |
| | | | 3000 | 782 | 1397 | 852 | 1442 | 937 | 1587 | |
| | | | 4000 | 837 | 1527 | 907 | 1597 | 1007 | 1752 | |
| 2500 | 64 | 73 | sea level | 502 | 867 | 537 | 912 | 587 | 1027 | |
| | | | 1000 | 532 | 942 | 562 | 977 | 632 | 1107 | |
| | | | 2000 | 567 | 1012 | 597 | 1147 | 687 | 1267 | |
| | | | 3000 | 612 | 1097 | 647 | 1172 | 737 | 1347 | |
| | | | 4000 | 677 | 1162 | 717 | 1247 | 817 | 1412 | |

1. According to Figure 1, what is the crosswind component for a 50-knot wind that is approaching at an 80° angle?

   A. 40 knots
   B. 45 knots
   C. 49 knots
   D. 52 knots

2. According to the following chart and Table 1, which takeoff speed is closest to what is required for a 2500 lb aircraft at liftoff?

| Mph | 46.0 | 57.5 | 69.0 | 80.5 | 92.0 |
|---|---|---|---|---|---|
| knots | 40 | 50 | 60 | 70 | 80 |

   F. 65 mph
   G. 74 mph
   H. 60 knots
   J. 74 knots

3. The operation manual for a particular aircraft notes that pilots should not operate the plane when the crosswind component is above 48. According to Figure 1, which of the following would be considered unsafe?

   A. headwind component 30
      wind speed: 45 knots
   B. headwind component: 40
      wind speed: 60 knots
   C. wind angle: 65°
      wind speed: 50 knots
   D. wind angle: 70°
      wind speed: 60 knots

4. Which of the following hypotheses is supported by Table 1?

   F. Pilots would need to add 50 ft to their ground roll to clear a 50 ft obstacle.
   G. When the temperature is doubled, the ground roll distance will also be doubled.
   H. As the temperature of the runway increases, pilots need to allow more room for their takeoffs due to an increase in friction.
   J. As the temperature of the air decreases its density is lowered, requiring slower takeoff speeds.

5. The above charts were created to be accurate under ideal runway conditions. For operation on an unpaved runway, pilots are expected to increase ground roll distances by 10%. For a 3000 lb aircraft at 2000 feet above sea level and 10°C, this would increase the ground roll distance by approximately:

   A. 8 ft.
   B. 80 ft.
   C. 90 ft.
   D. 150 ft.

## Research Summary

## Passage XI

Thermal expansion is the tendency of matter to increase in volume when heated. Some materials are *isotropic*, meaning that they expand equally in all directions. Other materials are *anisotropic*, meaning that they expand at different rates along different axes. Engineers must consider this factor in their designs, as failure to do so may compromise the stability of a structure.

The *coefficient of linear expansion* ($\alpha$) associated with each material can be calculated from the following formula, where $L$ is the length and $T$ is the temperature of the sample material:

$$\Delta L = \alpha L \Delta T$$

Note: The coefficient $\alpha$ is a constant, but anisotropic materials will have different $\alpha$ values for their horizontal and vertical axes. Additionally, $\Delta T = T_f - T_i$, where $T_f$ and $T_i$ represent the final and initial temperatures of the tube, respectively. All tubes began with a $T_i$ of 68°F.

| Table 1 | | |
|---|---|---|
| | | |
| tube material | $\alpha$ of tube ($10^{-6}$ in/in°F) | |
| | horizontal axis | vertical axis |
| aluminum | 12.30 | 12.29 |
| glass | 3.31 | 3.29 |
| wood | 1.70 | 17.00 |
| iron | 6.00 | 5.99 |

(In the above table, there is an allowed experimental variance of ± .02 for the $\alpha$ values.)

*Experiment 2*

In a commercial laboratory, scientists measured thermal expansion along the horizontal axis of three materials at various temperatures. All samples began with the same dimensions at room temperature (20°C). The results for the experiment are shown in Figure 2 below.

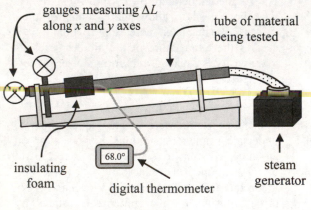

insulating foam

digital thermometer

68.0°

steam generator

Figure 1

*Experiment 1*

A group of students used the apparatus shown in Figure 1 to measure the expansion of several different materials at various temperatures. In each trial, hollow tubes with identical dimensions (at 68°F) were heated to 180°F from the inside using a steam generator. A thermometer located under an insulating foam sleeve tracked the temperature of the tube, and dial gauges measured expansion along the horizontal ($x$) and vertical ($y$) axes. The results of this experiment are shown in Table 1.

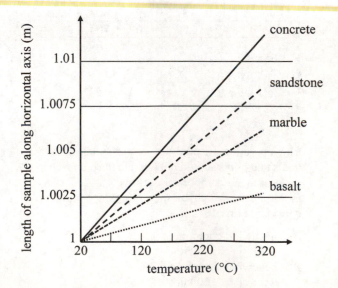

Figure 2

1.  According to Table 1, which of the following materials had the smallest α value for its vertical axis?

    A.  Aluminum
    B.  Glass
    C.  Wood
    D.  Iron

2.  Based on Experiment 2, if an engineer needs to build a foundation resistant to heat expansion, which of the following materials is most suitable?

    F.  Concrete
    G.  Sandstone
    H.  Marble
    J.  Basalt

3.  Which of the following is a dependent variable for Experiment 1?

    A.  Tube length after heating
    B.  Tube material
    C.  Temperature
    D.  $T_i$

4.  Based on Table 1, which material is most likely anisotropic?

    F.  Aluminum
    G.  Glass
    H.  Wood
    J.  Iron

5.  According to Figure 2, which material was closest to a horizontal axis length of 1.005 m at 200°C?

    A.  Wood
    B.  Concrete
    C.  Sandstone
    D.  Marble

6.  Material A and Material B are two different types of plastic. Researchers replicated Experiment 1 in every way, only changing the tube materials to Material A and B. They then used the formula $\Delta L = \alpha L \Delta T$ to calculate the unknown values. If Material A expanded more than Material B along the horizontal axis, and there was no change of phase, which of the following is true?

    F.  Material A had a larger α value for this axis.
    G.  Material B had a larger α value for this axis.
    H.  Both materials are the same for the vertical axis.
    J.  None of the above

SUMMIT
EDUCATIONAL
GROUP

## Research Summary

## Passage XII

Viscosity is a measure of resistance to flow in a liquid. A student ran 2 experiments to test viscosity of various liquids.

### Experiment 1

A student filled a graduated cylinder with honey and then surrounded this with a water bath (see Figure 1). The temperature of the water bath was used to control the temperature of the honey. Once the temperature of the honey reached a predetermined value, a steel ball was dropped into the graduated cylinder. The experiment was repeated three times. The time it took for the steel ball to fall to the bottom of the cylinder for each trial was recorded in Table 1.

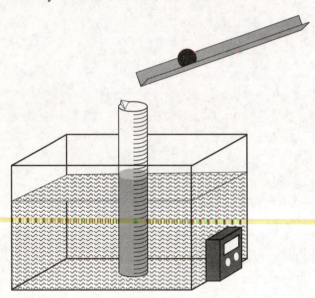

Figure 1

### Experiment 2

A student then decided to test the viscosity of multiple liquids all at a temperature of 296 K using a viscometer. The data was recorded in Table 2.

| Table 2 | |
|---|---|
| Substance | Viscosity (cP) |
| **Solvents** | |
| Ether | 0.233 |
| Chloroform | 0.58 |
| Benzene | 0.652 |
| Carbon Tetrachloride | 0.969 |
| Water | 1.002 |
| Ethanol | 1.200 |
| **Oils** | |
| Olive Oil | 84 |
| Castor Oil | 986 |
| Glycerol | 1490 |

| Table 1 | | | | | | | | |
|---|---|---|---|---|---|---|---|---|
| | Temperature of Honey (Kelvin) | | | | | | | |
| | 280 | 284 | 286 | 290 | 293 | 296 | 299 | 303 |
| | Time to reach bottom (seconds) | | | | | | | |
| Drop 1 | 7.8 | 6.3 | 5.7 | 4.9 | 4.5 | 3.5 | 3.0 | 2.2 |
| Drop 2 | 7.7 | 6.1 | 5.6 | 5.0 | 4.4 | 3.6 | 3.0 | 2.1 |
| Drop 3 | 8.0 | 6.4 | 5.5 | 5.0 | 4.7 | 3.4 | 3.1 | 1.9 |

1. If viscosity is a measure of resistance to flow in a liquid, which graph would best depict the relationship between the temperature of a liquid and its viscosity, as interpreted from the results of Experiment 1?

**A.**

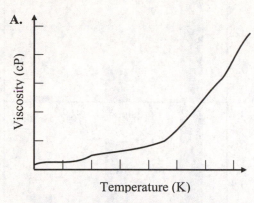

**B.**

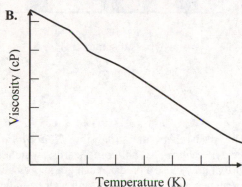

**C.**

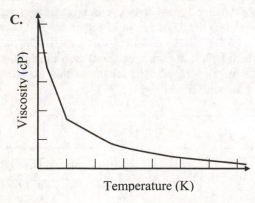

**D.**

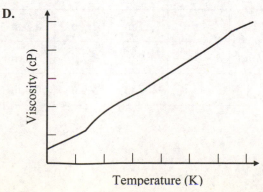

2. A liquid with a measured viscosity of 550 cP would most likely be categorized as a:

   **F.** solvent only.
   **G.** oil only.
   **H.** either solvent or oil.
   **J.** neither solvent nor oil.

3. In Experiment 1, which would NOT be a reason to run the drop of the steel ball three separate times?

   **A.** To figure out the maximum time for the steel ball to reach the bottom at a certain temperature
   **B.** To make sure the data actually shows a non-random pattern
   **C.** To find an average result for each drop
   **D.** To account for human error

4. Based on the results of Experiment 1, about how long would it take for a steel ball to reach the bottom of the beaker if the honey was at 270 K?

   **F.** 9 seconds
   **G.** 11 seconds
   **H.** 13 seconds
   **J.** 15 seconds

5. If the viscosity of benzene was measured at 300 K, what might the predicted value be?

   **A.** 0.541 cP
   **B.** 0.655 cP
   **C.** 0.681 cP
   **D.** 0.710 cP

6. Car oils are useful due to their high viscosities. When at the same temperature, oil used during an Alaskan winter would have to have what viscosity compared to that of oil used in Florida in the middle of August?

   **F.** Higher
   **G.** Lower
   **H.** Equal
   **J.** Approximately equal

## Research Summary

## Passage XIII

A team of scientists examined the escape behavior of the lizard *Rhotropus boultoni*. These studies were conducted on three separate islands off the coast of Africa, on which there only exists one lizard species. Island A is visited frequently by tourists, Island B restricts tourism, and Island C is protected and only visited occasionally by researchers.

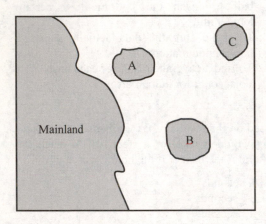

*Study 1*

Starting from a distance of 25 meters, researchers approached *Rhotropus boultoni* lizards with varying degrees of directness, at a constant speed. The *bypass distance* is defined as the minimum amount of distance between the researcher's path and the original position of the lizard. A bypass distance of 0 means that the researcher would have collided with the lizard if she continued on her path. The researchers conducted the experiment with 30 lizards per bypass distance, per island. The results of this study are shown in Figure 1.

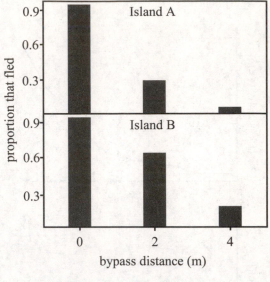

Figure 1

*Study 2*

The researchers measured the *flight initiation distance* of *Rhotropus boultoni* lizards, which is a measure of how close a predator can get to prey before the threatened animal flees. All trials were conducted with a 0 meter bypass distance, and researchers began approaching the lizards from 25 meters away. On each island, researchers conducted this experiment on 10 different lizards at each speed, and the values for each speed were averaged. The results of this experiment are shown in Table 1.

| Table 1 | | | | |
|---|---|---|---|---|
| | | *speed of approach (m/s)* | | |
| | | *1.0* | *1.4* | *1.8* |
| island | A | 1.5 m | 2.2 m | 5.2 m |
| | B | 1.9 m | 2.7 m | 5.6 m |
| | C | 2.2 m | 3.0 m | 6.3 m |

1. According to Table 1, under which of the following conditions was the *flight initiation distance* the same as it was on Island A at 1.4 m/s?

   A. Island A, Speed: 1.0 m/s
   B. Island B, Speed: 1.4 m/s
   C. Island C, Speed: 1.0 m/s
   D. None of the above

2. What is the most likely reason why the data for Figure 1 is the same for both Island A and Island B at a bypass distance of 0 m?

   F. The experimental data is incorrect.
   G. The researcher is not approaching the lizards directly, so few flee.
   H. The researcher is approaching the lizards directly, so all flee.
   J. The lizards are equally fast on both islands.

3. For the lizard populations on each island, as the speed of approach decreased, the *flight initiation distance:*

   A. increased only.
   B. decreased only.
   C. increased, then decreased.
   D. decreased, then increased.

4. The introduction and Figure 1 support which of the following statements?

   F. Lizards on islands with frequent tourism are more likely to flee.
   G. Lizards on islands with infrequent tourism are more likely to flee.
   H. Lizards on islands with frequent tourism never flee.
   J. Lizards on islands with infrequent tourism are less likely to flee.

5. Which of the following variables were held constant in both Study 1 and Study 2?

   A. The number of lizards studied
   B. The type of lizards studied
   C. The distance from which researchers began approaching the lizards
   D. Both B and C were held constant

6. The researchers conducted another trial of Study 2 on the mainland, which is more populated by humans than any of the islands. They created the following table with the observed flight initiation distances:

|  | *speed of approach (m/s)* | | |
| --- | --- | --- | --- |
|  | *1.0* | *1.4* | *1.8* |
| mainland | 1.7 m | 2.5 m | 5.4 m |

Which of the following statements does this data, along with Table 1, *most directly* support?

   F. The lizards only feel threatened by approaching humans.
   G. Increased exposure to humans correlates directly with flight initiation distance.
   H. Exposure to humans is not the only factor influencing flight initiation distance.
   J. The lizards on the mainland feel most threatened by approaching humans.

## Research Summary

## Passage XIV

A Leyden Jar is an example of an early parallel-plate capacitor. Capacitors are devices that store electrical energy in the form of opposing charges. This energy is released in a rapid burst when the positive and negative forces are allowed to discharge. Capacitors differ from batteries in that they cannot release energy at a slow, controlled rate.

In a parallel-plate capacitor, two metallic plates are separated from each other by a *dielectric* material. Dielectric materials insulate by rearranging their molecules to oppose outside charges, as seen below. The *permittivity* of a dielectric material is a measure of how much an electric field affects a material. The higher a material's permittivity constant ($\varepsilon$), the easier it is for a charge to pass through the substance. The *capacitance* ($C$) of a substance is a measure of its ability to store electrical energy.

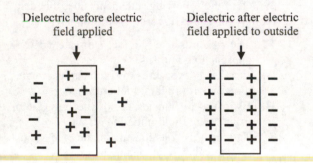

Dielectric before electric field applied | Dielectric after electric field applied to outside

A typical experimental setup for a Leyden Jar is shown in Figure 1.

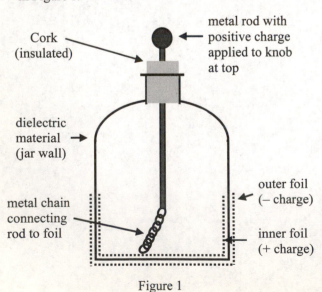

Cork (insulated)

metal rod with positive charge applied to knob at top

dielectric material (jar wall)

metal chain connecting rod to foil

outer foil (− charge)

inner foil (+ charge)

Figure 1

### Experiment 1

Experimenters determined the capacitances of six different Leyden Jars using the formula below. When the thickness of the jar ($t$) was increased, the area of foil overlap ($A$) was maintained. The results are shown in Table 1.

$$C = \varepsilon \times \frac{A}{t}$$

$C$ = capacitance
$\varepsilon$ = permittivity of dielectric (**constant**)
$A$ = area of foil overlap
$t$ = distance between foil pieces

| Table 1 | | | |
|---|---|---|---|
| | | thickness of jar wall: 10 mm | thickness of jar wall: 15 mm |
| dielectric material | dielectric permittivity ($\varepsilon$) | capacitance ($\times 10^{-12}$ farads) | capacitance ($\times 10^{-12}$ farads) |
| window glass | 7.80 | 78.00 | 52.00 |
| polystyrene | 2.60 | 26.00 | 17.33 |
| pyrex | 4.80 | 48.00 | 32.00 |
| silicone | 3.60 | 36.00 | 24.00 |

### Experiment 2

Using a similar setup to Experiment 1, experimenters attempted to identify the dielectric material used in unlabeled Leyden Jars in the lab. All jars were 15 mm thick. They recorded data in Table 2.

| Table 2 | | |
|---|---|---|
| dielectric material | dielectric permittivity ($\varepsilon$) | capacitance ($\times 10^{-12}$ farads) |
| Unknown 1 | 2.80 | 18.70 |
| Unknown 2 | 3.20 | 21.30 |
| Unknown 3 | 5.50 | 36.60 |
| Unknown 4 | 4.70 | 31.30 |

1.  Given the description in the first paragraph of the passage, capacitors are most likely used to:

    A.  power automobiles over long distances.
    B.  power the flash in a disposable camera.
    C.  measure the current of a circuit.
    D.  insulate a wire.

2.  According to Table 1, as dielectric permittivity increased, capacitance:

    F.  decreased only.
    G.  increased only.
    H.  decreased, then increased.
    J.  increased, then decreased.

3.  What is the best explanation for why the dielectric permittivity ($\varepsilon$) of the materials in Table 1 did not change when the wall thickness increased?

    A.  $\varepsilon$ is a constant.
    B.  $\varepsilon$ is too difficult to measure.
    C.  $\varepsilon$ did not change enough to be significant.
    D.  None of the above

4.  The researchers from Experiment 2 found the following chart in the lab:

    | material | dielectric permittivity ($\varepsilon$) |
    |---|---|
    | plexiglass | 2.78 |
    | porcelain | 5.52 |
    | mylar | 3.25 |
    | formica | 4.70 |
    | rubber | 2.82 |

    According to the chart, Unknown 1 is most likely to be:

    F.  porcelain.
    G.  mylar.
    H.  formica.
    J.  plexiglass or rubber.

5.  According to the formula for capacitance shown in Experiment 1, if the values of $\varepsilon$ and $A$ remain constant as $t$ increases, what is the change in $C$?

    A.  $C$ increases.
    B.  $C$ decreases.
    C.  $C$ stays the same.
    D.  There is not enough information to determine the change in $C$.

6.  If a Leyden Jar made of an unknown substance has an $\varepsilon$ value of 7.01, its capacitance is most likely:

    F.  less than that of silicone.
    G.  greater than that of window glass.
    H.  greater than that of window glass, but less than that of silicone.
    J.  greater than that of Pyrex, but less than that of window glass.

## Research Summary

### Passage XV

Vermicompost is produced by introducing worms to organic waste in order to break it down into nutrient-rich soil. This substance may be used as a natural and sustainable alternative to inorganic fertilizers. Agricultural scientists studied the effects of different concentrations of paper-based and food-based vermicomposts on strawberry (*Fragraria ananasa*) growth and yield.

*Experiment*

The strawberries were grown in raised soil beds with dimensions 2×5 m (10 m² per plot). There were 250 beds total, with 50 evenly-spaced strawberry plants per bed. All of the plants used were one year old, and ready to bear fruit. Concentrations of vermicompost mixed into soil were measured in tons per hectare (t/ha). Fertilizer and compost were mixed into the first 8 cm of each plot. The beds were treated in the following manner:

- *Group 1*: 50 beds inorganic fertilizer
- *Group 2*: 50 beds food waste vermicompost (concentration: 5 t/ha)
- *Group 3*: 50 beds food waste vermicompost (concentration: 10 t/ha)
- *Group 4*: 50 beds paper waste vermicompost (concentration: 5 t/ha)
- *Group 5*: 50 beds paper waste vermicompost (concentration: 10 t/ha)

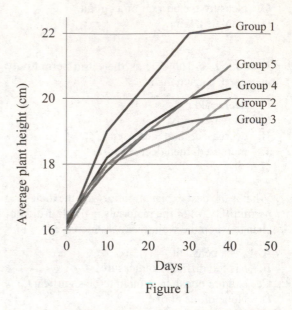

Figure 1

1. If a strawberry plant grew to a height of 23 cm, it was *most likely* in:

A. Group 1
B. Group 2
C. Group 3
D. Group 4

2. Which of the following groups had the highest percent of marketable fruit?

F. Group 1
G. Group 2
H. Group 3
J. Group 4

3. Many strawberry farmers prune their plants to keep them from growing too high. They say that shorter plants tend to grow more berries. Does this study support the farmers' observation?

A. No, because all of the groups had approximately the same yield.
B. No, because Group 1 had the largest berry.
C. Yes, because Group 1 had the highest crop yield.
D. Yes, because Groups 2 and 3 had the highest crop yield.

| Table 1 | | | |
|---|---|---|---|
| | Total berries produced (yield) | Weight of largest berry (in g) | % non-marketable fruit |
| Group 1 | 1200 | 24 | 19 |
| Group 2 | 1390 | 24.5 | 15 |
| Group 3 | 1500 | 22.5 | 15.5 |
| Group 4 | 1250 | 23 | 17 |
| Group 5 | 1240 | 25 | 15 |

| Table 2 | | |
|---|---|---|
| Nutrient composition of fertilizers (%) | | |
| | Inorganic fertilizer | Paper waste vermicompost | Food waste vermicompost |
| S | 2.0 | 1.8 | 2.6 |
| N | 10.4 | 1 | 1.3 |
| K | 2.4 | 6.2 | 9.2 |
| Mg | 3.8 | 4.5 | 4.4 |
| Fe | 4.2 | 6.2 | 23.3 |

4.  If a strawberry farmer were attempting to grow the most strawberries possible, he or she should add:

    F.  inorganic fertilizer
    G.  paper waste vermicompost (concentration: 5 t/ha)
    H.  food waste vermicompost (concentration: 5 t/ha)
    J.  food waste vermicompost (concentration: 10 t/ha)

5.  Runoff from some fertilizers has been named as a major source of water pollution. These fertilizers cause an excess of nitrogen (N) to enter marine ecosystems, resulting in the overproduction of algae. If a strawberry farmer were looking to fertilize a garden while minimizing the amount of N introduced to the soil, he or she should use:

    A.  Inorganic fertilizer
    B.  Paper waste vermicompost
    C.  Food waste vermicompost
    D.  A mixture of food waste vermicompost and inorganic fertilizer

6.  Which of the following was not studied in the experiments above?

    F.  Strawberry growth with no fertilizers added
    G.  Yield of strawberry plants under different conditions
    H.  Which plants produced the smallest berries
    J.  Neither F nor H were studied

## Research Summary

## Passage XVI

Students used two methods to calculate $V$, the total volumes of various objects made of aluminum.

*Experiment 1*

In Method 1, $V$ was calculated directly by water displacement. Table 1 lists measured variables and results for Method 1.

| Table 1 | | |
|---|---|---|
| | Mass (grams) | Volume (ml) |
| Object 1 | 1.05 | 0.42 |
| Object 2 | 3.24 | 1.30 |
| Object 3 | 6.28 | 2.51 |
| Object 4 | 10.84 | 4.34 |
| Object 5 | 11.25 | 4.50 |
| Object 6 | 14.69 | 5.88 |
| Object 7 | 17.20 | 6.88 |
| Object 8 | 19.84 | 7.94 |

| Table 2 | | |
|---|---|---|
| | Mass (grams) | Volume (ml) |
| Object 1 | 1.05 | 0.32 |
| Object 2 | 3.24 | 0.98 |
| Object 3 | 6.28 | 1.90 |
| Object 4 | 10.84 | 3.28 |
| Object 5 | 11.25 | 3.41 |
| Object 6 | 14.69 | 4.45 |
| Object 7 | 17.20 | 5.21 |
| Object 8 | 19.84 | 6.01 |

*Experiment 2*

The students then calculated density of aluminum to be approximately 3.3 g/ml. In Method 2, they calculated volume using the formula $V = M/D$ (volume = mass/density) and their estimated value of the density. Table 2 shows the results of Method 2.

The true volume of aluminum is calculated using the accepted value for density of 2.7 g/ml. The results of Methods 1 and 2 are graphed along with true volume in Figure 1.

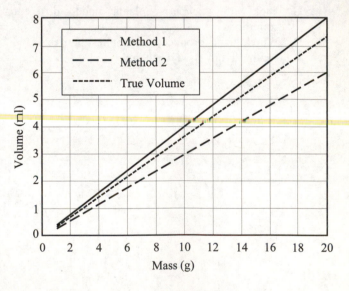

Figure 1

SUMMIT
EDUCATIONAL
GROUP

1. If an aluminum object has a mass of 4g, then the true volume will be approximately:

   A. 0.5 ml
   B. 1.5 ml
   C. 2.5 ml
   D. 3.5 ml

2. According to Figure 1, how do the results of both methods compare to the true volume?

   F. Method 1 produced more accurate results that were slightly higher than the true volume.
   G. Method 1 produced more accurate results that were slightly lower than the true volume.
   H. Method 2 produced more accurate results that were slightly higher than the true volume.
   J. Method 2 produced more accurate results that were slightly lower than the true volume.

3. How does the volume of an aluminum object with a mass of 10 grams compare to that of an aluminum object with a mass of 5 grams?

   A. ¼ as great
   B. ½ as great
   C. 2 times as great
   D. 4 times as great

4. Based on the information presented, which of the following statements can be concluded?

   F. As the mass of an object increases, density increases.
   G. As the volume of an object increases, density increases.
   H. As the mass of an object increases, the volume increases.
   J. As the mass of an object increases, the volume decreases.

5. If an object of unknown identity has a mass of 15 g and a volume of 4.5 ml, how does this relate to aluminum?

   A. The object has the same density as aluminum.
   B. The object has a density higher than aluminum.
   C. The object has a density lower than aluminum.
   D. The object would float in water.

6. Which of the following is the best approximation of the volume of an unknown substance with a mass of 15 grams and a density of 5 g/ml?

   F. 3 ml
   G. 4.5 ml
   H. 5 ml
   J. 6 ml

## Research Summary

## Passage XVII

Scientists studied the gravity on 3 planets by dropping pieces of paper in each environment.

*Experiment 1*

A flat piece of paper was held 10 meters above the ground and dropped. The distance traveled over time on three planets is represented in Figure 1. The acceleration due to gravity on these planets is represented in Table 1.

| Table 1 | | |
|---|---|---|
| Planet | Acceleration Due to Gravity (m/s$^2$) | Planet Mass (kg) |
| Saturn | 11.2 | 5.68 x 10$^{26}$ |
| Earth | 9.8 | 5.98 x 10$^{24}$ |
| Mercury | 3.61 | 3.2 x 10$^{23}$ |

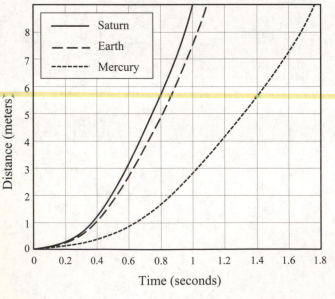

Flat Paper

Figure 1

*Experiment 2*

The paper was then crumpled into a ball and dropped again with the results in Figure 2.

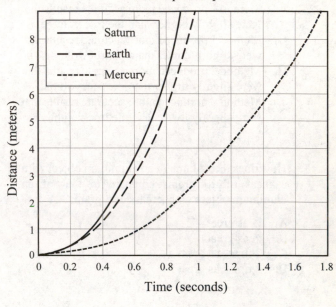

Crumpled Paper

Figure 2

1. Based on Figure 1, approximately how far did a flat piece of paper fall after 0.6 seconds on Mercury?

   A. 0.5 meter
   B. 1.0 meter
   C. 1.5 meters
   D. 2.0 meters

2. According to Figure 2, if a crumpled paper falls 3 meters in 0.6 seconds, it is falling on:

   F. Saturn.
   G. Earth.
   H. Mercury.
   J. the Moon.

3.  The acceleration due to gravity on the planet Uranus is 10.5 m/s². Based on Figure 2, a crumpled piece of paper's fall on Uranus' surface would be:

    A.  faster than the fall on the Saturn's surface.
    B.  slower than the fall on the Mercury's surface.
    C.  faster than the fall on the Earth's surface.
    D.  slower than the fall on the Earth's surface.

4.  What is the relationship between planet mass and acceleration due to gravity according to Table 1:

    F.  acceleration increases with mass.
    G.  acceleration decreases with mass.
    H.  as mass increases, acceleration first increases, then decreases.
    J.  acceleration is independent of mass.

5.  Based on the results of Experiment 1 and Experiment 2, which of the following conclusions can be made about Earth and Saturn, but not Mercury?

    A.  Flat paper falls faster than crumpled paper.
    B.  As the mass of a planet increases, objects fall slower.
    C.  Crumpled paper falls slightly faster than flat paper.
    D.  As the mass of a planet increases, objects fall faster.

6.  The planetary mass of Venus is 4.869 X 10²⁴ kg. The acceleration due to gravity on Venus would likely be closest to that of:

    F.  Saturn.
    G.  Earth.
    H.  Mercury.
    J.  It would be well below the acceleration of the planets in the study.

## Research Summary

## Passage XVIII

Experiments have shown that the rate of a chemical reaction can be affected by experimental variables, such as temperature and atmospheric pressure. In this study, two experiments were run to test the effects of these variables on the reaction rate of butyl chloride and water. When butyl chloride is dissolved into water, it undergoes hydrolysis, which breaks butyl chloride down to butyl alcohol and hydrochloric acid.

### Experiment 1

In the first experiment, butyl chloride was added to water to create a solution with a 1M concentration. Data was taken every 100 seconds to measure the amount of the butyl chloride present over the course of the reaction The experiment was performed at three temperatures: 20° C, 50°C, and 80°C. The data is represented in Table 1 below:

| Table 1 | | | |
|---|---|---|---|
| Time (seconds) | Concentration of Butyl Cloride [M] | | |
| | 20°C | 50°C | 80°C |
| 0 | 1 | 1 | 1 |
| 100 | 0.92 | 0.88 | 0.8 |
| 200 | 0.84 | 0.78 | 0.62 |
| 300 | 0.77 | 0.69 | 0.46 |
| 400 | 0.71 | 0.61 | 0.33 |
| 500 | 0.66 | 0.55 | 0.22 |
| 600 | 0.62 | 0.51 | 0.14 |

### Experiment 2

The same chemical reaction was repeated, also beginning with a 1M concentration of butyl chloride. In this experiment, all trials were performed at 20°C. The researchers ran the first trial with an atmospheric pressure of 1 atm and the second trial at 1.3 atm. Table 2 summarizes the results.

| Table 2 | | |
|---|---|---|
| Time (seconds) | Concentration of Butyl Chloride [M] | |
| | 1 atm | 1.3 atm |
| 0 | 1 | 1 |
| 100 | 0.92 | 0.93 |
| 200 | 0.84 | 0.85 |
| 300 | 0.77 | 0.75 |
| 400 | 0.71 | 0.71 |
| 500 | 0.66 | 0.65 |
| 600 | 0.62 | 0.61 |

1. In Experiment 1, a concentration of 0.135 M butyl chloride observed after 600 seconds would mean the experiment was probably run at:

   A. 20°C.
   B. 50°C.
   C. 70°C.
   D. 80°C.

2. The relationship between reaction rate and temperature shown in Experiment 1 is:

   F. as temperature increases, reaction rate increases.
   G. as temperature increases, reaction rate decreases.
   H. as temperature increases, reaction rate increases and then decreases.
   J. as temperature increases, reaction rate decreases and then increases.

3. Which of the following statements would support the hypothesis that reaction rates vary directly with temperature?

   A. Studies done on various other substances all showed a decrease in reaction rate as pressure increases.
   B. Studies done on various other substances all showed a decrease in reaction rate as temperature decreases.
   C. Studies done on various other substances all showed a decrease in reaction rate as temperature increases.
   D. Studies done on various other substances all showed a decrease in reaction rate as original concentration decreases.

4. Ideal conditions for a slow reaction rate would be:

   F. 0°C at 1 atm of pressure.
   G. 20°C at 1.3 atm of pressure.
   H. 60°C at 1 atm of pressure.
   J. 80°C at 1.3 atm of pressure.

5. The relationship between reaction rate and pressure shown in Experiment 2 is:

   A. as pressure increases, reaction rate increases.
   B. as pressure increases, reaction rate decreases.
   C. as pressure increases, reaction rate increases and then decreases.
   D. as pressure increases, reaction rate shows no significant change.

6. Which of the following figures best illustrates how the pressure of the reactant, butyl chloride, affects the reaction rate?

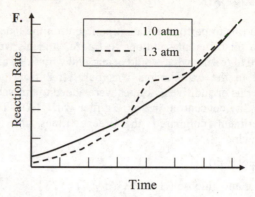

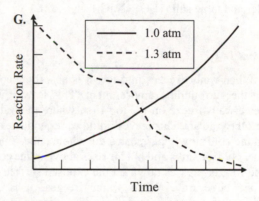

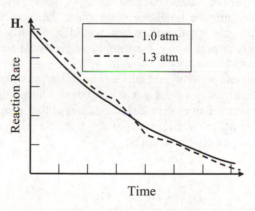

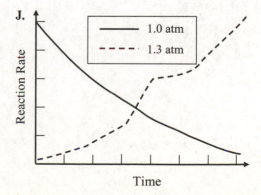

## Conflicting Viewpoints

### Passage XIX

Prior to performing an experiment on the time it takes for different solutions to freeze, students were asked to predict what would occur, and why. All water used in the experiments was pure, free from any minerals or additives. Solutes were added to the water with a concentration of 2g/liter of $H_2O$. The experiment compared the freeze times for the following:

Water ($H_2O$)

Water and glucose ($H_2O + C_6H_{12}O_6$)

Water and table salt ($H_2O + NaCl$)

*Student 1*

When water freezes into ice, it is absorbing cold from the surrounding environment. This is why ice cubes always freeze on the top first, where the water meets the cold air. This leaves liquid water underneath until the cold slowly permeates the whole cube. Since denser cold air sinks and hot air rises above it, the cold in the freezer presses down on the exposed surface of the ice cube tray. When water freezes, it is an endothermic process because energy is taken in by the ice to form the bonds between water molecules. A solution of sugar and water would not freeze as quickly as pure water, because the sugar would get in the way of the crystal structure of the ice. A solution of salt and water would take a shorter amount of time to freeze than would sugar water, but still longer than pure water. Salt molecules are smaller, so they disrupt the crystalline structure of ice less than the relatively gigantic glucose molecules.

*Student 2*

What we sense as "cold" is just very low kinetic energy in an object, or in the atmosphere. While it may seem as though cold air sinks, or is heavier, what is actually occurring is that the faster-moving particles bump into each other, transferring kinetic energy away from the more concentrated source. The contact between fast-moving molecules causes friction, which we sense as heat. This is related to water transitioning into ice because freezing is an exothermic process—as the bonds form between water molecules and they become colder, the energy that had once existed in the water is transferred to the air. The more kinetic energy present in a liquid, the more time it will take to freeze. Energy is never created or destroyed—it is just transferred or transformed. Since ice formation transfers the energy of the water to the surrounding air, it is an exothermic process. Water that has sugar added will take longer to freeze than a solution of salt and water. This is true because the sugar transfers its caloric energy to the water, giving it a higher energetic state than plain or salt water.

*Student 3*

Either solution with a solute added will take longer to freeze than would pure water. The salt water and sugar water will not freeze at the same rate, due to the relative sizes of the molecules. Salt, with the chemical formula $NaCl$, is a very small and simple molecule. Glucose is much bigger, with the formula $C_6H_{12}O_6$. Since a gram is a unit of measurement for mass, when we add 2 grams of salt to water, we are adding many more molecules to it than when we add 2 grams of glucose. The more distinct molecules are added to the water, the more time it will take for it to freeze solid, since the particles disrupt the formation of the crystalline bonds between water molecules.

1. According to Student 1, which of the following would take the shortest time to freeze?

   A. Water + glucose solution
   B. Water + salt solution
   C. Pure water
   D. Sea water

2. In order for the classroom experiment to result in meaningful data, which of the following factors must be controlled?

   I.   Initial temperature of water and solutions before freezing
   II.  Total amount of time liquids spend in freezer
   III. Volume of water or solutions before freezing

   F. I only
   G. II only
   H. I and II only
   J. I and III only

3. According to Student 2, water in the process of freezing:

   A. is endothermic.
   B. is neither endothermic nor exothermic.
   C. transfers the energy of the air to the water.
   D. transfers the energy of the water to the air.

4. Which of the students considered the size of the solute molecules as a factor that would affect freezing time?

   F. Student 1
   G. Student 3
   H. Student 2 and Student 3
   J. Student 1 and Student 3

5. Based on Student 1's explanation:

   A. freezing water takes in energy from the environment.
   B. the sugar solution would freeze fastest.
   C. bigger solute molecules affect freezing times more than smaller molecules.
   D. both A and C are true.

6. The Mpemba effect is a phenomenon where hot liquids freeze faster than cold liquids. This phenomenon most clearly contradicts a statement made by:

   F. The classroom teacher
   G. Student 1
   H. Student 2
   J. Student 3

7. The teacher of this class added another solution to the list of what will be tested. The size of the molecule added is smaller than NaCl, and it would be mixed with the same proportion of the others at 2g/liter of water. The substance added has no caloric content. Which student(s), if any, would predict that this would be the slowest to freeze?

   A. Student 1
   B. Student 3
   C. Student 1 and Student 2
   D. None of the students would predict this

## Conflicting Viewpoints

## Passage XX

Two scientific theories developed to answer the question, "Could the planet Mars support life?"

*Theory 1*

There is no conclusive evidence to support the belief that the planet Mars is capable of supporting living organisms. Mars lacks an atmosphere like Earth's. Its environment is hostile in temperature (down to negative 143 degrees Celsius) and there is no protection from fierce solar radiation.

Water, necessary for life as we know it, is found on Mars only in the form of ice, which has not proven to sustain life. Many compounds known to exist along with living organisms, such as carbonates, are undetected on Mars; the types that are detected there can also be produced by inorganic activity. Methane present in the atmosphere, on Earth an indication of living organisms, could just as easily have been produced by inorganic processes as by bacteria.

It is claimed that chondrules, found within a Martian meteorite, are wormlike bacteria of extremely small size, yet it is unlikely that life could exist on such a microscale. DNA and RNA, the building blocks of life, establish a minimum size requirement observed in all life on Earth. Since chondrules are below this limit, they most likely are an inorganic byproduct.

*Theory 2*

The explorations of NASA's Viking Mission on Mars amassed an extensive collection of soil and atmospheric samples. The evidence from these samples strongly suggests that the planet supports life.

To test for the presence of living organisms, Martian soil was blended with a radioactive material, carbon-14. If the soil were inhabited by living organisms, they would digest radioactive material. Chemical reactions between organisms and carbon-14 would produce certain gases. These gases were indeed detected by Viking researchers.

Atmospheric tests showed the presence of methane in the Mars atmosphere. Methane, abundant in Earth's atmosphere, is produced by organisms, though it can also be produced by inorganic means, like the tectonic shift of Earth's continental plates. However, the quantity of methane detected in the atmosphere surrounding Mars leads to the conclusion that some of it had to be produced by living organisms.

The litmus test for the existence of life is the presence of liquid water. Two theories suggest the existence of water on Mars. One states that the climate on Mars was warmer in the past. Higher temperatures would have meant the planet's current ice caps were at one point vast rivers and seas. Photographs that seem to depict ancient riverbeds support that theory. The second opinion is Mars has always been a cold planet covered in ice. But the ice, uniquely lower in density in solid than in liquid form, floated as a protective layer above liquid water, which flowed beneath.

The most conclusive piece of evidence for the existence of life on Mars was the discovery of chondrules within an ancient meteorite rock in Antarctica. Chondrules are living organisms formed within rocks when water is allowed to seep into the structure. The meteor not only contained chondrules, but fossilized worms, organic matter, and magnetite, a product of bacteria exposed to magnetism.

1. Both theories would agree that:

   A. liquid water existed on Mars at one time.
   B. liquid water is essential to life.
   C. chondrules are evidence of life.
   D. methane is evidence of life.

2. According to the Theory 1:

   F. methane does not exist on Mars.
   G. methane does exist on Mars and is evidence of living organisms.
   H. methane does exist on Mars but is not evidence of living organisms.
   J. methane is not discussed in Theory 1.

3. Finding a living organism on Earth smaller in size than a chondrule would:

   A. support Theory 1 only.
   B. support Theory 2 only.
   C. support Theory 1 and Theory 2.
   D. support neither Theory 1 nor Theory 2.

SCIENCE PRACTICE   371

4. Viking tested Martian soil with radioactive materials to see if:

   F. gases would be released.
   G. water would be found.
   H. methane would be found.
   J. chondrules would be found.

5. According to Theory 2, the existence of methane on Mars indicates that:

   A. organic matter exists on Mars.
   B. the soil is radioactive.
   C. there is tectonic activity on Mars.
   D. the methane was produced by inorganic means.

6. Proving tectonic shifting on Mars would:

   F. support Theory 1.
   G. counter Theory 1.
   H. support Theory 2.
   J. counter Theory 2.

7. The lack of magnetic fields on Mars disclaims what substance as evidence of life on Mars?

   A. Water
   B. Methane
   C. Magnetite
   D. Carbonates

## Conflicting Viewpoints

## Passage XXI

Three students discuss competing theories on why yawning occurs.

### Student 1

Contagious yawning is caused by *emphatic synchronization*, a means by which animals coordinate their behavior to mimic those around them. This trait is hereditary in creatures that travel in packs, since those which are more attuned to the actions of their fellow group members are more likely to survive and reproduce.

In a recent study, researchers monitored the responses of 12 infant and 21 juvenile chimpanzees after they watched a human sneeze or yawn. They observed that not a single chimpanzee of any age sneezed, and none of the infants yawned in response to the human's yawn. However, among the 21 juveniles, the researchers found that every single one produced a yawn within seconds of seeing a human do the same. It is likely that the infants did not yawn because they are not old enough to have developed a sense of empathy for others.

### Student 2

Yawning is a phenomenon that the body uses to keep the respiratory system healthy and balanced. When humans breathe in, we do not use our entire lung capacities. The average human male has the capability to hold around 6 liters — think, the equivalent of 3 large soda bottles — of air in his lungs. Since we do not generally breathe so deeply, it means that we must occasionally take deeper breaths, or yawns, to engage all of the alveoli within the lungs. Alveoli are air sacs that are essential to diffusing oxygen into the blood stream. If they are not engaged, these sacs may begin to stiffen or collapse.

Additionally, the deep exhalation during a yawn assists humans in dispelling excess $CO_2$ from their systems. Carbon dioxide is a waste product in the process of respiration. If an oxygen-dependent animal has too much of this gas in its bloodstream, this overabundance may lead to respiratory failure. It has been observed that many Olympic athletes yawn right before engaging in their events, which may be a conditioned response. Their bodies instinctively know that they will need more oxygen than they do at rest, so they subconsciously prepare for the exertion ahead.

### Student 3

Even though it deals with breathing and gas exchange, yawning actually has very little to do with getting oxygen into the bloodstream. The main purpose of a yawn is thermoregulation within the brain—a yawn is like the mind's air conditioning.

Yawns occur both spontaneously and contagiously. There have been studies that attempt to determine the underlying causes, but one factor has stood out. People are much more likely to yawn when their brains are warm, as long as they are in an environment where taking in the surrounding air would result in cooling. The brain does not just overheat as a result of physical surroundings; it can also grow warmer through cognitive arousal. This is why students may yawn during an important, stressful test, even if they are fully engaged and awake. Since the brain is doing work, it needs to cool down.

Contagious yawns can be explained as the result of two factors. First, the people or animals yawning are in a similar environment, so they are experiencing similar body and ambient temperatures. Second, mimicking the yawning behavior of others may increase an animal's chance of survival by keeping cognitive functioning at a high level. Even babies mimic various adult behaviors, such as laughter or facial expressions; this likely comes from the evolutionary necessity of learning from elders.

1.  Which of the following best explains why Student 2 mentioned soda bottles?

    A.  There is dissolved $CO_2$ within the drink as well as within the lungs.
    B.  They act similarly to alveoli.
    C.  They give the reader a reference for the amount of air lungs can hold.
    D.  They can be filled with oxygen.

2.  Student 1 would most likely agree that emphatic synchronization is:

    F.  useful for creatures that live solitary lives.
    G.  the underlying reason for spontaneous sneezes.
    H.  an inherited trait that is developed through maturity.
    J.  a way to strengthen the alveoli within the lungs.

3.  A recent study has shown that yawning decreases the amount of oxygen present in a person's lungs. This finding would most likely *weaken* the viewpoint(s) of:

    A.  Student 1 only
    B.  Student 2 only
    C.  Student 3 only
    D.  both Student 2 and Student 3

4.  Newborn baby humans, before developing what we recognize as "empathy," stick their tongues out in response to an adult doing the same. To what would Student 3 most likely attribute this behavior?

    F.  The babies are overheated.
    G.  The babies are exercising their facial muscles.
    H.  The babies are strengthening their respiratory systems.
    J.  The babies who imitate are more likely to survive to adulthood.

5.  Which student(s) would most likely agree that contagious yawning is an evolutionary consequence of social living?

    A.  Student 1
    B.  Student 2
    C.  Student 1 and 3
    D.  Student 2 and 3

6.  Which of the following situations is *most analogous* to Student 2's example of a conditioned response?

    F.  A member of the high school diving team recalls her coach's suggestions and performs a perfect backflip.
    G.  Alveoli in the lungs begin to shrivel if they are not engaged.
    H.  An adult otter automatically fluffs her fur for warmth before swimming in cold water.
    J.  A man yelps when he notices a large spider crawling on his leg.

7.  Which of the following findings would BEST support the viewpoint of Student 1?

    A.  In another study, infant and juvenile chimpanzees exhibit equivalent levels of empathy.
    B.  Colonies of meercats that engage in synchronous predator warnings do not have a higher life expectancy than those that do not.
    C.  Infant humans often laugh when they observe their parents yawning.
    D.  Teenage humans are more likely than infants to stretch after watching another person stretching.

## Conflicting Viewpoints

## Passage XXII

Although many mass extinctions have occurred throughout the Earth's history, the most massive one occurred between the Cretaceous period (K) and the Tertiary period (T). This time frame, known as the K-T Boundary, saw the extinction of the dinosaurs. Two theories explaining the cause are explained below.

*Theory 1 – Impact Theory*

The Impact Theory states that dinosaurs became extinct after Earth's huge collision with an object from outer space.

Evidence of what seems to be a gigantic crater dating from the K-T Boundary has been found on the Yucatan peninsula of Mexico. Samples of solidified clay from the time period have been chemically analyzed and discovered to be iridium-enriched. Iridium is rare in rocks of the Earth's crust but common to many objects found in the galaxy, so it is believed that the source was an asteroid that collided with the Earth 65,000,000 years ago.

This cosmic collision would have spewed huge amounts of dust into the atmosphere, blocking sunlight from the Earth. These conditions caused what is known as an "impact winter." In the darkness, temperatures dropped and water froze. Sun-dependent and water-dependent plants started to die out. The decline in vegetation led to the demise of herbivores, which in turn caused carnivores to become extinct. There have been findings in the Yucatan with markings which indicate the correct age and stresses, making it a likely place of impact.

*Theory 2 – Volcano-Greenhouse Theory*

The Volcano-Greenhouse theory explains that volcanic activity during the K-T Boundary begat a series of events causing conditions under which many living species could no longer exist.

Carbon dioxide, a substance which has great bearing on the existence of life on Earth, is the focus of the Volcano-Greenhouse theory. Carbon dioxide is a source of carbon, the elemental basis of life, and of free oxygen in the atmosphere. Carbon dioxide interacts with heat from the Earth's surface; along with other greenhouse gases in the atmosphere, it regulates temperature in both the air and oceans. Water remains in the liquid state and life flourishes.

There is evidence that the conditions leading to mass extinction, including rising climate temperatures, began as a disturbance in the carbon cycle. Volcanic activity is a major event known to disrupt carbon. A period of volcanic activity, known as Deccan Traps, coincides with the K-T Boundary and is thought to be the most violent in the history of the Earth.

Large amounts of volcanic activity released copious amounts of greenhouse gases (carbon dioxide and water vapor) into the atmosphere. The rate at which carbon dioxide was released exceeded the rate that plant life could absorb it. As carbon dioxide levels continued to rise, climate temperature also rose. Certain species adapted to this rapid and drastic change in climate, but many others, such as the dinosaur, were unable to adapt.

The Volcano-Greenhouse Theory directly links a known period of volcanic activity to a disruption of the carbon cycle and global warming caused by the greenhouse effect. The Impact Theory could explain the extinction of the dinosaurs through the lowering of temperatures, but does not explain other events that occurred during that time, such as changes in marine activity due to pH imbalance in the oceans from acid rain, reproductive failure of land animals, and changes in photosynthesis rates.

Furthermore, there is little evidence that an impact occurred at all during the K-T boundary. The Yucatan "crater" has not been proved to be such, and the element iridium found on earth, supposedly from an asteroid, is known to be emitted from active volcanoes today and cannot be considered evidence of the Impact Theory.

1. K-T boundary refers to:

   A. a time period during which dinosaurs first existed.
   B. a time period during which dinosaurs lived.
   C. a time period during which dinosaurs became extinct.
   D. a time period during which all living things died.

2. According to the Impact Theory:

   F. dinosaurs became extinct because of the toxic gasses emitted by violent volcanic eruptions.
   G. dinosaurs became extinct because of a rise in the Earth's temperature.
   H. dinosaurs became extinct because of cooling temperatures and a lack of sunlight that resulted from an asteroid collision.
   J. dinosaurs evolved into new species as a result of changed conditions on Earth.

3. What is one piece of evidence that would help settle the debate between the two theories?

   A. Finding evidence of atmospheric pressure changes that occurred during the K-T boundary
   B. Finding evidence of temperature changes that occurred during the K-T boundary
   C. Finding evidence of ocean level changes that occurred during the K-T boundary
   D. Finding evidence of volcanic activity that occurred during the K-T boundary

4. Which of the following statements does NOT support the Volcano-Greenhouse theory?

   F. Climate temperature being shown to rise during the K-T boundary
   G. $CO_2$ levels being shown to drop during the K-T boundary
   H. Extremely high levels of volcanic activity shown during the K-T boundary
   J. pH levels of the ocean changing during the K-T boundary period

5. Theory 1 and Theory 2 would agree with which of the following statements?

   A. High levels of iridium are found in rocks developed during the K-T boundary.
   B. Climate temperature was unnaturally cold during the K-T boundary.
   C. The concentration of greenhouse gases was extremely high during the K-T boundary.
   D. Water existed as a liquid during the K-T boundary.

6. Volcanic activity fits into the Volcano-Greenhouse theory because it:

   F. released large amounts of particles into the air.
   G. emitted $CO_2$ and water, which raised climate temperatures.
   H. also caused massively destructive earthquakes.
   J. released lava which destroyed living species such as dinosaurs.

7. Carbon dioxide affects all EXCEPT which of the following?

   A. Climate temperature
   B. Ocean temperature
   C. Living organisms (carbon source)
   D. Volcanic activity

# Answer Key

MATHEMATICS OVERVIEW

**Question Difficulty** – p. 16
1.  B
2.  H
3.  D

**Attractors** – p. 17
1.  B

MATH TOOLBOX

**Plugging In**
p. 25 Put It Together
1.  C
2.  K

**Choosing Numbers**
p. 26
100
D

p. 27 Put It Together
1.  E
2.  F

**Guesstimating**
p. 28
C
30

p. 29 Put It Together
1.  A

**Bridging The Gap**
p. 31
A
1.  Difference in contributions, number of people and cost
2.  Both contribution amount
3.  Average contribution per person = $20 at first
4.  $100/4 = $25 per person, $5 more than $20

p. 32 Put It Together
1.  C
2.  G

**Using Your Calculator**
p. 34
-25
25
-6
7/15
4/35
-1.75
2, -2
2 intersections
(-1,-3)  (2,0)

p. 36 Put It Together
1.  B
2.  F
3.  E

PRE-ALGEBRA

**Multiples, Factors, and Divisibility**
p. 42
multiples of 4: 4, 8, 12, 16...
1,24 and 2,12 and 3,8 and 4,6
no
2

p. 43 Put It together
1.  D
2.  H
3.  E

**Fractions**
p.44
17/15
21/10
2/21
2/5
3/2
30

p. 45 Put It Together
1.  C
2.  J
3.  D

## Ratios
p.46
>2/5
>
>3/5
>
>5
>
>1a + 2o = 45, and a = o

p. 47 Put It Together
> 1.  B
> 2.  G
> 3.  A

## Proportions
p. 48
>8
>
>4
>
>9.3
>
>$6/4.5 = 8/x$
>
>$6 \times x = 8 \times 4.5$
>
>$x = 6$

p. 49 Put It Together
> 1.  C
> 2.  K
> 3.  B

## Exponents
p. 50
>32
>
>$1/x^2$
>
>$x^{12}$
>
>1/8
>
>1/25
>
>$36x^2y^6$
>
>1
>
>10
>
>$x = 4$

p. 51 Put It Together
> 1.  A
> 2.  H
> 3.  C
> 4.  J

## Roots
p. 52
>5
>
>-2
>
>$8\sqrt{2}$
>
>4/7
>
>No
>
>$3\sqrt{2}$
>
>$\dfrac{\sqrt{2}}{2}$
>
>$2x\sqrt{3}$
>
>$\dfrac{x\sqrt{2}}{4}$ or $\dfrac{x\sqrt{8}}{8}$

p. 53 Put It Together
> 1.  C
> 2.  G
> 3.  A
> 4.  J

## Digits and Scientific Notation
p. 54
>$6.78 \times 10^{-13}$
>
>8,630,000

p. 55 Put It Together
> 1.  C
> 2.  G
> 3.  B

## Percents
p. 56
>75%
>
>25%
>
>450lbs
>
>45lbs
>
>95lbs, 19%
>
>56%

p. 58 Put It Together
> 1.  C
> 2.  H
> 3.  D
> 4.  J

**Checkpoint Review** – p. 60
1. E
2. G
3. C
4. J
5. B
6. G

**Absolute Value**
p. 62
1
-1

p. 63 Put It Together
1. B
2. H
3. E
4. K

**Sequences**
p. 64
27
3
4th position: 5
8th position: 5
multiple of 4 position: 5
101st position: 2

p. 65 Put It Together
1. B
2. J
3. C

**Averages (Arithmetic Mean)**
p. 66
83
320

p. 67 Put It Together
1. A
2. J
3. C

**Median and Mode**
p. 68
17
19.5
37, 38
6, 12, 18, 19, 21, 24, 24, 44, 47
21, 24

p. 69 Put It Together
1. C
2. J
3. C

**Combinations**
p. 70
6
first friend: 6, second friend: 5
6 × 5 × 4 × 3
360
point A: 4, point B: 3
4 + 3 + 2 + 1 + 0 = 10

p. 71 Put It Together
1. E
2. H
3. E

**Probability**
p. 72
20
16
16/20 = 4/5
8
1
1/8

p. 73 Put It Together
1. B
2. F

**Pre-Algebra Practice** – p. 78

1. C
2. H
3. C
4. H
5. D
6. H
7. C
8. G
9. E
10. G
11. E
12. G
13. D
14. K
15. D
16. K
17. B
18. F
19. E
20. H
21. D
22. G
23. D
24. J
25. C
26. H
27. D
28. K
29. C
30. F
31. D
32. J
33. B
34. K
35. E
36. G
37. D
38. J
39. D
40. H
41. A
42. H
43. B
44. F
45. D
46. K
47. D
48. J
49. E
50. H
51. E
52. J
53. C
54. J
55. C
56. H
57. B
58. J
59. D
60. J
61. C
62. K
63. D
64. K
65. B
66. K
67. B
68. H
69. E
70. H
71. E
72. H
73. C
74. K
75. D

ELEMENTARY ALGEBRA

**Algebraic Expressions**

p. 102

$7k^3 - 4k$

$-2x^2 + 14x - 2$

$3y^2 - 9y - 30$

$4x^2(2x - 3 + 5x^2)$

p. 103 Put It Together

1. A
2. F
3. A
4. J

**Equations**

p. 104

2

$3x - 4 = 8$

$3x = 12$

$x = 4$

p. 105 Put It Together

1. E
2. F
3. A
4. H

**Inequalities**

p. 106

$x > 8\dfrac{2}{3}$

No

No

Yes

E

p. 107 Put It Together

1. B
2. H
3. E
4. K

**Translation**

p. 108

$x$

$30 = 2(4 + x)$

$x = 11$

$j = 4n + 50$

450

Yes

p. 109 Put It Together

1. B
2. K
3. C
4. J

**Word Problems**

p. 110

Gallons used by Jeb, gallons used by Edith

Miles per gallon and distance traveled

600/12 = Jeb gallons, 600/50 = Edith gallons

Jeb = 50 gallons, Edith = 12 gallons

50 − 12 = 38 gallons

180 miles

10°C

p. 112 Put It Together

1. B
2. H
3. C
4. J
5. B

**Elementary Algebra Practice** – p. 118

1. B
2. G
3. D
4. H
5. D
6. J
7. B
8. G
9. B
10. G
11. C
12. K
13. C
14. H
15. C
16. H
17. D
18. J
19. E
20. H
21. E
22. H
23. E
24. G
25. A
26. K
27. D
28. G
29. E
30. H
31. A
32. G
33. B
34. G
35. D
36. J
37. E
38. K
39. B
40. H
41. C
42. J
43. D
44. J
45. C
46. K
47. B
48. G
49. C
50. K

INTERMEDIATE ALGEBRA

## Simultaneous Equations

p. 132

    2

    $(4x + 2y = 32) + (x - 2y = 3)$

    $x = 7$

    $10A + 2C = 5200$

    $A = 400$

p. 133 Put It Together

1. A
2. H
3. C
4. H

## Quadratic Equations and Expressions

p. 134

    $x^2 + 8x + 7 = 0$

    $(x + 7)(x + 1)$

    $x + 7 = 0, x + 1 = 0, x = -7, -1$

    $(x + 4)(x - 4)$

p. 135 Put It Together

1. A
2. J
3. E
4. J

## Radical Equations

p. 136

    $\sqrt{2x} = 5$

    $2x = 25$

    $x = 12.5$

p. 137 Put It Together

1. D
2. J

## Functions

p. 138

    $f(1) = 10$

    $f(a) = a^2 + 6a + 3$

    2 or -8

    7ш3 = 27

    $f(g(3)) = 11$

    $g(f(1)) = 9$

p. 139 Put It Together

1. A
2. J
3. E

## Logarithms

p. 140

    $a = 2$

p. 141 Put It Together

1. C
2. F
3. D

## Matrices

p. 143 Put It Together

1. B
2. G

## Complex Numbers

p. 144

    $i^5 = i$

    $i^6 = -1$

    $2i\sqrt{3}$

    $5i\sqrt{2}$

    $(1 + i)(1 - i) = 2$

    $i(2 + i)(3 - i) = 7i - 1$

p. 145 Put It Together

1. C
2. J
3. E

## Intermediate Algebra Practice – p. 150

1. A
2. G
3. E
4. G
5. C
6. G
7. A
8. G
9. E
10. J
11. C
12. J
13. D
14. F
15. C
16. G
17. B
18. H
19. D
20. J

21. C
22. J
23. D
24. J
25. A
26. K
27. C
28. F
29. A
30. K

COORDINATE GEOMETRY

## Coordinate Geometry Basics
p. 160
point D: (-3,2)
point E: (3,-3)

p. 161 Put It Together
1.  A
2.  F
3.  E
4.  G

## Midpoint and Distance
p. 162
distance = 5

p. 163 Put It Together
1.  D
2.  H
3.  D

## Slope
p. 164
-2/3
undefined
-2/3
3/2
0

p. 165 Put It Together
1.  D
2.  J
3.  A

## Linear Equations and Inequalities
p. 166
standard
$y = 3x - 3.5$, slope = 3, intercept = -3.5
$y = 3x$

$$y = -\frac{1}{3}x$$

-1/2

$$y = -\frac{1}{2}x + \frac{1}{2}$$

p. 168 Put It Together
1.  E
2.  F
3.  E
4.  J
5.  C

## Conic Sections
p. 170
$x^2 + (y - 3)^2 = 16$
FOIL: $x^2 + 6x + 9$
$x^2 + 6x + 9 + y^2 = 0 + 9$
Standard form: $(x + 3)^2 + y^2 = 9$

p. 172 Put It Together
1.  B
2.  G
3.  C

## Transformations
p. 174
(-1,-2)
(1,1)
(1,-1)

p. 176 Put It Together
1.  C
2.  G
3.  D

**Coordinate Geometry Practice** – p. 182

1. E
2. G
3. C
4. J
5. C
6. K
7. C
8. F
9. B
10. G
11. A
12. H
13. A
14. G
15. E
16. H
17. D
18. H
19. D
20. J
21. A
22. J
23. E
24. K
25. B
26. H
27. C
28. K
29. D
30. G
31. A
32. F
33. C

PLANE GEOMETRY

**Angles**

p. 196

$x = 90$

$a + b + c + d = 360$

$a = c, b = d$

$x + y + z = 180$

$a + b + c + d = 360$

$a + b + c + d + e = 540$

$a = 108$

p. 198 Put It Together

1. C
2. H
3. B

**Parallel Lines**

p. 201 Put It Together

1. D
2. J
3. B

**Isosceles and Equilateral Triangles**

p. 203 Put It Together

1. B
2. G
3. B

**Perimeter and Area of Triangles**

p. 204

area $= bh/2$

perimeter $= b + c + d$

48

p. 205 Put It Together

1. B
2. K
3. B

**Right Triangles**

p. 206

missing legs: $\sqrt{73}$ , 3

missing sides: 1 and 1, 3 and $3\sqrt{3}$

p. 208 Put It Together

1. D
2. G
3. B

### Similar and Congruent Triangles

p. 210

$DE$ = 10

$DE$ = $x$/2

15 and 86°, 12 and 53°

p. 211 Put It Together

1. B
2. J
3. C

### Quadrilaterals

p. 212

trapezoid: $\dfrac{b_1 + b_2}{2} \times h$

parallelogram: $bh$

rhombus: $bh$

rectangle: $2W + 2L$, $WL$

square: $4s$, $s^2$

perimeter: 36, area: 54

p. 214 Put It Together

1. B
2. H
3. E
4. J
5. C
6. G

### Circles

p. 216

area = $\pi r^2$

circumference = $2\pi r$

diameter = $2r$

$\pi$ = 3.14...

arc $AB$: $4\pi$

sector $AOB$: $12\pi$

p. 217 Put It Together

1. D
2. K
3. C

### Volume and Surface Area

p. 218

cube: $s^3$, $6s^2$

rectangular box: $lwh$, $2lw + 2lh + 2wh$

p. 219 Put It Together

1. E
2. J
3. D

### Plane Geometry Practice – p. 224

1. A
2. J
3. C
4. J
5. C
6. J
7. E
8. J
9. C
10. H
11. C
12. H
13. D
14. G
15. A
16. G
17. A
18. G
19. C
20. G
21. E
22. H
23. E
24. H
25. E
26. H
27. C
28. G
29. D
30. K
31. A
32. H
33. A
34. H
35. D
36. J
37. B
38. F
39. C
40. G

TRIGONOMETRY

## SOH CAH TOA
p. 240

$\sin^{-1}(3/5) = y$

$\cos^{-1}(3/5) = x$

$\tan^{-1}(4/3) = x$

p. 241 Put It Together
1. D
2. G
3. A
4. H

## Trig Identities
p. 244

-1/2

p. 245 Put It Together
1. D
2. G

## The Unit Circle
p. 246

$240° = 4\pi/3$

$\pi/2 = 90°$

$\cos 150° = -\dfrac{\sqrt{3}}{2}$

$\sin 150° = 1/2$

$405° = 45°, 765°, -315°$

$-210° = -570°, 150°, 510°$

positive

p. 249 Put It Together
1. E
2. F

## Graphs of Sine and Cosine
p. 251 Put It Together
1. E
2. F

## Laws of Sines and Cosines
p. 253 Put It Together
1. E
2. J

## Trigonometry Practice – p. 258
1. D
2. H
3. C
4. H
5. C
6. K
7. B
8. J
9. E
10. F
11. B
12. K
13. D
14. H
15. D
16. K
17. B
18. J
19. B
20. G
21. C
22. H
23. E
24. K
25. D

SCIENCE

SCIENCE OVERVIEW

**Attractors** – p. 273
1. C
2. J

DATA REPRESENTATION

**The Scientific Method**
p. 281
    Do different chemical burn with different colors?
    Student uses solutions of different diluted
    chemicals and burns the solutions.
    Student observes color of the flames.
    The metal in a chemical determines its color
    when burned.

**Interpretation**
p. 284
    39.2 m/s
    646.8 m
    The object hits the ground

p. 287 Put It Together
1. C
2. F
3. C
4. G
5. D

**Relationship**
p. 288
    as pressure decreases, volume increases
    inverse relationship
    years 30-32
    years 16-18
    when lynx peaks, hare population decreases
    ~10 years between peaks, next in year 42-46
    if hare population is 0, lynx will also fall to 0
    if lynx population is 0, hare population will rise
    (until resources are depleted)

p. 291 Put It Together
1. A
2. J
3. C

**Additional Data**
p. 292
    1500m below = 150atm
    20km above = ~0.05 atm
    1km below = ~1.3 atm
    alpha neutrino charge: 0
    D

p. 294 Put It Together
1. C
2. F
3. A
4. J

**Connection**
p. 296
    288 ft
    wet: 65 mph
    dry: at no speed shown
    emergency braking: will hit object

p. 297 Put It Together
1. B
2. H
3. D

**Checkpoint Review** – p. 298
1. D
2. J
3. B
4. J
5. B

RESEARCH SUMMARY

**Data**
p. 303 Put It Together
1. A
2. J
3. A
4. F
5. D

## Experimental Design
p. 304

directly manipulated: heat source

dependent: temperature of water

controlled: amount of water, type of heat source, room temp

part of the temperature change may have been due to the environment

p. 306 Put It Together
1. B
2. G
3. C
4. F
5. D

## Evaluation
p. 308

C

G

p. 310 Put It Together
1. C
2. J
3. D
4. G
5. D

## Checkpoint Review – p. 312
1. B
2. J
3. D
4. J
5. B
6. J

## CONFLICTING VIEWPOINTS

## Detail
p. 317 Put It Together
1. C
2. F

## Perspective
p. 318

A

C

H

B

p. 320 Put It Together
1. D
2. G
3. B
4. G
5. B
6. G
7. C

## Assessment
p. 322

C

D

p. 324 Put It Together
1. B
2. J
3. D
4. H

## Checkpoint Review – p. 326
1. A
2. G
3. D
4. G
5. B
6. J
7. A

## Science Practice – p. 332

Passage I
1. C
2. J
3. D
4. J
5. B

Passage II
1. C
2. J
3. A
4. H
5. B

Passage III
1. C
2. H
3. D
4. G
5. D

Passage IV
1. B
2. J
3. C
4. G
5. A

Passage V
1. C
2. J
3. C
4. J
5. A

Passage VI
1. B
2. G
3. A
4. F
5. B

Passage VII
1. B
2. J
3. C
4. G
5. B

Passage VIII
1. B
2. H
3. A
4. J
5. C

Passage IX
1. D
2. H
3. A
4. H
5. D

Passage X
1. C
2. G
3. D
4. H
5. B

Passage XI
1. B
2. J
3. A
4. H
5. C
6. F

Passage XII
1. B
2. G
3. A
4. G
5. A
6. G

Passage XIII
1. C
2. H
3. B
4. G
5. D
6. H

Passage XIV
1. B
2. G
3. A
4. J
5. B
6. J

Passage XV
1. A
2. G
3. D
4. J
5. B
6. J

Passage XVI
1. B
2. F
3. C
4. H
5. B
6. F

Passage XVII
1. B
2. G
3. C
4. F
5. C
6. G

Passage XVIII
1. D
2. F
3. B
4. F
5. D
6. H

Passage XIX
1. C
2. J
3. D
4. J
5. D
6. H
7. B

Passage XX
1. B
2. H
3. B
4. F
5. A
6. F
7. C

Passage XXI
1. C
2. H
3. B
4. J
5. A
6. H
7. D

Passage XXII
1. C
2. H
3. D
4. G
5. A
6. G
7. D

SUMMIT
EDUCATIONAL
GROUP

# Science Appendix

The **law of conservation of energy** states that the total amount of energy in a process will not change. In other words, energy cannot be created or destroyed; it must come from some source and must be transformed or transferred to another source.

**Kinetic energy** is the energy an object has due to its movement.

**Potential energy** is in a position that could give it kinetic energy. Imagine a stone resting in a slingshot or a book perched at the edge of a shelf.

**Temperature** is a measure of the average kinetic energy of molecules.

**Kelvin** is a unit of measure of temperature. 0°K represents absolute zero, the temperature at which there is no thermal motion. Kelvin and Celsius have the same degree intervals, but 0°K is equal to −273°C.

**Celsius** (or "centigrade") is a measure of temperature. 0°C is the freezing point of water, and 100°C is the boiling point of water.

**Sublimation** is the transition of a substance from the solid to the gas phase without the intermediate liquid phase.

An **element** cannot be broken down into a simpler substance through chemical reactions.

An **atom** is a single particle of an element. The nucleus of an atom is made up of protons and neutrons. Protons have a positive charge. Neutrons have no charge. The nucleus is orbited by electrons, which have a negative charge.

Chemical bonds join atoms to form **molecules**. Molecules are described by the number of each atom type. For example, $H_2O$ represents two hydrogen atoms and one oxygen atom. Energy is required to create chemical bonds. Also, energy is released when chemical bonds are broken. Heat is a common source of energy creating or resulting from chemical bonds. Because of this, chemical reactions often require or expend heat.

A **catalyst** increases the rate of a chemical reaction.

**Photosynthesis** is a process of converting light energy into chemical energy. The equation for photosynthesis is: $6CO_2 + 6H_2O + energy \rightarrow C_6H_{12}O_6 + 6O_2$. In other words, carbon dioxide, water, and energy are used to produce glucose and oxygen. In plant cells, this reaction occurs in the chloroplast.

**pH** is a measure of the acidity or basicity of an aqueous solution. Solutions with a low pH (less than 7) are **acidic** and solutions with a high pH (greater than 7) are **basic** or **alkaline**.

**Viscosity** is a measure of a fluid's resistance to deformation. For example, molasses and tar have much higher viscosities than water.

**Density** is the ratio of an object's mass to its volume.

**Calories** and **joules** are units of energy.

A **watt** (W) is a unit of energy transferred over time. For example, 1 watt is equal to 1 joule per second.

The **ohm** ($\Omega$) is a unit of electrical resistance.

**Electrical resistivity** measures how strongly a material opposes the flow of electric current.

**Electrical conductivity** measures how strongly a material conducts an electric current. For example, copper is commonly used for electrical components because it has high electrical conductivity.

A **battery** is often designated by |||.
The longer line represents the positive terminal.
In basic electrical systems, electrical current
travels in one direction, from a positive terminal
to a negative terminal.

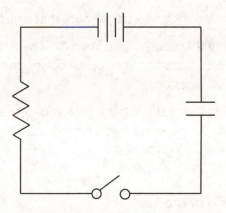

A **resistor** reduces electrical current flow and
lowers voltage levels within circuits.
A resistor is designated by ∧∧∧.

A **capacitor** stores electrical charge until it holds
as much as the battery supplying power.
A capacitor is designated by ||.

A **switch** can interrupt an electrical current and
break the circuit. A switch is designated by ✎o.

# Test Week Checklist

### Week of the Test

❑ By now, you know what you know.  Cramming won't help you learn anything new, and it will only add to your test anxiety.  If you want to study, review the Chapter Summaries.

❑ Take it easy, and try to get a week's worth of good sleep.  You want to be well rested for test day.

❑ If you are not testing at your own school, make sure you know where you're going.  Don't rely on an online mapping program the morning of the test.  If you need to, take a test run the weekend before.

### Friday night

❑ Again, you know what you know.  Do something relaxing and fun.

❑ Lay out everything you need to bring with you:

- Your admission ticket

- Official photo ID

- 3 or 4 sharpened No. 2 pencils with erasers

- Calculator with new batteries

- Watch

- A drink and a small snack that won't get your hands sticky

❑ Visualize success.  See yourself solving question after question.  Envision completing the last question, putting your pencil down, and closing the test booklet.  Let yourself feel the good feeling of a job well done.

❑ Go to sleep at the same time you've been going to sleep all week. Otherwise, you'll just toss and turn.  Don't worry if you have trouble sleeping.  You'll have plenty of adrenaline to keep your brain going during the test.

### Morning of the Test

❑ Have a backup alarm – either another clock or a parent.

❑ Eat a good breakfast.  Make sure to avoid heavy, fatty foods.

❑ Do something easy that you enjoy (take a walk or listen to music).  You want to go into the test awake and upbeat.

## At the Test

❑ Arrive about fifteen minutes early to the test center to find your room and settle in.

❑ Make sure to use the bathroom before you start the test. You only have a few short breaks during the test; you don't want to have to worry about a line at the restroom.

❑ Find your seat and sit for a minute. Continue to visualize yourself working successfully through the test, using all of the skills and strategies you've learned.

❑ During breaks, stand up and walk around. It helps you to stay focused.

❑ Pace yourself and keep your eye on the clock.

❑ If you start losing focus, try this concentration exercise: Every five questions, put down your pencil, stare at the ceiling, blink a few times, take several deep, slow breaths and then continue with the next five questions.

## After the Test

❑ Plan to do something positive and fun. You deserve it!